VICTIMOLOGY

VICTIMOLOGY

The victim and the criminal justice process

Sandra Walklate

London
UNWIN HYMAN
Boston   Sydney   Wellington

Published by the Academic Division of
Unwin Hyman Ltd
15/17 Broadwick Street, London W1V 1FP, UK

Unwin Hyman Inc.,
8 Winchester Place, Winchester, Mass. 01890, USA

Allen & Unwin (Australia) Ltd,
8 Napier Street, North Sydney, NSW 2060, Australia

Allen & Unwin (New Zealand) Ltd in association with the
Port Nicholson Press
Compusales Building, 75 Ghuznee Street, Wellington 1, New Zealand

First published in 1989

British Library Cataloguing in Publication Data

Walklate, Sandra
  Victimology : the victim and the criminal
justice system.
  1. Crime victims
  I. Title
  362.8'8

ISBN 0-04-445159-8
ISBN 0-04-445160-1 Pbk

Library of Congress Cataloging-in-Publication Data

Walklate, Sandra.
  Victimology : the victim and the criminal justice system / Sandra
Walklate.
    p.   cm.
  Bibliography: p.
  Includes index.
  ISBN 0-04-445159-8. — ISBN 0-04-445160-1 (soft)
  1. Victims of crimes. I. Title.
HV6250.25.W35 1989
362.88—dc20
                                  89-34061
                                    CIP

Typeset in 10 on 12 point Goudy and printed in
Great Britain by Billing and Sons, London and Worcester

Contents

Preface and Acknowledgements

The initial impetus for writing this book came from a general awareness of the way in which the victim of crime was increasingly figuring on academic, political and policy agendas. The actual motivation came not only from a real interest in these developments but from the opportunity to participate in the development of a new degree with colleagues within the School of Humanities and Social Science at Liverpool Polytechnic during 1986–7. Indulging what may have seemed a whim, they encouraged me to develop a course within the proposed Criminal Justice Degree on 'victimology'. In so doing Mike Brogden, Peter Gill and Joe Sim particularly contributed to the formulation of my thinking on that course, from which the ideas for this book subsequently emerged. My interest, however, in victims of crime, has a slightly longer history to it.

It began when, after several attempts to launch some research in the area, George Murphy (then chair of the South Liverpool Victim Support Scheme) opened the doors of victim support to me. Thanks are due to George for this and to victim support on Merseyside in general for sustaining my involvement in this area (and for the help they offered when we were subsequently 'victimized'). However, we may have ideas and motivation, but without a publisher we are unlikely to get very far. I would also like to acknowledge the support and help of Gordon Smith at Unwin Hyman, who took my act of bravado in Sheffield, July 1987, in showing him a rather sketchy outline, seriously, and who has since sustained a *real* interest in this project, uncommon, I am told, amongst editors.

In the process of writing I am indebted to a number of people. At the top of the list must be Tony Jefferson who has read and commented on almost every chapter in its draft form. His sustained critical comment was always valued, even if sometimes I did not like what he said! Other thanks are due to Mike Levi for responding to a request for information on victims of fraud. I apologize now, Mike, if I have used this in a way you would think inappropriate. Thanks are also due to Peter McMylor for loaning me his file of *Northern Echo* cuttings on the Cleveland child abuse crisis and for saying encouraging things in my subsequent attempt at tackling the victimization of children. Last, but by no means least, a mention is due to Mike Brogden who listened when the motivation to get on with the task in hand, waned.

The demand to complete this on a fairly tight schedule took its toll domestically as 'mother' pursued her 'obsession'. My children Lisa, Kenneth and Jessica always ensured that both they and I would be survivors and not victims of this project as did my partner, David. Thanks are also due to Billy (who always wanted to be mentioned in a book) and Carolyn Edwards who sometimes kept them all entertained while I fed the word processor. As always, the author takes full responsibility for what appears in the pages which follow.

Introduction

Despite the fact that the 'discipline' of victimology (the study of the relationship between victims and offenders) was founded in the late 1940s, the victim of crime has been largely neglected.

It is almost a commonplace to observe that there is now, however an increasing interest in victims of crime. This interest is not purely academic, though as shall be seen the academic world displays the same increasing interest. The concern with and, in some cases, for victims of crime is also reflected within the wider community of policy initiation and implementation as well as within the political arena. The purpose of this text is to examine this interest, both academic, political and policy; to assess its strengths and weaknesses and to equip the reader with a critical approach to the issues involved. A useful place with which to begin such an exploration is the kind of 'common-sense' knowledge we all have concerning victims of crime.

'Common sense' may equip us with a number of different images of the victim of crime. We usually think of a victim of 'mugging' as being someone elderly, usually female, who has been physically attacked in the course of being robbed. We think of burglary as either constituting the ransacking of an empty house during the day or an act of premeditated stealth during the night. We think of the victim of rape as being a female, usually young, who fought 'within an inch of her life' to resist her attacker (who was a stranger and attacked in a public place). These common-sense images have a number of common features. One of these features is the image of the victim they portray. It is not enough to be a victim of street crime; it is necessary to be an elderly, injured victim of street crime. In other words, someone who we assume could not defend themself. It is not enough to be a victim of rape; it is also necessary to show that in no way did one's own behaviour contribute to the event and that one fought strenuously to prevent its happening. Victims of a burglary may have to 'prove' to an insurance company that they took adequate preventive measures against such an event. Thus these common-sense conceptions indicate that in order to achieve the status of victim we must show that we have a legitimate claim: that is, that in no way did our own behaviour contribute to or exacerbate our victimization. This process of claiming legitimacy is enshrined in the notion of the 'innocent victim'. The more innocent a victim can show themself to be, the greater their legitimate claim for victim status.

As the following chapters unfold, the extent to which these questions of legitimacy and innocence have influenced both explanations of victimization and policy initiatives for victims will become clear. Chapter 3, for example, examines the notion of childhood innocence and its relationship to traditional explanations of child abuse. Chapter 5 raises the question of legitimacy when considering the nature of the claims made to the Criminal Injuries Compensation Board. The notions of 'legitimacy' and 'innocence', however, embrace a further process; that is, how the victimizing event is to be explained. If individuals can establish legitimate claims to the victim status, that is, possess the required qualities of innocence, it cannot be argued that they have precipitated their victimization. Thus, in circumstances where individuals cannot display the required qualities the explanation for their victimization may lie in their own behaviour; hence the notion of victim precipitation. For example, such a view of victimization was translated as 'contributory negligence' on the part of the female by Judge Bertrand Richards in January 1982 in passing a light sentence on a rapist.

Victim precipitation views of victimization not only relate to our common-sense images of the victim and some of the policy initiatives which have been constructed on behalf of victims of crime; they have also pervaded the academic study of victims of crime. Chapter 1 will examine the development of the academic study of victimology with particular reference to a critical evaluation of the concept of victim precipitation. But as we shall see, it is an image of victimization and crime prevention which still has considerable influence.

Our common-sense images of victims of crime have introduced us to a number of ideas which will be developed within this text. A further dimension to those images is reflected in the particular characteristics victims are assumed to have; victims of street crime are the *elderly*, for example. We shall be concerned to examine to what extent our common-sense knowledge matches with the available evidence on patterns of victimization.

Much of the early theoretical and empirical work within the field of victimology was conducted on the basis of officially recorded information. (See Wolfgang, 1958, on victim precipitation, for example, discussed in the next chapter.) Like criminologists, victimologists were unaware as to the 'true' incidence of crime or victimization; commonly referred to as the 'dark figure of crime'. The development of the criminal victimization survey has done much to change this situation. The first criminal victimization survey was conducted in 1966 in the United States, but this sample survey approach to uncovering the nature and extent of victimization has been much more widely utilized since then. It is now a regular feature of crime statistics in the United States, with surveys having been conducted in Canada, Australia, the Netherlands and the United Kingdom. The first of these in the United Kingdom was conducted on a relatively small scale by Sparks, Genn and Dodd (1977); and though the General Household Survey had included a question about domestic burglary since 1972, it was not until 1982 that the first British Crime Survey was conducted. This was repeated in 1984 and again in 1988.

Later to emerge, the British Crime Survey has not been without impact (particularly argued by Mayhew and Hough, 1988) and as with the information from other criminal victimization surveys has done much to fill out the picture of that 'dark figure of crime'. This does not necessarily imply that data gained in this way do not have associated difficulties. (See Chapter 2 for a detailed discussion of these methodological problems.) It has meant that an overall picture of the nature and extent of criminal victimization can be constructed looking to how that picture changes over time as well as gathering data on how people experience the police, their attitudes towards their offenders, general questions on lifestyle and more recently questions relating to particular policy initiatives involving victims and potential victims of crime (victim support schemes and neighbourhood watch, for example.)

This overall picture of criminal victimization has been important for a number of reasons. A data set is now available which informs us not only on the extent of criminal victimization, but also on the extent which goes unreported and on what kind of crime goes unreported. We now know, for example, that nearly all car thefts are reported and that the extent of serious crime which goes unreported is far less than people imagine or than the press would have us believe. (See the reports of the first and second British Crime Surveys, by Hough and

Mayhew 1983 and 1985.) However, it is also clear that much crime which comes into the category of sexual offence or personal violence which takes place in the home remains unreported. (See Chapters 2 and 3.) It is also clear that from this data alone the common-sense knowledge we have of victims of crime comes under some challenge. We can now state fairly clearly that the victim of personal violence in the street is most likely to be a young male who goes out drinking two or three times a week, not the elderly female we described at the beginning of this introduction. Having this clear information is not necessarily sufficient to undermine our common-sense knowledge since we may assume that the young male, not being frail, may also not be innocent. The assumptions which underpin the concepts of 'victim precipitation' and 'lifestyle' discussed in Chapter 1 may be one way in which our common-sense knowledge is sustained. However, as we shall see, our common-sense thinking about victims is very deep-rooted and may take more than just better information to shake off. Such deep-rooted assumptions are challenged by the feminist movement.

The feminist movement has contributed much to sociology and latterly criminology in encouraging a development of an understanding of the way in which patriarchy plays its part in sustaining some of the deep-rooted assumptions we have concerning women in general and the relationship between gender, crime and victimization in particular. Feminism has challenged particularly the victim precipitation view of crime with respect to rape (Chapter 1) and has contributed significantly to our understanding and explanation of child abuse (Chapter 3). It is also a movement which has influenced a more radical employment of the criminal victimization survey: the local crime survey.

The local crime survey approach, of which there have now been several examples, has been most notably influenced by the 'new realism' on Merseyside (Kinsey, 1984) and Islington (Jones, MaClean and Young, 1986) and by the feminist movement in the survey by Hall (1985). These empirical investigations have attempted to employ the criminal victimization survey approach much more sensitively in order to address a number of issues. First, they try to tease out a more accurate picture of the levels of sexual violence perpetrated against women. This has involved a commitment towards encouraging women to talk about their experiences of violence and has included within the survey's frame of reference that violence which occurs in the home as well as that occurring on the street. Thus these surveys claim to have addressed the questions raised by the feminist movement concerning the general statistical picture, whether official or survey-based, of violence against women. Secondly, they include a commitment to explore racial dimensions to crime, particularly racial harassment. Thirdly, they include a commitment to unfolding in greater detail the class dimensions to criminal victimization. Strategies have been employed to explore all these issues within a specifically local context; that context to date having been primarily the inner city.

This local approach has challenged the statistical baldness of the national survey approach which has a tendency to leave the impression that, for the most part, people's fears of crime are irrational. The 'new realist' approach aims to show that when examined in a local framework, with the issues indicated above in mind, people's fear of crime is anything but irrational. (See Young, 1988a on fear of crime; see the next two chapters for a fuller discussion of both the framework of the 'new realism' and the findings of the local survey approach.) This development has been a useful addition to understanding the nature and incidence of crime. It has been particularly useful in giving a clearer picture of how that criminal victimization may be concentrated and what that concentration might mean. It also significantly challenges some elements of the common-sense knowledge with which we started; at the end of this text it is hoped that the reader will have a different view of who is most likely to be a victim of violent crime, for example. However, both the national and the local survey approaches tell us little about two forms of victimization which for the most part still remain hidden from public view: the victimization of children and victimization by corporations.

The victimization of children, more commonly referred to as child abuse, is an all too common issue which receives media attention, particularly when the statutory services fail in their duty to protect a child from such abuse. Chapter 3 will be concerned to develop a view that such abuse, whilst difficult to measure and monitor, is a much more widespread phenomenon than perhaps we would care to believe. The reaction to the situation in Cleveland in 1987 is perhaps an indicator of our reluctance to accept the view that child sexual abuse is a much more common experience than official statistics portray. This chapter will offer a framework in which to understand our reluctance to see child abuse as a more prevalent problem as well as to understand the issue itself.

Chapter 4 moves from children to focus our attention on the victimizing activities of large corporations. Bhopal, for example, was seen largely as an accident, but Jones (1988) argues that technological and management issues made a gas leak almost inevitable.

This example highlights a number of reasons for considering the activities of business corporations. The first is that such activities do not normally figure in our everyday conceptions of victims of crime. They are even less likely than children to appear in such images. Secondly, they are activities which cannot be covered by the survey method and have therefore to some extent been neglected within the wider interest in victims of crime. Thirdly (and this is related to an explanation of the first two reasons), this is victimizing behaviour which for the most part goes on behind our backs. Common-sense knowledge is much more likely to tell us that victims of corporate activity are victims of disasters or accidents rather than victims of criminal activity. So if our attention was focused solely on what common sense tells us we would be in danger of neglecting these activities.

> Despite the scope of white collar crime and despite the fact that its depredations far exceed those of conventional crime it is totally left out of victim campaigns. And so are other socially harmful actions such as pollution of the environment, the production of hazardous substances, the manufacture and sale of unsafe products, and so on, although they cause more death, injury, and harm than all violent crime combined. (Fattah, 1986, p. 5)

It is not only that such issues have been left out of victim campaigns; victimology itself has neglected to explore and theorize this aspect of criminal victimization. In addition such issues lead to a consideration of the connections between the questions of criminal victimization and human rights explored more fully in Chapter 6.

So from discussing the findings of both the national and local surveys, this text will move into taking a closer look at both these forms of victimization, and will, it is hoped, offer some suggestions as to why they remain hidden from view and hidden from our common-sense thinking of the crime victim. However, this text is not only concerned with challenging our common-sense knowledge of victims of crime and adding to that knowledge, it is also concerned to analyse the political and policy initiatives which have emerged focusing on victims of crime.

Introduction

Both the major political parties had statements concerning services for victims of crime in their 1987 political manifestos. The current government has recently reinforced this political commitment in the form of funds for the National Association of Victim Support Schemes (NAVSS). It is the growth of this national association which illustrates the increasing practical and policy interest in victims of crime. It has grown from 30 schemes in 1979 to over 300 in 1987 (Maguire and Pointing, 1988, p. 4). It was much earlier, 1964 to be precise, when the United Kingdom became one of the first countries to establish a policy commitment to victims of crime in the form of the Criminal Injuries Compensation Board. The victim movement has gained considerable momentum since then. This momentum has not always been uniform across Europe. Van Dijk (1988) clearly indicates that victim initiatives have been concentrated in the United States, the United Kingdom, Canada, the Netherlands and France. In much of southern Europe there is little available to meet the needs of victims of crime.

> In the South of Europe another picture emerges. No state compensation funds have been established in Portugal, Spain, Italy or Greece. Victim assistance schemes are virtually unknown, too, mainly comprised of a few centres for victims of rape or spouse abuse. In the courts, however, the presence of the victim is very pronounced. Few victims in Greece, Spain, or Italy will abstain from suing their attackers for civil damages during criminal trial. In many cases the victim will express an opinion about the penal sentence as well. In this respect, crime victims in the south of Europe do not fit the academic stereotypes of the 'forgotten party'. (Van Dijk, 1988, p. 125)

In the United Kingdom the position of the victim has, historically, taken a very different path from that described above by Van Dijk. Chapter 5 reviews that history, contextualizing the current position of the victim in the criminal justice system.

The victim movement not only lacks uniformity across national boundaries; within the United Kingdom itself there are different strands to that movement. Chapter 6 will document the two main strands of the victim movement which are concerned to offer a service to victims of crime, namely, the initiatives which stem from the feminist movement and those which are related to the victim support movement. This chapter will also be concerned to document the current issues with which the victim support movement is involved and the question of that involvement with respect to human rights.

The victim support movement and the feminist movement are not the only sources of practical support in which the victim of crime figures. In the context of crime prevention a range of agencies and initiatives figures, all of which may make different assumptions about the victim of crime. At this level, the more that has been uncovered about the incidence of criminal victimization and the more it has been realized that the police cannot 'solve' the recorded levels of crime, the more attention has been paid to crime prevention, particularly in the form of harnessing the community in such strategies. Chapter 7 will pay particular attention to unwrapping the assumptions behind crime prevention strategies from the viewpoint of the victim of crime.

This text will then move from challenging our common-sense knowledge about victims of crime, to developing that knowledge, to furthering that knowledge in the general political and policy arena. Challenging our common-sense knowledge is of crucial importance if we are to move the interests of victims beyond individual victim blaming or community blaming to a level at which we can identify that victimization which we cannot always see, as well as that which we can. The purpose of this text is to encourage that deeper vision.

The chapters which follow, whilst addressing these various issues, can it is hoped be read separately or as part of an unfolding thesis. Chapter 1 is essentially an introduction to the concepts which have informed the theoretical thinking of those involved in victim-oriented research. Chapter 2 concerns itself with the methodological difficulties of measuring criminal victimization and then proceeds to review what is known about the extent, nature and impact of being a crime victim. Chapters 3 and 4 unfold two issues not covered by the criminal victimization survey: namely the victimization of children and victimization by corporations. These two chapters will also be concerned with the methodological difficulties of measuring victimization of this sort as well as proceeding to offer a review of what is known about and an explanation of victimization of this sort. The next two chapters change track a little and move to looking at first of all the position of the victim in the criminal justice system both historically and contemporaneously and then the role of the voluntary sector in providing for the victim of crime. These two chapters will be concerned to develop further the current position of the victim in society. Chapter 7 will be concerned with the assumptions which underpin crime prevention initiatives from a victim-oriented perspective. To conclude, a review of the questions raised by the text will be offered in the context of the recent concerns of victim-oriented research.

1
Key concepts in victimology: an overview

Introduction

The main purpose of this chapter is to equip the reader with an overall appreciation of the concepts which have informed the work of those who have addressed the question of the victim of crime. In so doing it is necessarily going to be selective in the material presented but it is hoped that that selection will equip the reader with enough knowledge to address these concepts critically. An attempt will be made to pay some attention to the historical development of victimological work, beginning with the ideas of Von Hentig and Mendelsohn and ending by addressing the current work which has been informed by interest in the victim. In this way it is hoped to contextualize the empirical findings of the criminal victimization research; the focus of Chapter 2. We shall begin by examining early victimological work which was concerned to construct victim typologies.

Victim typologies

The usual place with which to begin an overview of victimology is with the work of Von Hentig, and this overview is no exception. Von Hentig's book *The Criminal and his Victim* (1948) was in fact intended as a textbook in criminology. In the last chapter of this book he considers some of the ways in which the victim plays a role in the perpetration of a crime. He states that:

> Experience tells us that ... relationships between perpetrator and victim are much more intricate than the rough distinctions of criminal law. Here are two human beings. As soon as they draw

1

near to one another, male or female, young or old, rich or poor, ugly or attractive – a wide range of interactions, repulsions as well as attractions, is set in motion. What the law does is to watch the one who acts and the one who is acted upon. By this external criterion, subject and object, a perpetrator and a victim are distinguished. In sociological and psychological quality the situation may be completely different. It may happen that the two distinct categories merge. There are cases in which they are reversed and in the long chain of causative forces the victim assumes the role of determinant. (von Hentig, 1948, pp. 383–4, quoted by Sparks, 1982, pp. 1920)

This rather lengthy quote more than adequately encapsulates the concerns which von Hentig was interested in. His approach focused on the role of the victim in the perpetration of a criminal event. In so doing he was primarily interested in how the victim may contribute to the creation of a crime. In pursuing this interest he created thirteen classes of victim: the young, the female, the old, the mentally defective, immigrants, those belonging to 'minorities', 'dull normals', the depressed, the acquisitive, the wanton, the lonesome and heartbroken, the tormentor and the 'fighting' victim (see von Hentig, 1948, last chapter). These classes refer to psychological as well as sociological variables which can be related to situations or persons. There is no necessary inference that von Hentig is suggesting some people are born victims. There are perhaps clearer tendencies within his work towards a notion of 'victim proneness': that some people and some situations are more likely to constitute the circumstances in which victimization occurs. (This theme will be returned to.) It must be noted that this typology, and the one which follows, were both speculative. They were not constructed on the basis of empirical evidence, unlike some of the work to be discussed, but were probably intended as a spur to further research.

Mendelsohn's typology (quoted in Schafer, 1976, p. 154) classifies victims with respect to their culpability for a crime. By this Mendelsohn appears to be referring to the extent to which the victim made a 'guilty contribution to the crime' (ibid.). This notion of culpability adds some weight to the extent to which the victim contributes to the perpetration of crime. It is a notion which moves away from simply describing the variables which contribute to a situation, to, by implication, assigning responsibility for the occurrence of an event. This notion of making victims responsible, to whatever extent, for their own victimization, 'blaming the victim', has been a considerably problematic one for victimology as will be seen below. (It is likely that the legal background from which Mendelsohn came led him to using this term without, perhaps, appreciating the consequences it might have outside the legal setting.)

Mendelsohn had six categories, ranging from the 'completely innocent' (such as young children) to the 'most guilty victim' (such as the aggressor who is subsequently killed). As later chapters will illustrate, whilst problematic, this notion of culpability, or the assignation of guilt and innocence, is a powerful concept in explanations of, particularly violent, criminal incidents. It takes on a particularly powerful and emotive form in the concept of 'victim precipitation'.

Victim precipitation

The concept of 'victim precipitation' was formulated most precisely by Wolfgang (1958) in his book *Patterns in Criminal Homicide*. He offers this definition of the concept:

> The term victim precipitation is applied to those criminal homicides in which the victim is a direct, positive precipitator in the crime. The role of the victim is characterised by his having been the first in the homicide drama to use physical force directed against his subsequent slayer. The victim precipitated cases are those in which the victim was the first to show and use a deadly weapon, to strike a blow in altercation – in short, the first to commence the interplay of resort to physical violence. (Quoted by Fattah, 1979, p. 202)

Using this definition Wolfgang classified 26 per cent of the cases of criminal homicide he studied from police records as being victim precipitated. He concluded his study by arguing that his evidence supported the view postulated by von Hentig that, in some instances, the victim was the determinant of criminal events.

Several researchers subsequently subjected Wolfgang's notion of victim precipitation to further empirical investigation in cases of homicide. Others attempted to apply the concept to other crimes involving interpersonal violence. Hindelang, Gottfredson and Garofalo (1978) suggest from their survey results that the rate of injury was much greater for victims who used force as a 'self-protective' measure than for those who did not and that the younger people and males were most likely to do this. They do not go on to give the notion of victim precipitation any great prominence in their theorizing, however. Normandeau (1968) changed the concept somewhat so that it could be applied to the crime of robbery. He argued that some victims created, through their own behaviour, 'temptation-opportunity situations' (ibid., p. 110) which precipitated the crime. In addition there have been attempts made to use this concept in the context of rape.

Amir's study of rape developed the notion of victim-precipitation in a very broad fashion:

> the victim actually – or so it was interpreted by the offender – agreed to sexual relations but retracted ... or did not resist strongly enough when the suggestion was made by the offender. The term also applies to cases in which the victim enters vulnerable situations charged sexually. (Amir, 1971, p. 262 quoted by Morris, 1987, p. 173)

Using this broad definition, Amir could identify only 19 per cent of his sample of cases known to the police as being victim-precipitated. Apart from the empirical difficulties of this study, relying on officially recorded reports of rape, feminists have been particularly concerned to point out the way in which the notion of victim precipitation builds on the commonly held view that the victim of rape must have 'asked for it'.

There are considerable dangers inherent in giving academic legitimacy to such a view which, it has been well established, carries considerable weight from the police handling of rape, through to the cases which reach the courts (there translated as 'contributory negligence', see Jeffreys and Radford, 1984). This culminates in the impact such a view has on women who have been raped. They blame themselves. Which is hardly surprising, since everyone else has blamed them too. These dangers stem from translating a fairly precisely formulated concept focused on criminal homicide to a much more broadly and loosely defined notion applied to rape. Fattah (1979) argues that the fact that the concept may have been poorly formulated and loosely operationalized does not offer grounds for dismissing its validity. He suggests that the concept, as originally formulated by Wolfgang (1958), is sound. He goes on to suggest that the concept itself meets a need to understand, dynamically, why a particular crime occurred, in a particular context against a particular victim.

Whilst appealing for greater clarity of definition in the use of the concept, Fattah (1979) is also aware that some of the problems associated with the use of this concept derive from the way in which terms such as 'guilt' and 'culpability' have been used in victimological writing. (See Mendelsohn, for example above.) Fattah states:

> The use of explanatory concepts such as victim-precipitated, victim-facilitated, victim-initiated, victim-induced, and victim-invited criminality to describe the victim's role in the causative process should in no way be interpreted as an attempt on the part of the social scientist to blame the victim or to hold him responsible for the crime. (Fattah, 1979, p. 202.)

In some senses this defence of victim precipitation is couched in very traditional social scientific terms of value freedom. Social scientists are not to be held responsible for the way in which others might read the work they produce. In its own terms such a defence is perfectly logical. Fortunately, an increasing number of social scientists, many of them feminists, have found it impossible to engage in the issues pertinent to social science without being cognisant of the way in which the social scientific enterprise displays a particular, male-dominated way of viewing the world. They have thus striven to develop conceptual frameworks more in keeping with a social science which embraces value commitment rather than value freedom; that is, a commitment to recognize the hidden assumptions underpinning the construction of theory and practice which do not relate to women's experiences but only to men's. In this way concepts such as victim precipitation are severely criticized for the way in which they lead to blaming the victim whether that was the intention or not. That most of those who would reject such a concept in the context of rape, in particular, are also feminists is, of course, no accident. That others still regard the concept as having some value will be illustrated later in this chapter and will also be a recurring theme of subsequent chapters.

There is, however, a further problem with the concept of victim precipitation, particularly associated with Fattah's (1979) defence of it. If its value lies in its ability to explain why this particular victim was victimized in these particular circumstances, then, in these terms, it does not take the explanatory potential of victimology very far. Victimology remains confined to offering explanations of individual events by reference to their individual precipitating characteristics.

It cannot, by relying on this concept, offer explanations of recurring patterns of victimization.

The next key concept to be considered here takes as its frame of reference personal crime; but attempts to develop a conceptual framework with which to understand such patternings. This is the notion of lifestyle.

Lifestyle and victimization

Hindelang, Gottfredson and Garofalo (1978) constitute the main proponents of the lifestyle approach to victimization. This concept is intended to relate a series of hypotheses concerning the nature of personal victimization. A series of hypotheses, it is argued, are grounded in victimization data. Garofalo (1986) points to the similarities of this approach to that of Cohen and Felson (1979) who proposed a 'routine activity' approach to victimization. The main focus of attention will be directed here, however, to the work of Hindelang, Gottfredson and Garofalo.

The proponents of the lifestyle approach are keen to point out that they are presenting a model of personal victimization in which the concept of lifestyle refers to 'routine daily activities, both vocational activities (work, school, keeping house, etc.) and leisure activities' (Hindelang, Gottfredson and Garofalo, 1978, p. 241). The model proposes that any individual is constrained by role expectations and structural characteristics, the nature of which will be connected to demographic variables: age, sex, race, etc. Individuals adapt to these constraints and their adaptations are reflected in their daily routines; lifestyle. There is a direct link, the proponents argue, between an individual's routine daily activities and exposure to high-risk victimization situations. Personal victimization follows from such high-risk exposure. (For a more detailed discussion of these assumptions and the concept of lifestyle, see ibid., pp. 241–50.) For personal victimization to occur, it is argued that several factors must come together:

> First, the prime actors – the offender and the victim – must have occasion to intersect in time and space. Second, some source of dispute or claim must arise between the actors in which the victim is perceived by the offender as an appropriate object of the victimization. Third, the offender must be willing and able

to threaten or use force (or stealth) in order to achieve the desired end. Fourth, the circumstances must be such that the offender views it as advantageous to use or threaten force (or stealth) to achieve the desired end. The probability of these conditions being met is related to the life circumstances of members of society. (ibid., p. 250)

This general picture of the conditions to be met for a personal victimization to occur is detailed by eight propositions. At the risk of boring the reader, there is some value in listing these propositions.

(1)   The probability of suffering a personal victimization is directly related to the amount of time that a person spends in public places (e.g. on the street, in parks, etc.) and particularly in public places at night.

(2)   The probability of being in public places, particularly at night, varies as a function of lifestyle.

(3)   Social contacts and interactions occur disproportionately among individuals who share similar lifestyles.

(4)   An individual's chances of personal victimization are dependent upon the extent to which the individual shares demographic characteristics with offenders.

(5)   The proportion of time an individual spends among non-family members varies as a function of lifestyle.

(6)   The probability of personal victimization, particularly personal theft, increases as a function of the proportion of time that an individual spends among non-family members.

(7)   Variations in lifestyle are associated with variations in the ability of individuals to isolate themselves from persons with offender characteristics.

(8)   Variations in lifestyle are associated with variations in the convenience, the desirability and the vincibility of a person as a target for personal victimizations.
(For a fuller discussion of each of these propositions see ibid., pp. 250–66.)

Before examining in detail the relative strengths and weaknesses of these propositions, it may be of value to consider what one of the proponents of the model sees as the major weaknesses of the model and how they might be addressed.

Garofalo (1986) suggests three main weaknesses in the original lifestyle model. First, that the lifestyle concept suggests hypotheses which are true by definition and therefore trivial. Someone who does not go out cannot be exposed to street crime and is therefore very unlikely to be a victim of such an incident. Garofalo suggests two responses to this weakness. The first involves employing a distinction made by Gottfredson (1981) between absolute exposure to risk and probabilistic exposure to risk. The first of these is necessary for a victimization to occur; there must be some form of contact between a person (or property) and an offender for a victimizing incident to take place. However, such events do not happen every time a person (or property) comes into contact with an offender. Other factors must be present for the incident to happen at a given place and given time. This is probabilistic exposure. It is the process of this probabilistic exposure that the concept of lifestyle can elucidate. The second response, he suggests, is to use the lifestyle concept as a way of assessing levels of risk which are above or below the average norm for society, suggesting the work of Smith (1982) as an illustration of this approach.

The second criticism addressed by Garofalo (1986) suggests that the lifestyle concept is so vague as to be unfalsifiable. Garofalo's answer to this criticism is less than convincing. He recommends that the concept be more rigorously defined and that adequate theory testing take place in the context of victimization surveys. The problem here is how it might be possible to operationalize the concept of lifestyle so that it avoids being vague and yet at the same time is meaningful. Questions can be, and have been, asked concerning drinking habits and use of public transport, for example, and subsequently related to chances of victimization; but do questions such as these relay anything meaningful with respect to lifestyle? In other words, are daily or weekly routine activities necessarily the complete lifestyle picture? (This comment is developed more fully below.)

The third criticism he addresses suggests that the lifestyle approach is inadequate for policy initiatives. It is not possible to argue convincingly that people should change their lifestyles. (Though some do; see Chapter 7.) Garofalo lists a number of ways in which public policy impinges upon lifestyle and subsequently would feed into the lifestyle-exposure model (ibid., pp. 151–2).

The main modifications suggested by Garofalo in the light of these criticisms of the lifestyle model include heightening the way in which structural constraints are related to the associations people make which

8

may not be necessarily mediated by lifestyle. This requires making a closer examination of the way in which economic variables, for example, are related to housing opportunities which may relate to associations and risk. He also includes consideration of 'reactions to crime' – fear, evaluation of risk, beliefs about crime – as being a further dimension to appreciating lifestyle and exposure. Finally he suggests that two factors, target attractiveness and personal idiosyncrasies, which are unrelated to lifestyle, need to be placed somewhere in the equation which culminates in a victimizing event.

So, whilst Garofalo's (1986) modifications to the lifestyle model may or may not meet the criticisms he considers have been made of it, the question as yet unanswered is what do we make of this type of empirically grounded theoretical approach to the study of victimization? Its first strength lies in the fact that it is an empirically grounded approach. Its concepts and propositions are derived from data and can be used to inform further data-gathering processes. This statement is not intended as an empty comment. It is clear that the lifestyle-exposure model has enabled sense to be made of empirical observations which 'common sense' might dictate as being contradictory. Proposition 4, for example, which states that the chances of personal victimization are related to the extent to which the victim shares demographic characteristics with the offender, might, on the surface, contradict common sense. After all, victims are innocent and offenders are evil and it is often assumed that these two can be differentiated in ways additional to the legal relationship they have with one another. Victims of burglary, for example, are home owners with something of great value to steal. Victims of street crime are defenceless, elderly people more often than not female. The evidence suggests otherwise. The first British Crime Survey, informed in some respects by the lifestyle-exposure model, clearly indicates that victims of street crime are young males who go out drinking two or three times a week. (See Hough and Mayhew, 1983, and Chapter 2.) These are also the characteristics of offenders. Information such as this does much to facilitate a questioning of the way in which the matter of legitimate victim status and criminal injuries compensation is addressed (see Chapter 5) even if, to date, it has done little to change this or the way in which the media approach the issue of criminal victimization. Without this empirical base, however, such a questioning process could not begin.

By implication the discussion of the empirical feature of the lifestyle model has also drawn on its second strength: the requirement to be empirically informed as accurately as possible. This approach was concomitant with the move away from relying on officially recorded crime as a data source for victimology as well as for criminology. Thus whilst Wolfgang's conceptualization of victim precipitation was applied to officially recorded homicides, the lifestyle-exposure model of criminal victimization was created from data from criminal victimization surveys. The advantages and disadvantages of the survey method in the context of criminal behaviour are discussed in great detail in the next chapter; suffice it to say here that the availability of the lifestyle-exposure model makes it possible to examine fairly complex relationships in personal victimization, household victimization and multiple victimization. It is arguably the case that the criminal victimization survey might look considerably impoverished without the theoretically informative approach of this model. This does not of course mean that the survey approach as conceived by the Home Office is not without its limitations (see below). But merely to suggest that its value, particularly in policy terms, might have been less without the work of Hindelang, Gottfredson and Garofalo.

The third strength of this model lies with the realistic and questioning policy implications which can be derived from it. Garofalo (1986) lists some of these implications; encouraging the elderly in greater participation in the community might also result in their greater exposure to risk and subsequent victimization, developing policies to include women positively in the workforce might also expose them to greater risks as conceived by the model. Implications such as these are challenging because they clearly indicate that policy, lifestyle and exposure to risk are connected and that those connections do not necessarily have to be explored to the detriment of lifestyle; that is, by inhibiting lifestyle. They do demand that the challenges of such policy initiatives need to be considered in terms of the equation suggested by the model rather than in a vacuum; and that some of the implications of that process may not be very palatable but, nevertheless, have to be considered (see below).

The final strength of the model can best be appreciated by comparing it with the concept of victim precipitation discussed above. It has been seen that victim precipitation offers a rather individualistic framework for understanding victimization. The event is to be explained by reference to the victim, the offender and what passed between them. Whilst this framework may permit the creation of types of events which can be couched in terms of the nature of their precipitation and the roles played by the parties involved, rather like the creation of precedents in the legal sense, it does not permit the insertion of variables which lie beyond the control of the participants, variables which the lifestyle-exposure model refers to as structural constraints. These constraints – the family, the economic system, for example – are beyond the control of the individual (though the lifestyle model suggests that individuals adapt to them) and yet are, nevertheless, precursors to their being in a particular place at a particular time precipitating or not precipitating a particular event. Whilst it may be possible to dispute the way in which Hindelang, Gottfredson and Garofalo (1978) have postulated the nature of these constraints, they are nevertheless present. This constitutes an advance for victimology from the individualistic bias of the victim precipitation approach.

Having considered the main strengths of this approach it is now time to turn to some of its weaknesses. Three will be considered here, none of which was addressed by Garofalo (1986). The first weakness is associated with the concept of lifestyle. It will be recalled that this was defined by reference to the routine daily activities both vocational and pleasurable which people engage in. By implication, it seems, the focus of concern within this model is those features of our routines which are measurable, which can be articulated and of which we are aware. This in itself is reasonable, except that it omits to consider an important feature of everyone's daily activities. It clearly omits that which is taken for granted. In other words that which is so much part of our daily lives that either we do not think to articulate it or we are not even aware of its routine presence. What relevance does this omission have for victimology? In key respects it is crucial. It is crucial for black people who are so used to being routinely subjected to racial harassment that they would not think it worth articulating to an interviewer even if it was recognized by them as being a criminal incident. It is crucial for a woman, routinely subjected to violence by her partner so that again she might not think it to be of relevance in a criminal victimization survey. It is crucial to a child brought up in close relationships which, routinely, involved the criminal victimization of that child. All of these are examples of personal victimization, but personal victimization not handled by the model in part because the conceptualization of lifestyle contained within it has been translated in a way which renders it difficult to get at the processes illustrated. The key problem lies in the interpretation of the concept; lifestyle as a process as opposed to lifestyle as a measurable, objective entity. The process approach addresses questions pertaining to lifestyle which are important for victimology but which the model, as conceived here, cannot address.

This first weakness is closely related to the second. This is most clearly identified in the first proposition of the lifestyle model. This proposition states that the probability of suffering a personal victimization is related to the amount of time a person spends in public places. It clearly emphasizes the public as being the focus of concern for the model. It thus excludes from consideration the extent to which the world of the private, the home, the family, is an arena for personal victimization. This exclusion is further endorsed by proposition 6. This suggests that the more time an individual spends outside the family the greater the chances of personal victimization. The exclusion of the private domain severely limits the lifestyle model in what it can reveal about personal victimization. Work done on child abuse both physical and sexual, and work on domestic violence, both clearly state that the private world is very much an arena in which personal victimization occurs and which is the concern of victimology. (See Chapter 3.) (Feminism has contributed much to our understanding of these processes. Its contribution is discussed more fully below. At this juncture it is sufficient to be aware of the limitations of this particular model.) This limitation carries over into the question of policy. Increased participation of women in the labour force might reduce their overall level of victimization rather than necessarily increase it as Garofalo (1986) seems to imply, if their current levels of victimization in the private domain were included in the equation.

The third weakness to be addressed here stems from the model's functionalist overtones. This is a weakness not peculiar to this particular work within victimology. The model postulates structural constraints, role expectations and the way in which individuals adapt to these. The functionalist overtones are most clearly observed in the notion of adaptation. This implies that individuals, whilst active in the construction of their daily routines, do little to resist or question them. These overtones are derived from the way in which the structural constraints invoked are interpreted by the authors of this approach. The structural constraints are legal, economic, educational, familial. The demographic variables are descriptive categories; race, sex, age, income, marital status, education, occupation. These are not conceived as ageism, sexism, racism. In other words they are not conceived as critically implicated in sustaining a particular power structure in society. They are not ideologically constructed. This is, of course, in keeping with functionalism which would focus, for example, on sex role differentiation and its function in the family rather than sexism. This ultimately functionalist framework is a weakness because it limits our thinking about the process of victimization. Questions of power relationships not only matter in terms of addressing what is conventionally understood as personal victimization (violence in the street rather than the home or the workplace), but also encourage us to rethink the construction of that convention. Garofalo (1986) rightly points out that corporate crimes are excluded from consideration (ibid., p. 149). There is no reason for this to be the case other than that our theorizing fails to include corporate crime as personal victimization. Why it should have been so excluded, in this model, is connected to the way in which the relationship between lifestyle and structural constraints has been conceptualized.

This lifestyle-exposure model of victimization is fairly sophisticated in its theoretical formulation and the hypotheses it generates in terms of crime prevention. It has displayed, and still has potential to display, in great detail, the nature of personal victimization provided that that victimization is understood as that which is publicly identifiable and can be articulated. The model moves forward from victim typologies and the notion of victim precipitation, in setting victimization in a fairly narrowly defined structural context.

From the discussion so far, then, what might be included in a list of key concepts for victimology? Sparks (1982) attempts to construct such a list. Our understanding of the more current issues on victimology's agenda willl progress if some attention is paid to the concepts outlined by Sparks. They constitute what might be termed conventional victimology.

Conventional victimology; key concepts

Sparks (1982) lists six features of the victimization process which he believes to be important at a theoretical level. These six features build on some of the material already highlighted in this discussion and draw together some threads of the more recent developments in victimology.

His list begins with the notion of precipitation. For Sparks this concept is clear enough and could be applied to incidents of interpersonal violence including rape, though there might be some operational difficulties in doing this (ibid., p. 27).

The second feature Sparks refers to as facilitation:

> even if the victim does not take anything that could be called an active part in the crime, he or she may still facilitate its commission by deliberately, negligently or unconsciously placing himself or herself at special risk. (ibid., p. 27)

Sparks likens this notion to that employed by Normandeau (1968). It is a view which suggests that those who fail to protect themselves when they know, for example, that burglary rates in an area are high, are increasing, through their own behaviour, the chances of being burgled (a view increasingly being displayed by insurance companies, who will not, in some areas, agree to house contents insurance cover unless preventive measures, stated by the company, are undertaken by the client).

The third notion listed by Sparks is the notion of vulnerability. This notion is derivable from some of the classes of victims listed by von Hentig. It refers to a state in which the victims do nothing to put themselves at special risk but find themselves at risk because of the attributes they possess: being frail, being very young, etc. There are, however, different categories of vulnerability: ecological vulnerability, to do with the environment, similar it seems to Oscar Newman's 'defensible space'; status vulnerability, to do with belonging to a particular group in society; or role vulnerability, to do with particular situations from which withdrawal is not easy. This notion and the former one of facilitation are both related to the fourth in Sparks's list; namely opportunity.

Sparks (1982) states that 'an absence of opportunity is a sure-fire method of crime prevention' (ibid., p. 29). At one level the absence or presence of opportunity is obvious; without video recorders there would be no video recorder thefts. The notion of opportunity also implies, however, risk management behaviour. An old person who rarely goes out is unlikely to be a victim of street crime. It is in this sense that Sparks regards the notion of opportunity as having explanatory potential, rather like the lifestyle concept of the previous discussion.

The fifth characteristic listed by Sparks (1982) is attractiveness. Some houses are more attractive than others to prospective burglars;

namely those in which there is little opportunity for surveillance and access appears easy. (See Bennett and Wright, 1984; the case for subsequent 'target hardening' is made by Forrester, Chatterton and Pease, 1988.) Some, it appears, promote such attractiveness in the form of conspicuous displays of wealth. (See Nkpa, 1976.) Ultimately an attractive target is one which promises greater benefits to the offender.

The last feature of victimization discussed by Sparks he calls impunity. By this he means that some people are chosen as victims precisely because they are less likely to report an incident; homosexuals, for example.

The point of this list as far as Sparks is concerned lies in the features' usefulness to explain:

> variations in proneness to victimization among different types of persons, places, organisations, situations etc., where proneness in turn is defined in terms of differences in the a priori probability of victimization or a crime taking place. Thus precipitation, facilitation, vulnerability, opportunity, attractiveness, and impunity all imply the probabilities of crime or victimization are higher with some situations than with others. (Sparks, 1982, p. 33)

Sparks goes on to suggest that these six concepts may be used to analyse changes in victimization rates which may be related to changing lifestyles, social control arrangements, etc. He also evaluates the survey method as a way of addressing these theoretical questions. In particular he goes on to suggest that there are special topics for future research within victimology in which these concepts may be used informatively. Before considering these special topics suggested by Sparks, a brief critical evaluation of his conceptual list will permit a better appreciation of why this might be termed conventional victimology.

There are a number of threads which are intertwined in these concepts. The first thread is that of individual responsibility. This is illustrated in a number of ways. Sparks in discussing the notion of precipitation does so in a fairly broad fashion. For example:

> a woman's husband repeatedly brutalizes her over a long period of time; terrified and distraught, she kills him in his sleep. It

15

does not seem unnatural to regard this as a case of precipitation. (ibid., p. 27)

And:

> It is characteristic of victim-precipitated crimes, of course, that they tend to take place between persons who are known, related, or married – or even friendly – to each other or between persons who have associated together for some period prior to the crime. (ibid.)

This broad understanding would seem to constitute a considerable advance on the way in which the notion of victim precipitation has traditionally been employed. However, the next sentence serves to undermine some of the optimism which might have been generated by this:

> In part, this is a matter of opportunity; persons who never encounter one another cannot (logically) be involved in victim-precipitated crime, or indeed, any other kinds of crime. (ibid.)

So the explanation for this broad range of activities which might be encompassed by the notion of precipitation lies within a further concept: opportunity. And whilst this is again broadly conceived (there can be no cheque card frauds without cheque cards, for example), it does little to advance our knowledge at a level which moves beyond the correlating of particular incidents with particular variables. The concept of facilitation is similarly constructed and so on. In other words, the concepts suggested by Sparks are still rooted in an individualistic frame of reference. A frame of reference which focuses attention on the way in which attributes of an individual's relationships or behaviour either consciously or unconsciously contribute to the person's own victimization, thus implying individual responsibility. (He also suggests that these concepts might be applied to places, locales, or particular situations.) This thread, whilst possibly having advantages in enabling the assessment of particular crime prevention programmes along those same six dimensions, and possibly highlighting the way in which a number of features of the victimization process may interact with one another, still constrains the vision of victimology.

In this way these concepts hold much in common with the lifestyle model. Rather like the lifestyle-exposure model, Sparks has failed to conceptualize the nature and impact of much broader structural features of society, particularly those features which are power-based, which exist above and beyond individual people, places, or situations.

A second thread which runs through these concepts, which again makes them similar to the lifestyle model, is the way in which these concepts lend themselves to policy-oriented initiatives. This second thread derives from the first since policy initiatives are easier to suggest and implement if one makes assumptions concerning the role of the victim in the construction of crime. Again, the victim does not have to be a human being, it can be property. A property's 'attractiveness' can be evaluated, hardened and thus modified. Such a focus moves attention away from the crime-inducing process to the victim creation process. This is a danger of victim-oriented research commented on earlier in the form of 'victim blaming' and by Antilla (1974). It is a danger which is implicit in the range of concepts discussed here. The ultimate problem associated with this danger is its relationship with crime control strategies; is it the victim creation process which must be modified and changed in order to prevent further victimization, or is it the offending process which must be tackled, or is it a mixture of the two? The 'nothing works' view of dealing with offenders may latch on to crime control through victims as an alternative strategy without necessarily considering the implications of that strategy for the victims themselves. (See Chapter 7.) It is important at least to consider this question.

The third thread which runs through this list of concepts stands more as an observation on them. Sparks (1982) uses a number of examples to illustrate these concepts. The examples used by Sparks all come from what can generally be understood and identified as conventional crime; ranging from petty shoplifting through to homicide. None of his examples comes from the arena of corporate criminal activity. It would be interesting to speculate what propositions might look like which incorporate the concepts of precipitation, facilitation, vulnerability, opportunity, attractiveness and impunity in the context of corporate crime. A moment's reflection might suggest some validity in engaging in such speculation. This is really a question of omission on the part of victimology in general rather than a particular criticism of Sparks. His work merely illustrates its conventionality in the examples it uses and how that conventional thinking structures the concerns of victimology in a particular way.

Thus conventional victimology can be seen to consist of three tendencies: a tendency to individualistic analysis of the victim–offender relationship, a tendency to hold the victim responsible to a certain extent especially in terms of policy formation, and a tendency to work within that which is conventionally understood as criminal. To this extent, it reflects some parallels with the 'common-sense' thinking about victims referred to in the introduction. This group of concepts, despite their conventional nature, was used by Sparks to suggest further areas of work of interest to those addressing the question of the victim. It is to an examination of those areas of interest that we now turn.

Issues for further research

Sparks identifies three topics for future research in the area of victimization: multiple victims, high-risk victims and high-harm victims.

Multiple victims (which, for this discussion, also include series victims) pose particular problems for the criminal victimization survey. If the survey is designed to count incidents multiple victims, despite being statistically uncommon, are likely to distort the incidence of victimization to a greater level than would be expected if they were excluded from the survey. If the survey is designed to count households or individuals, how many incidents of victimization for a multiple victim are counted? Despite these computational problems, multiple victims are interesting according to Sparks because they might 'help to illuminate the extent to which attributes of victims themselves may help explain their victimization' (ibid., p. 115).

Genn (1988) tackles the question of multiple victimization from a different viewpoint. She produces an illuminating case study analysis of multiple victimization from the earlier survey conducted by Sparks, Genn and Dodd (1977). In so doing she presents a challenge to the victim survey approach and conventional victimology:

> Our approach could not adequately record or reflect conditions
> of life where fights, verbal abuse, sexual assault, and property
> theft were commonplace, and where the use of violence in
> the resolution of conflict was virtually automatic. In these

social situations, questions like 'Have you been threatened
with violence in the last 12 months?' or 'When did you
last have any contact with the police?' become, frankly, an
embarrassment. (Genn, 1988, p. 99)

This echoes some of the comments made earlier in this chapter in
the context of lifestyle concerning the difficulties in conceptualizing
and capturing what are essentially social processes. The question of
multiple victimization is interesting not so much because it may
illuminate victim attributes, which Sparks suggests, but also because
it causes a rethinking of not only how the survey method may or may
not be employed to identify such victims, but because it illuminates
criminal victimization as a process. A process in which some people
are continuously involved. This kind of awareness has led some to
construct the 'local' crime survey as a way of addressing this issue.
(See below.)
    The second of Sparks's (1982) issues was that of the high-risk victim.
He identifies the high-risk victim by membership of particular types of
institutions. The two which he talks about are prisons and secondary
schools, particularly public schools. In some senses both these institutional types have been subjected to a range of different types of
empirical investigation by sociologists. However, these investigations
have not necessarily concerned themselves directly with criminal
victimization. Sparks argues that in general there is little concern
with the criminal victimization features of 'inmate life'. Crime is a
problem outside the institutional walls. 'Too little is known at present
about the extent to which victimization – not only sexual attacks and
assaults but also robbery, theft, extortion – is a fact of life in prison'
(ibid., p. 128). What is interesting about this observation by Sparks
is not so much the question of what is or is not known about criminal
victimization within institutions (recent feminist research indicates the
extent to which girls may be sexually harassed and victimized by boys
in mixed secondary schools; see Mahoney, 1985) but the fact that in
addressing this issue one of the key questions becomes the patterns of
power and leadership which facilitate such exploitation. One might be
tempted to suggest that this was always the key question whether on the
inside or the outside; the total institutional framework of the prison or
the public school merely renders the processes involved more acute.
    The third issue for Sparks is the high-harm victim; those for
whom the chance of victimization is relatively rare but for whom

the impact might be especially serious. The elderly have frequently been identified as a group for whom it has been traditionally thought that criminal victimization constitutes a serious problem. Mawby (1988a) has attempted to assess the extent to which the elderly might be thought of as a 'high-harm' group. Whilst the evidence does clearly indicate that the elderly are less at risk of criminal victimization than other age groups, with females less at risk than males (ibid., p. 103), however, once victimized, it appears they may perceive themselves as being more vulnerable.

> It is clear from this that the elderly rated the crimes they experienced as more serious, and having a greater effect on them, than did younger victims. Undoubtedly, crimes were more significant intrusions into lives of the elderly than they were for younger respondents; in these terms the elderly were indeed more vulnerable. (ibid., p. 108)

The other group for which there may be the 'high-harm' effects mentioned by Sparks (1982) are children. This group, and the problems associated with the measurement of the criminal victimization of children in the form of child abuse, are the concern of a specific chapter of this book, Chapter 3. Children, however, may also constitute a high-harm group in their reaction to conventional crime. In a small survey conducted by the author, not primarily focused on children, it was found that in households where a victimizing event had occurred, usually a burglary, and where there were children, it was the children who displayed disturbed sleep or behaviour patterns (Walklate, 1984). This has been referred to more recently as 'indirect victimization' (Morgan, 1988) and is currently the topic of a research project.

There are a number of reactions which might be posited to these special topics highlighted by Sparks (1982). Each in its own right is interesting. Taken together, however, they constitute a point at which it is of value to consider the way in which the question of criminal victimization has been tackled outside of this conventional framework particularly when consideration is given to how the question of 'high-harm' victimization of children might be addressed. Feminism has contributed much to our understanding of some of the issues involved in this process and it is to that theme alongside the emergence of the 'new realism' that we shall now turn in beginning to construct an alternative to this conventional victimology.

Feminism and 'new realism'

Feminist research over the last fifteen years or more has revealed a wealth of information concerning women's experiences. One of the themes of feminist research has been women's experiences of male violence. This theme has focused on rape, physical violence in the home and more recently child sexual abuse. Some of the implications of this research have been included in the discussion so far and some are the subject of later chapters in this book. It is the general feminist framework which is of interest at this point.

There are a number of questions which the feminist position raises for victimological research. These questions concern: the concepts of victimology – do the concepts adequately convey women's experiences?; and the measurement process – can the techniques adequately uncover the essential nature of women's daily lives? Feminist research consistently shows that very little of women's experiences of rape and sexual assault, for example, comes to the attention of officialdom. The national crime survey approach has uncovered little more. (The details of this are discussed in the next chapter.) Stanko (1988) talks in detail of the way in which much of the violence against women is hidden from view; from the official agencies and the crime surveys alike. She concludes by stating that

> Unless policing and crime survey researchers lend credence to the concept and reality of gender stratification, violence against women will, on many levels, remain a hidden, but all too real part of women's lives. (ibid., p. 46)

In addition feminist researchers would argue that the formal structured interview strategy, asking questions which focus on the public dimensions of criminal activity, does little to tease out the experiences of women which are of relevance to a criminal victimization survey.

The local crime survey approach claims to have taken to heart the questions posed by feminist research and simultaneously to have constructed an approach which places the victims in their material context (Young, 1988a, p. 173). These local crime surveys have been informed by the 'new realism'. What does this approach imply?

To date, the 'new realism' within criminology has placed the victim at the centre of the stage. Realist criminology, it is argued, embraces the reality of the criminal process: the offender, the victim, informal social control and the state (Jones, MaClean and Young, 1986). To date, most has been heard about the necessity for an 'accurate victimology' (Young, 1986, p. 23) and the way in which it is possible to institute an accurate victimology from 'problems as people experience them' (ibid., p. 24).

Young (1988a) argues that the extent to which crime risk figures conceal or reveal anything about the real incidence of risk is a function of a number of mechanisms. He uses the example of the victimization of women to illustrate the way in which a realist approach would uncover these mechanisms. First it involves recognizing the way in which the actual impact of known crime on women is trivialized: the mechanism of concealment. Secondly, it involves recognizing that the impact of crime on women cannot be assessed without taking into account the levels of sexual harassment women experience: the mechanism of compounding. Thirdly, it involves recognizing that the relative powerlessness of women makes them more unequal victims: the mechanism of vulnerability. Finally, it involves recognizing that crime is a product of a particular set of relationships: the mechanism of patriarchy. (See ibid., pp. 174–5.) The way in which this approach, theoretically informed in this manner, is to be achieved empirically is the local crime survey.

The local crime survey is described in the following way:

> local studies are not only considerably more focussed than the national studies but embrace a much greater part of the whole process of criminalisation – namely the pattern of victimization, the impact of crime, the actual police response to both victim and offender, the public's requirements as to an ideal police response and the public's notions of appropriate penalties for various offences. (Jones, MaClean and Young, 1986, p. 5)

The analysis of such local data is also important. Analysis by subgroup enables the differences in experiences of crime to be more precisely highlighted (Young, 1988a, p. 171). The extent to which this marriage between the new realism and feminism has been applied and has achieved its aims is discussed in detail in the next chapter. The purpose here is to evaluate the differences and the similarities between this approach and conventional victimology.

On the surface the similarities are obvious. Both approaches have focused their efforts in using the survey method, though the new realists would argue that their use of the survey technique is more sensitively and theoretically informed. (Conversely the Home Office would argue that without the British Crime Survey initiative, funding for such local surveys would have been, to say the least, much more difficult to secure; Mayhew and Hough, 1988.) Both have focused for the most part on crime as it is conventionally defined; though again the realists would argue that they have tapped incidents of racial harassment and violence against women more successfully than the Home Office based surveys. One of the key differences between conventional victimology and realist victimology is the political commitment of the latter. This is displayed most strongly in the way in which the data from local surveys is read. (See Chapter 2 and Brogden, Jefferson and Walklate, 1988, Chapter 8.)

The new realist is concerned to see crime through the eyes of the public; to take what the public defines as problems as being the points to tackle. Policy initiatives and suggestions flow from this view of the world. As yet, new realism has told us little about how the state is to be conceptualized in this process, though that is part of the new realist agenda. This has resulted in the observation made by Sim, Scraton and Gordon (1987): that the realist position and the policies which flow from it 'accept rather than challenge the terrain of the powerful ... remaining politically conservative in its conclusions about what can be done about the state' (ibid., p. 59). Much the same observation could be made about conventional victimology. It remains to be seen, in the chapters which follow, how far this marriage between new realism and feminism really embraces the concerns of the latter and how far the former has progressed the cause of crime victims or victimology.

Conclusion

From the concepts and themes discussed here it is hoped that the reader has some appreciation of the issues which, at a theoretical level, have informed victimological research. From this overview it can be seen that whilst some issues have been addressed in a relatively more sophisticated manner and been explored empirically through the use of the criminal victimization survey in a relatively more sophisticated way, some questions have consistently remained untackled by victimology. These questions pertain primarily to the conceptual framework in which victimology has traditionally operated. That framework has been challenged by feminism; by opening up the questions of rape, violence against women and child abuse; and by the new realism in embracing some of the questions raised by feminism and by putting to the fore the material conditions of victimization. These themes have consistently presented themselves as issues which conventional victimology has not fully formulated. There is one remaining question which none of these frameworks has, as yet, adequately addressed; the production of victims through corporate criminal activity. In the chapters which follow it is hoped to document the extent to which both conventionally informed survey work and realist informed survey work have achieved their aims, as well as to address some of the questions which feminism, corporate crime and an historically informed appreciation of the victim pose for victimology.

2
Documenting victimization

Introduction

The purpose of this chapter is to offer a review of the extent and nature of criminal victimization as revealed by the recent survey research. There is no easy way of presenting what is, in the first instance, a mass of statistical data. For the purposes of this review the material will be discussed paying attention to the general incidence of victimization and to the incidence of fear and risk from crime as revealed by these surveys. Additionally some attention will be paid to the overall impact of victimization. First of all, though, some cautionary comments on the difficulties of using the survey method as a way of counting the incidence of criminal victimization.

How well can surveys count victimization?

The question posed assumes that the survey method can count incidents of victimization; we must ask whether or not this is a fair assumption. The criminal victimization survey concerns itself with measuring criminal incidents for which there are clearly identifiable victims. Thus it focuses on crimes against individuals and their property. There are a number of difficulties in using this method for counting, for example, corporate crime, crimes between consenting parties and drug offences, some of which are associated with the requirement in the way in which the technique has been used for identifiable victims. Some would argue that in the cases of homosexuality and drug use the question of there being a victim as such is debatable, since offender and victim are often one and the same person. In the case of corporate crime the difficulty lies in the fact that people are not generally aware of their victimization from this source of criminal behaviour. These sorts of criminal activity do not, for the most part, fit with the crime focus adopted by the criminal victimization survey. It focuses attention on conventional crime: crimes against the person (meaning for the most part 'street crime') and crimes against property. It might be argued, then, that the criminal victimization survey offers a fuller picture of criminal victimization from specified criminal incidents – specified incidents which are also the most likely to be recorded by the police should they come to their attention. They are, therefore, useful for making comparison with police statistics in estimating the extent of these specified incidents.

It is, however, important to note that different surveys operationalize the definition of these incidents in different ways. They do not all comply with the legalistic definitions of police work, neither do they all necessarily confine themselves to those incidents which are by definition notifiable to the police. For some crimes, like car theft, this does not pose any particular problems; the survey respondent, the survey and the police are all likely to concur in their definitions of such an incident. This may not be so in the case of an assault. Technically an assault might happen at a school, in a pub, or in circumstances where no injury had occurred. In all these examples, had the police been called, the incident might not have been pursued because of the circumstances of its occurrence. This may have the effect of producing a greater discrepancy between respondent, survey and police definitions of such incidents. Hough and Mayhew summarize the relationship between police statistics and crime survey statistics in the following way:

> police statistics count one category of actions: those reported to them which could be punished by a court and should occupy the attention of the criminal justice system. The [British Crime Survey] counts a second category of actions which according to the letter of the law and regardless of the value in so doing, could be punished. (Hough and Mayhew, 1985, p. 5)

There is still a difficulty here, of course, in so far as it is not possible to know precisely whether the events being identified by respondents are, in fact, strictly speaking illegal. So, whilst criminal victimization surveys provide a good deal of information about certain types of crime, as reported by the victims of these crimes, it is not always possible to make a direct comparison of estimates of crime with police statistics because of the definitional and operational differences between the two measures. Crime surveys, then, attempt to count those offences against individuals and property which could be legally punished. How well does the survey technique match this task?

Like all social surveys the initial sources of error for the crime survey may be found in examining the sampling process, a process designed to ensure the representativeness of the sample interviewed. The sampling frame, the list from which the respondents are drawn, can involve some difficulties in achieving this. Sparks, Genn and Dodd (1977) used the electoral register as their sampling frame and comment on the inadequacies of this, in particular, which arise as a result of people who had moved on from their listed address (ibid., p. 220). The British Crime Surveys also use the electoral register and readily admit that this might mean certain sections of the population, particularly ethnic minorities and the young, who are most likely to fail to register to vote, are missed in the survey. The Islington Crime Survey used the 1981 census to generate households as the sampling unit, rather than the electoral register which generates individuals. This strategy left the interviewer to select at random (using a grid) a member of the household to interview.

Whichever sampling technique is chosen, at the end of the day there is still a problem of ensuring an adequate response rate. Even a representative sample can become unrepresentative if there is not an adequate response from all the chosen sample units; this may bias the sample in favour of one type of respondent. The 1984 British Crime Survey (BCS) achieved a response rate of just under 80 per cent, the Islington Crime Survey (ICS) aimed for a 70 per cent response rate. These are good response rates, but nevertheless a proportion of the chosen sample is still missing. In terms of representativeness, little is obviously known about the non-respondents, though when using the electoral register it is possible to say something about where non-respondents live. Block and Block (1984) suggest that such non-respondents may include a high number of victims. Additionally these surveys, like many other social surveys, specifically exclude those under the age of 16 and those people in institutions in constructing their samples. These too may include a high number of victims. (See Chapter 3 on children as victims.)

The end result of the sampling process is a sample size for which sampling errors can be estimated; that is, the degree to which the sample can be assumed to be representative. The BCS process produces a sample size of around 11,000 from the population of England

27

and Wales. The more local crime surveys vary in sample size from 1,722 in Islington to 2,382 across Merseyside. It is possible to offer a statistical estimate for each of these samples relative to population size; an estimate of sampling error which increases the rarer the crime. Such statistical procedures enable sampling error to be incorporated into the way in which the data is read. Other errors, however, enter into the survey method technique from a number of less controllable sources: namely, errors which relate to what is being counted within the survey, errors which are associated with the respondent and errors which are attributable to the interviewer. Each of these will be discussed in turn.

Errors which derive from the counting procedure within a survey can occur in a number of ways. First of all it is important to be clear on the units for which the data are being gathered. For example, the 1984 BCS asked respondents about their personal experiences of thefts, assaults, sexual offences, etc., but when it came to household crimes respondents were asked about the experience of others in the household. The ICS used the household as the unit of analysis, so that when it came to personal crimes

> it was decided that in order to capture enough cases of vic-
> timization for valid comparisons between subpopulations to be
> made, that the interviewers would ask about other members of
> the household. (Jones, MaClean and Young, 1986, p. 43)

Jones, MaClean and Young argue that this process is still likely to yield an underestimate of incidents (ibid., pp. 231–2); a conclusion supported by Skogan (1986a, p. 83). This does pose some problems, however, in fairly comparing the data from these two sources in the case of personal victimization. Additional counting problems arise from definitional issues; that is, how incidents have been defined within the survey.

It has already been established that there are definitional problems in comparing crime survey findings with police statistics; in addition, different surveys use different ways of operationalizing the variables they are interested in. Some (notably the Australian surveys) use legalistic language in posing the questions; the BCS opted for more everyday language in the questions posed to respondents, the replies being translated into more legalistic categories after the data had been gathered. Obviously whichever way is chosen, considerable interpretation on the part of the interviewer and/or the researcher may take place, particularly when it comes to borderline cases. The question of definition raises more fundamental issues, however, when a closer examination is made of how to operationalize and count, in particular, sexual assaults. (See below.)

Errors which can be associated with the respondent have been well documented in survey research. It is useful, however, to document the issues which are particularly pertinent to crime surveys. It was assumed initially that the survey would be a useful tool in uncovering incidents of victimization, since it was felt that crimes were salient events; people would remember them and talk about them. It has been revealed that this is not necessarily the case. Respondents may not have the knowledge the survey assumes (particularly a problem if the survey questions an individual about other people's experiences of crime). Respondents forget incidents or purposely choose not to relate them. Skogan (1986a) reports recall rates of over 70 per cent for incidents involving strangers and as low as 22 per cent for incidents where the parties were related (ibid., pp. 85–6). Respondents get tired if the interview procedure is lengthy. They may of course remember incidents, but remember them inaccurately or incompletely. This is a particular problem when it comes to recalling the timing of an event. Sparks, Genn and Dodd (1977) found that when they compared respondents' timing of events with police records, only 55 per cent recalled the month in which the event occurred accurately. Recalling the timing of an event may not, however, distort the data as much as the phenomenon of 'telescoping'. This refers to the way in which a respondent draws on events outside the reference period of the interview. One attempt to solve this problem has been to 'bound' the reference period of the interview; that is, to draw together for the respondent a time period which has within it salient features, benchmarks, in order more accurately to locate the time period under discussion. The BCS uses Christmas as the bounding period. (This data consequently covers a calendar year and can be more easily compared with police statistics.) The ICS instructed its interviewers to establish clearly a bounded time for the respondents by asking them to recall events at the same time in the previous year, and then proceeding to discuss any criminal events which occurred from that time to the date of the interview. (For further details on this see Jones, MacClean and Young, 1986, pp. 257–9.) Sparks, Genn and Dodd (1977) seem to come down on the side of a twelve-month reference period as being the most productive for crime surveys, taking into account the cost which would be incurred in pursuing a shorter time-span.

It is not only the timing of events which may be inaccurately recalled, other details – for example, estimating the cost of goods stolen – may be subject to inaccuracies. Additionally respondents may fail to recognize an event which has happened to them as being relevant to the question, and may even make up incidents. Whilst it is difficult to estimate the effects of these sources of error, the BCS seems to feel that overall effect of them probably results in an underestimate of crime. There is some evidence to suggest that when it comes to specific types of offence, there are differences in recall between different groups of respondents. This is discussed more fully below in the context of assaults.

The next source of error is associated with the interviewer. The effect of the interviewer on the general interview process has again been well documented, and obviously some of the errors which arise are more likely to occur with poorly trained and ill-supervised interviewers. Interviewers may differ in how they understand the purpose of the survey, in how they understand and present the questions; some interviewers are better at probing than others; some accept 'don't knows' better than others. Sometimes interviewers make mistakes in recording answers. Where these errors, arising from the interviewer, seem to have the most impact on victimization data is in those areas which require sensitivity to verbal and nonverbal cues and sensitive probing; namely assaults, sexual assaults, rape and interfamilial disputes. The impact of particular interviewers, whose skills may not be so great in these areas, will diminish when more interviewers are employed and more training, supervision and feedback are available. However, it is interesting to note that, as with the other problems so far discussed, this difficulty is most pertinent when exploring specific kinds of victimization, particularly experiences which involve violence and sexual offences. To a certain extent these categories overlap, in that a sexual offence may also involve violence. To illustrate this, the problems associated with counting each of these types of offence will be discussed in turn.

The first problem in counting violence is definitional. The police recording of assault is categorized under the broad heading of 'violence against the person'. The BCS makes a distinction between three subcategories of assault: serious wounding, other wounding and common assault which results in very minor or no injuries. The problem is when does pushing and shoving become an assault, and when does common assault turn into a more serious attack? (See Hough, 1986, p. 121.) The BCS 1982 found a clear relationship between the length of a respondent's education and willingness to report violent offences (Hough, 1986, p. 119), a finding also commented on by Sparks, Genn and Dodd (1977). This seems to represent a response bias; that is, it cannot necessarily be inferred that the more educated lead more violent lives. It may be that the interview process elicits a different kind of response from the more educated (Sparks, 1981, does argue that interviewing is a middle-class game), or it may be that the more educated have a lower threshold of tolerance for such offences. (See Hough, 1986.) The survey method may well therefore underestimate the extent of such offences because of this bias. Additional difficulties arise when the definition of assault is extended to include racial assaults, police assaults and incidents of domestic violence (Jones, MaClean and Young, 1986, pp. 60–3). The difficulty is not so much a conceptual one, since despite the fact that police records are not kept in this way the evidence does indicate that these are important categories of assault to include. The question is whether the survey method can capture, as an event, what is likely to be a process; that is, an everyday life experience which the respondents themselves may not even define as criminal. In discussing the categorization of racial assaults Jones, MaClean and Young state:

It would seem ... that some segments of the population are so over-exposed to this kind of behaviour that it becomes part of their everyday reality and escapes their memory in the interview situation, indicating that our estimate is probably low. (ibid., p. 63)

The same problem of underestimate may apply to domestic assault with the added likelihood that respondents would feel embarrassed or ashamed to report such incidents, especially with the possibility that their assailant might be present during the interview. (The presence of others, particularly partners, of course, may pose interviewing problems on a general level as well as in this specific context.) This category of assault is also least likely to be reported to the police. (The difficulties of exploring offences against women are discussed more fully below.) The question of assaults by the police is a category difficult to follow through in comparison with police statistics and it is, therefore, routinely collected. The police keep records only of official complaints made against them and whilst such incidents may be reported they invariably are not pursued officially. Hough (1986) concludes by saying that surveys are probably of least value when it comes to trying to establish a 'yardstick' for the volume of violence, though they may well inform explanations of violence through developing an understanding of whom they show to be at risk and why. Caution may therefore be necessary in interpreting the findings on this issue.

The second specific offence area which raises problems for the survey method in an acute form is that concerned with offences against women. Whilst any offence may be committed against a woman, the dimensions of which the analysis by Worrall and Pease (1986) begins to illustrate, the offences of rape and attempted rape are gender specific. It is at this point that the problem of definition arises. The legal definition of rape is concerned with a specific form of penetration, by the penis into the vagina, without the consent of the female or being reckless to that consent. This legal definition of rape poses a number of problems for feminists and other researchers in this area. It focuses on one type of behaviour (and as it has been interpreted in the courts one type of coercion, the physical), it puts the burden of proof on the female and it excludes rape within marriage. (For a fuller discussion of the implications of these problems see, for example, Box, 1983, Chapter 4.) It also excludes the application of the definition of rape by women on men and by men on men. This legal framework has implications for victimization surveys which attempt to identify the incidence of rape and sexual assault.

The 1984 BCS uses the term sexual assault to cover a range of offences which apply to women interpreted in the following way:

> Only women were asked about their experiences of sexual offences. The sexual offences which were counted as crimes in the survey comprised rape (and attempts), woundings with a sexual motive, and indecent assaults which involved no injury. Women were also asked about other forms of sexual harassment which were not counted as crimes. (Hough and Mayhew, 1985, p. 105)

This interpretation, whilst taking what the respondent says at face value, is ultimately categorized to mirror police use of such categories, that is, the legal definition (ibid., p. 4). The ICS, acknowledging that the categories used by the police do not reveal the range or severity of sexual assaults, uses four categories: sexual assault, sexual assault with more than one assailant, rape or attempted rape, rape or attempted rape with more than one assailant. Here it is stated that 'for an assault to be recorded as a sexual assault there had to be an indecent assault in which physical contact was made' (Jones, MaClean and Young, 1986, pp. 70–1). The ICS also argues that it adopted a range of methodological innovations designed to maximize the willingness of respondents to disclose such experiences. These strategies included considering how interviewers were used and trained and paying attention to the structure of the interview schedule (ibid., p. 69). This constituted an attempt to respond to the feminist criticism of victimization surveys which argues that such surveys seriously underestimate the incidence of rape and sexual assault. And indeed the ICS revealed a higher incidence of such victimizations than the two sweeps of the BCS. (See below.) The definitional difficulty still remains, however; first in understanding what exactly is being counted and secondly whether the strategies adopted by the ICS are themselves sufficient (or are indeed in any way 'special') to meet the feminist critique.

Stanko (1987) points to the way in which the everyday experiences of women are marked by feelings of insecurity and the likelihood of experiencing male violence. To focus on the public experience of this overlooks the all-embracing private dimension. To date, the survey method has had greater, though still limited, success in uncovering public incidents of sexual assault; that is, incidents which involve strangers (see the discussion in Sparks, Genn and Dodd, 1977, p. 50, for example). The private domain is much more difficult to penetrate by formal interview means, not only because of the nature and dynamics of the interview procedure but also because this involves penetrating those everyday realities of women's experience. Kelly suggests that this requires reconceptualizing the nature of sexual violence in terms of a continuum:

> Using the concept of a continuum highlights the fact that all women experience sexual violence at some point in their lives. It enables the linking of the more common, everyday abuses women experience with the less common experiences labelled as crimes. It is through this connection that women are able to locate their

own particular experiences as being examples of sexual violence.
(Kelly, 1987, p. 59)

This broadens the understanding of women's experiences and is certainly at odds with the legal definition with which this section started. This broader understanding does help, at an explanatory level, in understanding other features of the survey data particularly with respect to, for example, women's fear of crime. (See Stanko, 1987.) Whether this understanding of sexual assault can meaningfully be explored within a large survey methodology is highly suspect. It requires in-depth longitudinal interviewing to be adequately explored.

A final comment on the exploration of sexual assaults in victim surveys. They have all focused on sexual assaults against women. Very little seems to be known about homosexual assaults by men on men, or sexual assaults by women on men, or by women on other women. Whilst it might be argued that such incidents are comparatively rare, an understanding of them would nevertheless contribute to our understanding of the more conventionally understood sexual assault.

Given this catalogue of difficulties for the victimization survey, is there any reason to proceed with them? The Home Office obviously thinks so. Hough and Mayhew argue that many of the problems will remain constant over time and that the victimization survey should not be viewed as a perfect measure, just better than police statistics alone (Hough and Mayhew, 1985, pp 6–7). Certainly, the victimization survey is no better and no worse off than other areas of research which employ the survey technique when it comes to respondent and interviewer biases. The sum total of these is likely to be an under-estimate of what is being recorded. There may be some definitional translations to be made from the responses received but all things considered more may be revealed about burglary, attempted burglary, thefts from vehicles, etc. It is obviously more difficult to be quite so positive about this research strategy when the difficulties outlined here concerning violent offences and sexual offences are considered. Again the overall conclusion to be reached is that the survey method probably underestimates the incidence of these offences, but to what extent is a far more difficult question to answer. In some respects a case can be mounted suggesting that the survey technique is inappropriate in these areas, though alternative research strategies would, at the end of the day, be much more costly. The most appropriate recommendation would seem to be to treat the survey findings in these areas with particular caution. Despite these caveats, survey method research has begun to reveal more information concerning the incidence of certain types of victimization, who is most likely to be a victim, and what the general impact of this victimization is. It is to those findings that we now turn.

How many victims? Who are they?

The first British Crime Survey suggested that about four times as many property offences and about five times more offences of violence occur than are recorded by the police (Hough and Mayhew, 1983, p. 32). This general under-recording of crime in official statistics is not peculiar to England and Wales. Elias (1986) comments that, with the exception of homicide, criminal victimization surveys in the United States have revealed that official records of crime have underestimated actual victimization from 300 to 500 per cent. (ibid., p. 38). Whilst the United States probably has a higher crime rate that any country in Europe, with one murder occurring every twenty six minutes (ibid., p. 47), Hough and Mayhew go on to point out that much of this 'dark figure of crime' in England and Wales was generally less serious than that which was recorded in official statistics. The first British Crime Survey showed that

> a 'statistically average' person aged 16 or over can expect: a robbery once every five centuries (not attempts), an assault resulting in injury (even if slight) once every century, the family car to be stolen or taken by joyriders once every 60 years, a burglary in the home once every 40 years. (Hough and Mayhew, 1983, p. 15)

This way of expressing the likelihood of victimization is not very meaningful but can be used to compare victimization risks with other events which people might encounter, like, for example, fire or accidents in the home. (The chances of robbery are smaller apparently than the chances of being admitted to hospital as a psychiatric patient; ibid., p. 15.) Expressing risks of victimization in this way and offering such comparisons masks the patterning of victimization. These patterns are revealed when other variables are controlled for; in particular, the variables of age, race, sex and place of residence.

The first British Crime Survey revealed that the risk of car theft, for example, increases if someone owns a car, if that car is parked in the street at night in an inner city area, if the owner lives in a council house and the car is used frequently. In the case of assault, this survey also suggested that those most likely to be assaulted were male, under 30, single, went out several times a week, drank, and assaulted others. It also uncovered only one incident of rape (attempted) and suggests that this indicates the rarity of such attacks by complete strangers. The findings of the second crime survey echo those of the first with the additional opportunity to make some estimates concerning the extent to which crime had increased. (10 per cent on crime survey estimates compared with 12 per cent on police statistics). These general findings, particularly from the first survey, informed the construction of the local surveys conducted on Merseyside and in Islington. These surveys have developed our understanding of the influence of variables like age, race, sex and place of residence on levels of victimization.

The Merseyside Crime Survey (MCS) reveals that the incidence of crimes against the person is only marginally higher on Merseyside than in the rest of England and Wales, but that in the case of burglary it is three times higher than in the rest of the country. (Kinsey, 1984, p. 5). From the general sample Kinsey states that 44% of people on Merseyside had been victimized in the previous year; and that the least victimized were women over 50 (29 per cent), and the most at risk of victimization were men under 30 (60 per cent) (Kinsey, 1985, p. 14). Additionally, it is argued:

> There can be no doubt that both in terms of the quantity and the impact of crimes examined the poor suffer more than the wealthy. The problems appear critical for the 20% of the Merseyside population living in the poorest council housing and especially in the District of Knowsley where 48% of the population (six times the national average) live in such areas. (ibid., p. 16)

The Islington Crime Survey reveals considerably more detail about such patterns. It found that young people, black people and men were most at risk from burglary, particularly if they lived in the Mildmay area (Jones, MaClean and Young, 1986, p. 47). The risk of theft or robbery in Islington seems to decrease with age, but blacks are more likely to be victimized in this way than whites, and women are, on average, more at risk from this event than men. The ICS is particularly more detailed in its description of the incidence and risk of assault. The survey estimates that 2,569 domestic assaults occurred in Islington in the time period covered by the survey, (22 per cent of the total number of assaults), 870 racist assaults (7 per cent of the total) and 400 police assaults (3.5 per cent of the total) (ibid., p. 97). The report states that:

> Younger people are on average thirteen times as likely to be assaulted as people in the over 45 years of age category. Black people on average are almost twice as likely as other people to be victims of assault and women half as likely again as men to be assaulted. (ibid., p. 65)

Clearly, incorporating an understanding of domestic violence, in particular, begins to alter somewhat the influence of gender as a variable in the patterning of victimization as compared with BCS findings. These survey findings also indicate a much higher incidence of sexual assault than those of the BCS sweeps. (From samples of 11,000 on each occasion the BCS revealed one incident of attempted rape and 17 and 18 sexual assaults respectively.) The ICS estimates 1,200 cases of sexual assault in Islington in the time period of the survey, with the under-45 age group being approximately eighteen times more likely to be victimized than older women (ibid., p. 73). Race may also be a variable here, though it is difficult to assess to what extent and whether white women were reporting incidents more readily than women from other groups. The data also suggest that the higher the income the more likely women were to be subject to sexual violence (ibid., p. 74). (Does this relate to the question of lifestyle raised in Chapter 1?)

These survey findings obviously considerably moderate the initial assessment of risk of victimization from the first British Crime Survey, and to a large extent contradict the popular media image of crime victims as being elderly females. A contradiction again inherent in the survey findings in the United States:

> Overall, the greatest victims of common crime, when we combine the various measures of risk and likelihood, are precisely the most likely offenders, or at least those most likely to be apprehended: poor, young, nonwhite males. (Elias, 1986, p. 61)

What these survey findings do not explain is why the patterns of victimization occur in the way that they do.

It has been seen from Chapter 1 that victimologists have employed the concept of 'victim precipitation' as a way of explaining victimization. And it was argued that whilst some crimes might be explained by reference to the behaviour of the victim, this is hardly a way of explaining the patterns identified here, particularly the locational variations of victimization. Chapter 1 also indicated that the concept of 'lifestyle' might offer some understanding of victimization patterns; do the elderly go out less and are therefore less at risk? Whilst there is some evidence to support the lifestyle model in general, Clarke *et al.* (1985) suggest that victimization rates are still low for the elderly when lifestyle is controlled for. The role of lifestyle in contributing to victimization remains unclear. A further question to address in trying to understand the patterning of victimization is to what extent fear of crime plays a part in precipitating changes in behaviour. The extent to which crime surveys answer this question is the next consideration.

Who is afraid of crime and what impact does that fear have?

The difficulties here, of course, rest in identifying what is meant by fear of crime and finding a suitable way of tapping that fear. Maxfield offers this understanding of fear of crime: 'Fear therefore involves a personalised threat rather than abstract beliefs and attitudes about crime as a problem' (Maxfield, 1984, p. 3). He goes on to suggest that the questions chosen by the BCS to tap fear, focusing on fear of personal safety on the street and worry about crime, provide a broad view of fear of crime. This is despite the probability that men are likely to under-report any feelings of fear for their personal safety (ibid., p. 4).

Within this broad framework, the first BCS reveals that burglary and street crimes seemed to worry people most, with 60 per cent of elderly women who lived in inner city areas saying that they felt very unsafe when out on foot after dark. In pursuing these questions from the 1984 BCS data, Maxfield concludes by saying that fear for personal safety is a feature of residents of densely populated, urban areas, with 41 per cent of women in inner cities feeling very unsafe walking alone at night in their neighbourhood. (The threat of sexual assault seems to be of particular concern here.) As far as worry about household crime is concerned, this seems to be more uniformly distributed throughout the population.

In asking the same sorts of questions about fear of and worry about crime, the MCS reveals that one in three said they worried about going out on their own after dark. Overall elderly women worried the most. Whilst the level of anxiety in the home was less, one in four still expressed feeling unsafe in their own homes, with this occurring twice as much in the inner city area as compared with the more affluent suburbs (although the ICS data suggested that the 'better off' women were more likely to report incidents of assault). Women expressed being more worried about household crime than men. When asked whether they felt there were risks for women who go out in this area after dark, over a third of respondents believed it fairly likely something would happen to them. Again, there are locational variations in this ranging from 14 per cent in Ainsdale (a residential part of Southport) to 76 per cent in Granby (an inner city area) (Kinsey, 1985, pp. 20–3). The ICS found that the majority of the sample worried about being burgled and about half worried about being a victim of robbery in the street. Women felt there were risks for them out on the street after dark and were more likely to feel unsafe in their own home. Black women felt more unsafe in their own home than out on the street.

Drawing these findings together they suggest that gender, age, race and location are important variables related to worry and fear of victimization; fears and worries which the local 'new realist' crime surveys argue are not unfounded. Kinsey states:

> Merseysiders in general worry a lot about crime but those under the greatest social and economic pressure also suffer most from crime; they worry more, perhaps too much, but they do have the most to worry about. (Kinsey, 1985, p. 24)

This range of findings is again echoed in the American literature. (See Elias, 1986, pp. 61–5.)

Again, Jones, MaClean and Young (1986) argue that the perceptions of risk revealed in their survey data relate to the actual risk of events happening. The BCS data do not address this question in the same detail as the ICS, especially with respect to the variables of gender and race, but do support the overall view that in areas of a high incidence of crime there are also high anxiety levels (Hough and Mayhew, 1985, p. 52). The question remains as to whether there is any connection to be made between these fears and behaviour.

Connecting fear of crime to behaviour is not necessarily a straight-forward process. Skogan (1986b) proposes four models of crime-related behaviour. First is the sociological model. This takes two forms. The first is a Durkheimian form which sees crime as a threat to social stability and integration; therefore the community responds to do something collectively about the problem. The second form is expressed in the views of Conklin (1975) who suggests that the likely response to such threats is a withdrawal from the community. The second model is a utilitarian one in which people find their level of acceptable risk by balancing the costs and benefits of their activities. In the third model, the psychological, people are 'motivated to act by a desire to lower their risk in the face of potentially severe consequences, when they think it is likely to work' (Skogan, 1986b, p. 183). The final model, the opportunist model, suggests that what people can do about crime depends upon the nature of the opportunities which face them. Skogan argues that none of these models has been fully explored, and each of them may be more or less relevant to different crime-related behaviours.

Of the four models discussed, Skogan (1986b) suggests that the behavioural response, risk management behaviour, seems to be directly related to fear of crime. This involves the individual in taking pre-cautionary action against criminal victimization, a suggestion echoed in Maxfield's (1984) discussion of BCS data. He states that fear for personal safety is a major limiting factor on personal mobility; people stay off the streets and avoid night-time activity, which is perceived as risky. Such risk management behaviour, however, is not necessarily connected to fear when it comes to the household. Measures taken to protect against burglary, Maxfield comments, are particularly lacking. (There may be a clearer connection here to be made between this and Skogan's opportunistic model; the wealthier, whilst being less at risk, have more resources to act on their perceptions in investing in security systems than the less well off. The ICS supports this and the BCS data suggests that property protection is more related to income than any other variable.)

The connection between fear of crime, precautionary behaviour, age and gender appears from BCS data not to be that clear. Maxfield reports that feeling unsafe reduces night-time activity for old and young alike (Maxfield, 1984, p. 30), stating that

Males, younger persons, and those who were single, divorced or separated more often spent evenings outside their home than did

others, but even among these groups night-time activity declined
as fear for personal safety increased. (ibid., p. 33)

The local crime surveys, however, make a stronger case for the importance of these variables. Kinsey says, for example:

> The picture which has emerged is one of people of the inner city
> – especially the women – living under curfew. While, as has been
> seen, the actual chances of victimization are less than many people
> believe, nonetheless, in Granby, for example, three quarters of
> those interviewed believe there are real risks for women who go
> out at night and half said they often or always avoid going out
> after dark. (Kinsey, 1985, pp. 23–4)

Similarly, Jones, MaClean and Young state:

> In either event, it is clear [from Table 4.10] that women generally,
> and particularly older and black women, feel it is necessary to
> restrict their behaviour and avoid certain situations as a precaution
> against crime. *In this sense, the Islington Crime Survey helps to illustrate
> that a 'curfew on women' appears to be implicitly operative.* (Jones,
> MaClean and Young, 1986, p. 169; italics in original)

In discussing these findings, alongside their findings on sexual harassment, Jones, MaClean and Young suggest that there may be a
connection between women's fear of personal safety and gender roles
(ibid., p. 183). It is here that a particular difficulty is highlighted in
explaining the relationship between fear and behaviour; the connection
is not necessarily a mechanistic or linear one. Once this is recognized,
the conclusion does not necessarily follow that it is crime which produces
the curfew on women. Fear of crime may just be the expression of other
perceptions, of the neighbourhood, for example, which have yet to be
fully explored.

In conclusion then, it can be seen that the most concrete connection
the survey data suggests between fear of crime and behaviour is with
respect to perceptions of personal safety. It may be, however, that fear
of crime is just one way of expressing worries about all kinds of things
to do with broader assumptions of decline. (See, for example, Hall *et
al.*, 1978.) It seems that there is still much to be learned about the
expression of fear in relation to crime and the kinds of behavioural

patterns the victimization surveys have to date described. Behavioural changes are, however, not the only way in which victimization or the fear of victimization may have an impact on individuals. The impact of victimization may take its toll in other ways and it is to the available evidence concerning this that we now turn.

The impact of victimization

The impact of victimization may be measured by reference to 'objective' and 'subjective' criteria. Objective measures concentrate on material losses: valuables taken; days lost from work; the 'cost' of physical injuries. Subjective measures concentrate more on the psychological impact of crime. Janoff-Bulman and Hanson-Frieze (1983) suggest that a theoretical framework for understanding the psychological impact of victimization needs to take into account the extent to which a victimizing experience calls into question three fundamental assumptions with which human beings operate on a day-to-day basis: that we are invulnerable, that the world is a meaningful place and that on the whole we view ourselves in a positive light. A victimizing experience renders us vulnerable, may be something that we struggle to make sense of and may result in our questioning our own contribution to that event. We may develop a range of strategies to cope with these effects over a period of time. Our ability to develop such strategies may depend on the nature of the event, the nature of the perpetrator and features of our own lives. Considerable evidence has been gathered focusing on the impact of rape and the impact of serious physical assaults. Here attention will be focused on referring to the 'routine' way in which people respond to victimization, along both the 'objective' and 'subjective' criteria outlined above as they have been employed by the criminal victimization survey.

Whilst some detailed information is available on the impact of burglary (Maguire, 1982) and the experience of victims of crimes of violence within the criminal justice system (Shapland, Willmore and Duff, 1985), the second British Crime Survey, 1984, included, for the first time, general questions concerning the impact of crime which were directed towards a sample of the general population. It is important to note that when the findings of the more specific studies are compared with the general findings of victimization surveys, there is a tension between them.

The BCS conclusions are based on data from victims who may not have reported the event under discussion to the police. The more specific surveys are concerned with events which have been reported to the police. The different nature of these populations is important when considering the findings concerned with the impact of crime. The more specific studies, by definition, are dealing with the impact of events which are deemed serious by respondents and police alike. The BCS findings discuss the impact of events with respondents who deemed such an event too 'trivial' to report to the police as well as with those victims of more 'serious' events. In order to take account of the possible differences which might derive from these different populations, Maguire and Corbett (1987) analyse the impact of crime not only by reference to BCS data but also by reference to a sample of respondents of more serious crimes who had been referred to victim support schemes. In-depth interviews were conducted with the latter. This leads Mawby and Gill, who also use the 1984 BCS data to consider the impact of crime, to suggest that the greater impact reported from Maguire and Corbett's in-depth data may be attributable to the technique itself 'encouraging victims to magnify the effects' (Mawby and Gill, 1987, p. 20). Whether this is the case or not, Maguire and Corbett's in-depth data do allow an appreciation of the possible longer-term effects of criminal victimization to be developed. With these qualifications in mind, what are the findings with respect to the victims' response to crime?

Hough and Mayhew conclude: 'But many victims of even relatively serious offences seemed able to cope without significant practical or emotional problems' (Hough and Mayhew, 1985, p. 52). However, when those who were 'very much affected' by the incident are examined more closely Maguire and Corbett's in-depth data reveal a third more such cases than the BCS data. Within both these data sets, for the category of events most likely to be reported to the police, at the top of the list in the impact they cause appear burglary with loss, snatch theft and robbery, wounding, and additionally threats and major vandalism (Maguire and Corbett, 1987, p. 45). These are also the kinds of incidents most likely to pass through a victim support scheme from which Maguire and Corbett's in-depth sample was drawn. (The disparity in overall findings is therefore probably explained by this.)

A further feature of the event likely to heighten the impact on the victim is whether the offender was known to the victim. This relationship is considered in a little more detail by Mawby and Firkins (1986) and Mawby and Gill (1987). They report that 53 per cent of victims whose offender was well known to them were 'very much affected' by the event, which rises to 62 per cent for crime by neighbours and 81 per cent for spouse-related crimes. They conclude that it is personal crimes by spouses which most affect victims (Mawby and Gill, 1987, p. 24). These are also offences which are least likely to be reported to the police, though Mawby and Gill do not comment on this. As well as offence characteristics there appear to be certain victim characteristics which contribute to the observed variations in the general impact of crime.

Women report being 'very much affected' by criminal victimization more often than men (though whether this difference is real in general terms is difficult to assess; it may be that men are more reluctant to report being affected). Households headed by non-manual occupations and those who were separated, widowed, or divorced report being very much affected. The variables of age and living alone appear to be important in this respect when combined with other variables (Maguire and Corbett, 1987, p. 50; Mawby and Gill, 1987, pp. 21–3). Thus the vulnerable are likely to be women, the divorced or separated, those living alone, the less well off.

The kinds of effects experienced again vary according to gender and whether or not the event had been reported to the police. Emotional problems were more likely to be reported by females than by males. Men and victims of burglary were most likely to report feeling angry. 'Difficulty in sleeping' and 'feeling unsettled' seems to be a common response with female victims of burglary, who are most likely to report the first of these problems. Other responses such as 'fear' and 'shock' were also identified in Maguire and Corbett's data (1987, pp. 53–6). Maguire and Corbett also report on the longer-term emotional effects. They report that from three to six weeks after the event, a quarter of their sample stated that they were still considerably affected by it, with a third of those with children saying that they (the children) were still frightened or upset (ibid., p. 62). In looking at the effects three months and twelve months later, Maguire and Corbett conclude that:

> Taken together, the evidence we have suggests that, although some unpleasant memories, unease and nervousness may remain for quite a long period, the majority of victims of most types of crime recover from the worst psychological effects within a few weeks – the 'crisis' period according to crisis theory. However, a substantial minority – perhaps as high as 20 per cent – of victims

of serious violent crime, and a small percentage of other offences do not recover in the same way. The event causes lasting changes in their personality and behaviour. (ibid., pp. 69–70)

As was indicated at the start of this section, the experience of victimization may have both objective and subjective effects. Maguire and Corbett have arguably identified some of the ways in which the psychological mechanisms involved in repairing the impact of an event can take considerable time; the victim may need the help of others (here victim support) to talk through the event, perhaps make sense of it, to regain some control over their everyday existence. Rape Crisis for example, encourages women to see themselves as survivors rather than victims (see Chapter 6). The objective effects will be considered next.

Hough and Mayhew conclude:

A minority of BCS victims sustained substantial financial losses and few were seriously injured. Four out of ten of those who had a burglar in their home received some insurance compensation, and 6 per cent who claimed on insurance said they were better off. (Hough and Mayhew, 1985, p. 52)

At the same time they report that four out of ten victims of burglary did not have cover for the property damaged or stolen, and a fifth of those covered did not claim. In terms of aggregate losses it seems that vehicle theft cost about £160 million in 1983, burglary about £100 million and snatch thefts about £13 million. (It is interesting to compare these aggregate costs with those incurred by corporate crime; see Chapter 4.) Such costs are not borne equitably amongst the population. Jones, MaClean and Young state that when all the material factors are taken into account, 'it is the lower income groups who are hardest hit by crime' (1986, p. 200). This is so despite their initial losses possibly being less than those higher up the income scale, because the lower income groups are less likely to be insured and are more likely to lose pay for time off work to rectify the impact of the event. There are additional costs borne in terms of inconvenience and time taken up in making insurance claims, replacing the contents of a handbag (keys, credit cards, etc.), dealing with house repairs and dealing with a range of organizations (Maguire and Corbett, 1987, pp. 60–1).

To conclude, victimization is likely to have its greatest subjective impact when the offender is known to the victim, particularly if that offender is a spouse; when the victim is female, when the victim is divorced or separated, when the victim lives alone, when the victim is older, when the victim is less well off. The longer-term effects are likely to occur in cases of crimes of violence and in households where there are children. Victimization has its greatest material impact on the lower income groups.

Conclusion

The foregoing discussion has highlighted the main difficulties associated with the criminal victimization survey and has indicated where these difficulties pose more or fewer problems in interpreting the data from such surveys. In the first instance the Home Office surveys have been useful primarily for indicating the extent of household victimization, with the local surveys suggesting somewhat more detailed information concerning personal victimization. Both data sources have provided some information concerning the distribution of such victimization. As has been seen, these data sources have also provided a means by which a general picture of the relationship between fear of crime and behaviour has been constructed, though this as yet has not been fully explored. A picture of the impact of victimization has also been painted.

This review of these survey findings so far has treated the Home Office survey approach and the local crime survey approach as if they are much the same animal. However, as was indicated in the previous chapter, the local crime survey approach sees itself as significantly different on a number of dimensions. It sees itself as taking the meaning of crime for the victims seriously, as having embraced feminism, and as having a greater political commitment. It is useful to consider how far the local crime survey approach has achieved its aims, in the first instance, and, secondly, to consider the wider political implications of both the Home Office surveys as well as the local crime surveys.

There are a number of ways in which one might begin to assess the extent to which the local crime survey approach has achieved its aims. If one of the implications of the goals set (that is, to take feminism seriously, to take the meaning of criminal victimization seriously, etc.) is to adopt strategies which would get closer to people's everyday experiences of crime and in doing so to count more incidents of victimization, then the local crime survey approach has achieved the latter. It has revealed more incidents of violence against women and racial harassment in particular than the Home Office approach. How it has achieved this remains a little mysterious. We are told about the nature of the sampling procedure, the sampling units, the weighting process (none of these strategies is particularly novel in survey methodology); and it is clear that if you want to know more about the criminal victimization of blacks, for example, then you make efforts to talk to black people. Special claims are made for the way in which interviewers were chosen, trained and deployed; though this process is not detailed. These are certainly strategies which would need careful consideration to achieve greater sensitivity to the issues of sexual assault and racial harassment. In addition, it is also necessary to pay attention to how questions are worded. This is a key part of the strategy adopted by Russell (1984) in her much acclaimed study of sexual exploitation. (See Chapter 3.) The ICS (1986) gives no information concerning the questionnaire so it is not possible to judge the extent to which any strategies similar to those of Russell were employed. Some special efforts were made it seems but precisely what they comprised is a little uncertain. Young (1988a) states that it is not only the data-gathering process which is important in the local crime survey approach, but also the way in which the data are analysed. Constructing a sample with, in particular, subset analysis in mind certainly increases the sensitivity of the general measuring instrument. Two questions remain, however. Whilst more incidents were uncovered (though how is not completely clear), does this information constitute uncovering the meaning of criminal victimization? And, secondly, how does the analysis process referred to by Young (ibid.) relate to the political commitment of the local survey approach?

The answer to the first question depends very much on how the concept of meaning is interpreted. One way to understand this term would be to document clearly the range and extent of criminal victimization which occurs for particular populations. To measure and identify the fact that victimization is such a common occurrence, and involves such a range of costs, both behavioural and financial, that people's lives are significantly altered by the process is important. This is certainly, it would seem, what the local crime survey has illustrated, and in so doing it has captured a much more meaningful picture of the impact of crime for some sections of the population than could be achieved by a national survey approach. However, there is at least one other way in which one could interpret the concept of meaning; one which is arguably more in keeping with a feminist position, for example. Stanko (1987) argues that to understand some of the figures associated with gender and fear of crime it is necessary to explore the extent to which our notions of personal safety are gender constructed. By suggesting this we are moving away from the context of crime *per se* to a position in which we try to understand much more fundamental and overarching daily strategies in which fear of crime is then located. In this sense meaning is something so routine, so taken for granted, that it may not be possible to articulate it in a formal interview. It demands exploration by in-depth interviewing, observation, secondary analysis of diaries, etc. It is this fundamental structuring of women's lives as compared with men's which the ICS does indicate may contribute to its findings but about which it can say little. (See above, p. 41.) A feminist might reply by saying that until these processes have been incorporated, then we are nothing more than a little further down the road in describing women's experiences and no nearer explaining them. The same argument can also be constructed in trying to understand the impact which race has in terms of criminal victimization. So how far the question of meaning has been tackled (and feminism embraced) depends on how that concept is defined. The local crime survey seems to achieve an understanding at one level perhaps but not the other.

The question of the political commitment associated with the local survey approach also relates to the question of whether the data gathered achieve the goals set. This critique has been more fully developed elsewhere (see Brogden, Jefferson and Walklate, 1988, pp. 186–9). It rests primarily on appreciating how the data from the local crime survey approach have been read. There is a tendency to gloss some aspects of the survey data. For example, whilst 'people in the highest income bracket are the most vulnerable to crime' (Jones, MaClean and Young, 1986, p. 59) the poor are still emphasized. 'The poor, it appears, are worse off when their victimization rates are highest *and* when they are not. With political championing of that order, who needs surveys' (Brogden, Jefferson and Walklate, 1988, pp. 188–9). There are times, then, when the political commitment overrides the data. This is perhaps the appropriate moment at which to examine some of the political implications of each of these survey approaches which have informed our discussion so far.

The Home Office survey approach and the way in which its findings are presented leave the reader with the view that crime is a pretty rare occurrence and that people's fear of crime is somewhat irrational as a consequence. This lends credence to the political view, commented on by Kinsey, Lea and Young (1986) and Phipps (1988), particularly in the Labour Party in the late 1970s and early 1980s, that the crime problem was much exaggerated by the police and the media, and that they were, in fact, the real problem. The Home Office approach also leaves the reader feeling that somehow the statistical chances of being victimized are fairly evenly distributed; and that we are 'all equal in our capacity to resist' (Kinsey, Lea and Young, 1986, p. 72).

The evidence discussed above from the local crime survey approach, in particular, clearly amends that view. Arguably, the Home Office approach has usefully justified, in political terms, the use by the Tory Party of the issue of law and order as a platform for voicing very individualistic and private responses to the possibility of criminal victimization. (See Phipps, 1988.) There is no need for massive state intervention to alleviate the plight of victims if victimization is a rare occurrence and we all have the same capacity to resist. This stems ultimately from the Tory Party view that crime has nothing to do with social disadvantages of deprivation. The local crime survey approach seriously challenges the basis of this viewpoint. The data it provides clearly permit a more socialist response to the problem of crime, which as Phipps (1988) has pointed out the Labour Party has taken some time to consider. The local crime survey approach not only reveals the nature and extent of the patterning of criminal victimization, it also encourages serious consideration to be made of the extent to which there is both intra-class and intra-racial criminal activity and victimization; something those on the left have found difficult to embrace. The local crime survey findings have also been used to construct political and policy initiatives with respect to policing. However, whilst it is argued in the introduction to the Islington Crime Survey that victimization surveys developed in the United States from social democratic origins to guide public policy, they have been absorbed politically in the United Kingdom much more effectively by the right than the left. This does not mean that there is nothing on offer to the left from this source of data, as the work cited here clearly displays. Though in keeping with the general tenor of this chapter, caution would be recommended with respect to what one might hope to achieve in policy terms by resting one's case on people's perceptions of and attitudes towards crime and their victimization. Human beings may have such perceptions but may not always base them on full or accurate information; particularly if they, themselves, are not being victimized.

The Home Office survey approach lends itself to a conservative reading of its data; the local crime survey approach lends itself (without the political commitment of its proponents) because of its inherent structure to a radical reading of its data. To date, for the most part, the conservative seems to be winning the day in the general political arena.

Overall conclusions

This general summary of the findings of the recent criminal victimization surveys has drawn attention to the fact that victimization is not randomly distributed throughout the population. Age, gender and place of residence are significant variables when it comes to calculating chances of being a victim of household or street crime. These variables may have a compounding effect on each other. Variables such as these and our understanding of their impact do not stand in isolation from the wider social context. They, in many ways, act as a reflection of the way in which structural features of society have a real impact on the day-to-day lives of human beings. In the chapters which follow, the concern will be to develop an understanding of that impact more fully and an appreciation of the connections to be made between it and the wider social structure.

This chapter, however, whilst unwrapping some of the ways in which the effect of these variables is beginning to be documented has not revealed anything concerning aspects of victimization which remain much more hidden from public scrutiny; namely the activities of corporations and the victimization of children. Much has been made towards the end of this chapter of the way in which the new realist approach aims to take seriously the meaning that criminal victimization has for individuals who are victimized. This assumes to a certain extent that individuals recognize their victimization. However, it is also important to recognize, and take seriously the processes which carry with them a whole range of meanings for our everyday lives, but which nevertheless go on 'behind our back'. The consequences felt from the activities of corporate crime, for example, in comparison with the kinds of day-to-day events highlighted in this chapter, which may in experiential terms and on the surface seem to be more real in their consequences, are small. We need to consider and balance the concerns of this chapter with an understanding of this kind of process. The victimization of children, probably the most difficult issue to document, serves to reinforce the way in which the vulnerable are not only likely to experience the material consequences of structural sources of victimization, but also may be subjected to experiences which derive from their personal powerlessness. This too needs to be measured against the more conventional focus of the issues of this chapter. The chapters which follow will be concerned to pursue these issues further.

3

The victimization of children

Introduction

Chapter 2 offered a summary of what is known in general about the process of victimization and an understanding of the difficulties which need to be faced in making sense of that information. That chapter also drew attention to features of the victimization process which the criminal victimization survey has not addressed. One of those features, the victimization of children, is the concern of this chapter. Following the pattern of Chapter 2, this chapter will be concerned, initially, to develop an appreciation of the difficulties of measuring the incidence of such victimization. This problem involves not only addressing the question of how to measure such incidents (by retrospective sample surveys of adults, for example) but also developing an understanding of what it is which is being measured; that is, what is meant by victimization in this context. This question will it is hoped permit us to examine the historical processes which have contributed to changes in the understanding and definition of child victimization. These historical changes set the scene for the way in which two strands within the process of child victimization have been constructed; namely the 'battered child syndrome' and the sexual abuse of children. A distinction will be made in this chapter between child physical abuse and child sexual abuse in the first instance, though as we shall see this distinction in some instances is somewhat arbitrary. This chapter will weave together these issues with a view to drawing attention to the structural processes which form our understanding and explanation of them, and the need for their development within victimology.

Measuring the victimization of children

It is in some respects self-evident that measuring the incidence of child victimization is closely connected with how such victimization has been defined; the broader the definition the higher the incidence of victimization likely to be identified. Whilst this might sound like a truism it is nevertheless a crucial problem to address if an understanding of child victimization is to be developed. It is useful and necessary, therefore, to take each of the strands of child victimization to be focused on here and examine the relationship between definition and measurement. First of all, the 'battered child syndrome' or child physical abuse.

Child physical abuse

The label 'battered child syndrome' is now somewhat dated. It was coined in a series of papers published in 1962 by Dr C. Henry Kempe who identified a clinical condition of intended injury inflicted by parents or foster parents on a child in their care. The identification of this syndrome had a considerable impact on the medical profession in America. Following a visit by Kempe to the National Society for the Prevention of Cruelty to Children (NSPCC) in the United Kingdom, the society established a Battered Child Research Team in 1968, a report of which, published in 1969, suggested that 60 per cent of a sample of children who had been injured at home had received injuries previously undetected. Whilst much of the purpose of this was arguably to raise the consciousness of professionals working with children, it reflects a narrow definition of child physical abuse which focused on the more serious forms of child abuse. It excluded incest unless this occurred with some other form of ill treatment. It is specifically concerned with the commission of an act, which is currently more likely to be referred to as 'ill treatment' rather than 'battering'. This, it is suggested, distinguishes abuse from neglect:

> The relationship between abuse and neglect is unclear. Neglect is certainly not less serious than abuse, for both neglect and abuse are potentially damaging to a child's growth and development. Leaving a youngster in dirty diapers, without adequate nourishment or stimulation, is at least as detrimental to a child

as the administration of bruises and broken bones. Physical abuse, however, frequently triggers intervention more rapidly than does neglect, commission being perceived as more life-threatening and 'evil' than is omission. (Bourne, 1979, p. 4)

This emphasis on action rather than inaction moves away from the notion of intent implied in Kempe's work and in so doing potentially embraces a wider range of behaviours which may include more serious forms of neglect but not any form of maltreatment. Maltreatment, depending on how it is defined, might include the vast majority of children and would not be very useful for social work practice; a key determinant in constructing these conceptual frameworks. From this brief discussion it is hoped that the reader begins to get a feel of the definitional difficulties this topic provokes.

Using a fairly narrow definition, then, the studies conducted by Creighton (1980, 1984) using the child abuse registers of the NSPCC suggest that there has been a steady increase in the number of injuries being notified to the registers but that the number of fatal or serious injuries reported has reduced. The vast majority of children recorded sustained minor soft tissue injury. (See Jones *et al.*, 1987, p. 34.) Studies of this sort are useful at one level. The child abuse registers have been collecting data using a fairly rigorous definitional approach for some time, and such a data source can provide a measuring stick with which to compare other data sources. Another data source sometimes used to indicate the incidence of child abuse is the statistics on the number of children taken into care. Taylor (1988) suggests that whilst the figures for children taken into care may be on the increase this is more a reflection of social workers' response to handling cases rather than necessarily an increase in abuse. Parton (1986) suggests that the overall number of children admitted to care decreased between 1980 and 1983! Though, alongside Taylor, he argues that this too is a reflection of social work practice rather than a measure of child abuse cases (ibid., p. 527). Lea, Matthews and Young (1987) report an increasing trend in child abuse referrals in Islington between 1983 and 1987. Again they argue that this is not in itself a cause of concern since it reflects an increase in public awareness following the Jasmine Beckford affair. The main difficulty is, of course, that not only do these particular figures relate to social work practice and public awareness but that child abuse figures in general, including the NSPCC register, rely on cases coming to the notice of 'the professionals': social workers, teachers, GPs, hospital doctors, in the first instance. The question remains as to whether figures such as these reveal the 'real' incidence of child abuse within this fairly narrow framework, or whether there is a 'dark figure' of child abuse which these processes fail to uncover. If there is such a figure, how can it be identified ?

One of the first studies of child abuse conducted in the United States of America by Gil (1970) included a public opinion survey on child abuse. He used the following definition of abuse:

> Physical abuse of children is intentional, non-accidental use of physical force, or intentional, non-accidental acts of omission, on the part of a parent or other caretaker in interaction with a child in his care, aimed at hurting, injuring, or destroying that child. (Gil (in Lee, 1978), 1970, p. 48)

He reports that 15.9 per cent of the respondents (a sample of the general population) reported that they had come near to abusing their own children and that 0.4 per cent had injured a child in their own care. It is suggested that both figures are under-reports, and for Gil they are a reflection of the 'culturally sanctioned use of physical force' in American society (ibid., p. 50). The question of culturally sanctioned behaviours raised by Gil is an important one particularly in the arena of child-rearing practices.

The studies by the Newsoms (1965, 1978) revealed the nature and extent of the use of corporal punishment on children and the variations between the social classes in this respect; particularly between working-class and middle-class parents, the use of the 'smack' being more prevalent amongst working-class mothers than their middle-class counterparts. The question is when does the 'smack' become excessive physical punishment become abuse, and for whom? Not such a trite question as it might seem. Whilst it may be possible to reach some common agreement between professionals and members of the public alike when particular cases of severe abuse come to light which involve scalded feet or fractured skulls, it is not so easy when dealing with cases which involve bruising as a result of corporal punishment or shaking. The injuries are identifiable; offering an explanation of the causes is harder for they are not so clearly identifiable.

The Newsom studies, amongst others, have also highlighted the tendency for middle-class parents to use psychological as opposed to physical sanctions, yet as the quote from Bourne above illustrates, at the end of the day there is little serious concern given to this kind of damage to a child. Much more attention has been given to identifying families at risk of abusing their children by focusing on variables such as socio-economic status and social deprivation; these variables are also more likely to be associated with physical punishments. This is rather like the lifestyle approach to victimization discussed in Chapter 1 but applied in the context of social work practice. Arguably at the end of the day, the physical is more measurable in the sense that one can photograph the damage and can assess what is needed for bones to be repaired, or for a child to grow in accordance with what might be expected for its age, height, etc. (Though again this last question of children who 'fail to thrive' depends on the nature of the cultural context as to whether this label can be applied.) Thus whilst Gil (1970) raises an important question it is a question which opens a further range of complex issues. Because it is complex, information from sample surveys like Gil's needs to be treated carefully, but also because it is complex, there are a range of reasons why cases of child abuse may fail to come to the attention of the professionals. Some of these reasons may relate to the question of the cultural context of the behaviour referred to by Gil. On the whole, however, there appears to be little agreement on the general issue of whether there is a 'dark figure' of child abuse. Peckham (1978) suggests that the bulk of cases will never come to official notice and Bourne states:

> Though the number of official cases is clearly increasing, it is doubtful that more child abuse and neglect exist now than in the past. What has changed is not the amount of abuse but the fact that abuse is now a salient social problem. Because we recognize it as an issue; because the law requires that, if recognized, it be reported to a state agency; because of intense media interest, there seems to be an increase in occurrence. In fact, the increase is more perceptual than real. (Bourne, 1979, p. 6)

If the view is that this is an area of relationships which to say the least is difficult to identify and measure, and if it is as Bourne suggests a change in attitude which has produced the apparent perception that child abuse has increased, how is it that this change has taken place, and are we right to accept the conclusion offered by Bourne?

Maria Colwell, Paul Brown, Darryn Clarke, Jasmine Beckford are just a few of the children's names which have hit the newspaper headlines in the last twenty-five years as cases in which the social services failed to protect the child. They have also been cases in which the newspapers have painted a particular view of the worsening social problems which face contemporary society. A brief historical excursion may enable these cases to be viewed in a different light.

Parton (1985) provides a valuable and interesting historical overview of the emergence of child abuse as a cause for concern. He highlights changes taking place within the nineteenth century as being of particular importance in understanding this process; in particular, changes in the economic base which produced more modern images of age groups and the social construction of childhood as a protected stage in the life cycle. There was also, in the nineteenth century, a growing concern that violence and delinquency were the outcome of childhood ill treatment.

The Society for the Protection of Women and Children from Aggravated Assaults was founded in 1857 and acted as a forerunner for concerns voiced later in the nineteenth century. It was not until 1882 that a Society for the Prevention of Cruelty to Children was formed in Liverpool (at a meeting of the Royal Society for the Prevention of Cruelty to Animals!) and the national society received its royal charter in 1895. The Prevention of Cruelty to and Protection of Children Act in 1889 was a success for the NSPCC and marked a turning-point in attitudes towards the treatment of children. The act made it an offence for anyone over 16 who was in charge of a girl under 16 or a boy under 14 to ill-treat, neglect, or injure them in any way likely to cause them harm or suffering to health. Within five years of this legislation 5,792 people had been prosecuted and 5,400 convicted for such offences (Parton, 1985, p. 35). Other pieces of legislation consolidated this act but increasingly became more concerned with the child as an offender to the extent that Parton argues:

> Under the 1969 Children and Young Persons Act, children in trouble with the law were treated in virtually the same way as children who were not offenders. In the process of conceptualizing and treating all problems to do with children

57

as being essentially the same, *any reference to children as victims was lost.* (ibid., p. 45; italics added)

The point being made here is that historically children appeared as victims only for a very short period alongside the appearance of childhood as a separate and protected stage in the life cycle. During the twentieth century this way of viewing children largely became entangled in also viewing them as offenders. Indeed one criterion used by social workers in deciding whether a case is child abuse or excessive physical punishment is whether or not the child could be deemed to have committed an offence!

It appears that Kempe was discovering the 'battered baby syndrome' in the 1960s because the question of child cruelty had itself largely been neglected in the interim. The case of Maria Colwell and the media coverage of it did much to heighten public awareness of an issue which had always been there. Additionally it did much to heighten concern with social work practice, which subsequent cases have also done.

A good deal of the research which has been conducted on child abuse has been concerned with problems of practice; identifying cases of abuse and cases at risk of abuse, and the management of abuse cases. Little work has been concerned to assess the validity or otherwise of Bourne's assertion with which this discussion began. On the basis of the evidence presented by Parton (1985) it would seem that Bourne is correct to argue that child abuse is now a salient social problem and that the increase in numbers may be more apparent than real. It is, however, not possible to be certain on the issue of whether there is more or less child physical abuse until a way is found of penetrating the potential 'dark figure' of child abuse. There appears, recently, to have been more success in identifying the nature and extent of child sexual abuse, to which we shall now turn.

Child sexual abuse

Like child physical abuse, child sexual abuse is not a new phenomenon. All societies have at some time operated with incest taboos but the extent to which such taboos are rigidly enforced depends on the cultural context of the behaviour. The Egyptian pharoahs believed incestuous relationships were a way of maintaining the purity of the royal lineage. More importantly, however, because of the status of incest as a taboo it is a behaviour which is surrounded by secrecy for all participants, including the unwilling participants. And it is interesting to note that incest did not become a criminal offence until relatively recently in 1908. Despite its criminal status, not until very recently has incest in particular, and the sexual abuse of children in general, begun to shed its veil of secrecy. This unveiling is largely as a result of the work done by the feminist movement in sensitizing a range of professional bodies (including the media in the case of the Childline initiative launched by Esther Rantzen) to the nature and extent of child sexual abuse. However, as with child physical abuse, it is important to clarify what exactly is being discussed.

Russell (1984) states that:

> Researchers and practitioners have reached no consensus on the child sex acts that constitute sexual abuse, nor on the age that defines a child. Nor do they agree about which is the most appropriate concept: child sexual abuse; sexual victimization; sexual exploitation; sexual assault; sexual misuse; child molestation; sexual maltreatment; child rape. (ibid. p. 177)

Additionally she comments that these terms have been frequently limited to describing behaviours which occur between adults and children and have not been concerned with behaviour between children and their peers. Russell's study (1984) uses the terms sexual abuse, exploitation and victimization interchangeably and includes behaviour between peers. Morris (1987) equates child sexual abuse with incest. This equation depends on how incest is defined; and though the two terms may be seen to be frequently connected, they are not necessarily so related. West prefers the general term paedophilia which he then goes on to define as:

> significant erotic arousal on the part of a phyically mature adult to pre-pubertal children or to children in the early stages of pubertal development. (West, 1987, p. 40)

This definition excludes the behaviour which might occur between peers which is included by Russell (1984) and also excludes physical attraction to physically developed adolescents, on the grounds that in the current climate this can hardly be viewed as deviant (West, 1987, p. 40). These definitions again illustrate what a problematic area this can be to make sense of (difficulties echoed by Kelly, 1988). One way to make sense of it is to draw out what might be considered to be the common elements in these definitions and focus attention on those commonalities.

All three definitions are concerned, to varying degrees, with behaviour between adults and those yet to be legally defined as adults. In other words all three draw our attention to relationships which are structured in terms of age. It is this element of child sexual abuse which will be of concern here. Therefore like West (1987) this study will not consider behaviours between children as peers but consideration will be given to all other behaviours which involve children under 16 and adults. The question of incest will therefore be contextualized within a wider framework of sexual behaviours.

Definitional problems are not the only difficulties to be faced in this area. It is also necessary to be clear on what particular studies are actually measuring. Kelly states:

> Further confusion arises when, in attempting to get the issue of child sexual abuse on the public agenda, the likelihood of a child experiencing some form of sexual abuse before the age of sixteen is transformed into the numbers of children currently being abused or who will experience abuse in any one year. (Kelly, 1988, p. 66)

Thus it is important to distinguish between 'incidence', the number of cases of abuse within a specific time period, and 'prevalence', the likelihood of an individual experiencing abuse whilst under the age of 16. A distinction clearly made by Russell (1984) but not always so clearly made by other feminist writers. Stanko (1988) points out that Russell's concern with 'lifetime experiences' clearly embraces the idea that these are experiences a woman will never forget. Fattah (1986) feels that this kind of position may introduce the 'danger of delaying the natural healing process' (ibid., pp. 9–10). Whichever position is adopted they clearly feed into how child sexual abuse is approached, measured and explained. (See below.) One last comment on the question of definitions. Studies also vary according to whether they have adopted 'official' definitions of sexual abuse or definitions of abuse constructed by those being abused. This is particularly important in considering the question of incest. There is a tendency to confuse incest with other forms of sexual abuse. Kelly (1988) argues that it is valuable to retain a distinction between incest, child sexual abuse by a member of the child's own household, and the wider continuum of sexual abuse experienced by women, since this allows incest to be contextualized. In agreement with Kelly an attempt will be made here to clarify this spectrum of experiences.

The studies which have been conducted on the question of child sexual abuse have tended to use retrospective social surveys and/or in-depth interviewing of specific samples rather than relying on official data sources for their information. Official data sources on this issue, it is argued, are likely to be even more limited than official records of child physical abuse, because of the secret and hidden nature of the behaviour. The experience of child sexual abuse, rather like being a victim of crime, is assumed to be the kind of event adults will be able to recall. As will be seen, people (though mostly women) develop very effective strategies of 'forgetting' such incidents.

These studies have, nevertheless, revealed a startling incidence and prevalence of child sexual abuse. The study by Russell (1984), whilst conducted in San Francisco using a sample of 930 women, provides a useful starting-point for our purposes since clear attempts were made methodologically to overcome any unwillingness to respond to the survey. Russell used face-to-face interviews, avoided the use of emotive terms like rape and incest, and carefully selected and trained interviewers. In addition Russell makes a clear defini-tional distinction between extra-familial child abuse and incestuous child abuse. These were defined as follows: extra-familial child abuse

> One or more unwanted sexual experiences with persons unrelated by blood or marriage, ranging from attempted petting (touching of breasts or genitals or attempts at such touching) to rape, before the victim turned 14 years, and completed or attempted forcible rape experiences from the ages 14 to 17 years (inclusive). (Russell, 1984, p. 180)

and incestuous child abuse as

> Any kind of exploitative sexual contact or attempted sexual contact, that occurred between relatives, no matter how distant

61

the relationship, before the victim turned 18 years old. (ibid., p. 181)

Using these definitions she found that within her sample 31 per cent had experience of extra-familial sexual abuse before the age of 18, of which 20 per cent had experience before the age of 14. Out of the sample 16 per cent reported having experienced incestuous child abuse before the age of 18, and of these 12 per cent had been sexually abused by a relative before the age of 14 (ibid., p. 183). Taking these findings together, Russell argues that the overall prevalence of sexual abuse within the female population on these figures is a quarter before the age of 14 and one third by the age of 18. These figures are perhaps the most detailed and definitionally clear ones available to us.

A sample survey conducted by MORI in 1984 of 2,000 of the British population revealed that 8 per cent of males and 12 per cent of females remembered having been involved in a sexual incident with an adult before they were themselves 16. (West, 1987, p. 42). Finkelhor (1979) found that amongst his sample of college students, 8.6 per cent of the males had been sexually abused as children as compared with 19.2 per cent of the females. In the survey conducted by Nash and West (1985) of 421 women in Cambridge, 94 had at least one childhood incident to report with half of these incidents recalled as having taken place before the age of 12, and 25 per cent constituting a 'significant experience with an older person' (West, 1987, p. 42).

These figures, despite the lack of clarity associated with some of them, emphasize the prevalence of child sexual abuse, suggesting that around one in four girls and one in ten boys are likely to experience some form of child sexual abuse either within the family or with adult figures outside the family before they reach the age of 16. (See Kelly, 1988, p. 66.) Feminists in particular would argue that these figures are an underestimate since they do not necessarily reflect what women themselves find abusive.

Women as survivors of incest, in particular, develop strategies of coping with these events which lead either to their being excluded from the definitions which are offered (because it is too painful to admit to a behaviour as being incestuous) or to their being erased from the memory. In addition Kelly (1988) makes clear that for some women incidents which are often excluded from these discussions, flashing, for example (see also McNeil, 1987), can be equally as painful as the more usually recognized form of sexual abuse, as can being subjected to verbal sexual harassment.

Incest, then, lies at one end of a continuum of behaviours which women may be subjected to both as adults and children. Whilst it is useful to contextualize child sexual abuse in this way it is also necessary to develop an understanding of who perpetrates such behaviours. This is important since it helps unfold the potentially different patterns of behaviour which are known for child physical abuse as opposed to child sexual abuse and contributes to an understanding and explanation of these figures.

The perpetrators of child victimization

It is clear that children are physically victimized in school by other children (bullying) and are subjected to sexual abuse and harassment of one form or another in school by their peers (see Mahoney, 1985). The concern here is, however, the way in which the figures discussed above are a result of adult behaviour with children. In this sense, child physical abuse will be examined first of all.

Identifying the perpetrators of child physical abuse has been dominated by what Parton (1985) calls the 'disease model' approach. Much time and effort has been devoted to discovering whether parents who abuse their children have particular personality traits or psychopathic disorders, or were themselves abused as children. He argues there is little concrete evidence to support any of these hypotheses.

Other studies have concerned themselves with identifying the structural characteristics of abusing parents. Gil (1970) observed in his national survey of abused children that 30 per cent lived in households headed by females; in 46 per cent of the cases the child's own father lived at home and in 20 per cent of the cases the child lived with a stepfather (Gil (in Lee, 1978), 1970, p. 49). When he examined the incidents these children were subjected to, he found that in 50 per cent of the cases the mother or stepmother was the perpetrator and in 40 per cent the father or stepfather (ibid., p. 50). Given that 30 per cent of the households were headed by women this means that men were over-represented in incidents of abuse in his survey. In a case study analysis of sixty cases conducted by Steele and Pollock (1968) fifty of the incidents were perpetrated by the mother and seven by the father. In creating a typology of abusing parents Jones et al. (1987) suggest, in their four types of primary child abuse, that mothers are more likely to be responsible for child specific abuse and obsessional abuse, fathers more likely to be involved in over-discipline abuse especially of older children, and both parents likely to be responsible for the rejection abuse of a particular child. (They go on to discuss types of secondary child abuse; see Jones et. al., 1987, Chapter 6.) The main point to be discerned from these findings, apart from reminding the reader of the complexities of the issue we are concerned with and the fact that these findings refer only to those cases which have come to the attention of the professionals, is that child physical abuse appears to be perpetrated by both male and female adults who find themselves in the parenting role. This is in stark contrast to the findings concerning the perpetrators of child sexual abuse.

In reviewing the evidence concerning the likely participation levels of the sexes in child sexual abuse, Russell concludes that 'Women rarely use children for their own direct sexual gratification' (Russell, 1984, p. 228). This does not mean that sexual abuse by women never occurs; it happens in about 5 per cent of the cases involving girls and 20 per cent of the cases involving boys (ibid., p. 231). Wilson (1983) in discussing incest states that 90 per cent of the victims are female and 95 per cent of the offenders are male (ibid. pp. 120–1). Nash and West (1985) report from their Cambridge study that of those who had had early sexual experiences with an older male, the perpetrator was a father or stepfather in 9 per cent of the cases, another relative in 9 per cent, a teacher or vicar in 4 per cent, a family friend in 24 per cent, an older boyfriend in 5 per cent; in 49 per cent of the cases there was no significant relationship (West, 1987, p. 55; the last figure being apparently inflated because it includes exhibitionist encounters outside the home). Russell (1984) reveals that one in six of those interviewed in households headed by a stepfather was abused by him, in comparison with one in forty for households headed by the natural father. Dominelli quotes figures from Berliner indicating that 'Fathers/stepfathers commit the bulk of incest offences (75%). The remainder are apportioned amongst male cohabitees (7%) and uncles, grandfather, and brothers (17%)' (Dominelli, 1986, p. 8). Taken together these figures paint the clear picture that child sexual abuse is most likely to be perpetrated on female children by male adults who are well known to the child. Dominelli (1986) goes on to say that the bulk of these offences occur when the child is under 12. This requires closer examination.

Russell's (1984) figures have already been cited. They give an indication of the experience of child sexual abuse before the age of 14. It is arguable, however, that the recent dispute concerning child sexual abuse in Cleveland was particularly controversial because of the youthfulness of the children involved; in one case allegedly involving a 9-month old baby. It is worthwhile, for this and other reasons, to spend a short time considering the questions raised by the Cleveland affair.

Cleveland; a cause for concern?

The situation in Cleveland arose, initially, as a result of the adoption of a new medical technique (new to Cleveland) in the diagnosis of child sexual abuse: the examination of the anus for signs of dilatation, referred to as reflex anal relaxation and dilatation (Butler-Sloss, 1988, p. 2). This technique was used and reported by Dr Wynne and Dr Hobbs in 1986 in the *Lancet* and Campbell quotes them as saying:

> Buggery in young children, including infants and toddlers, is
> a serious, common and under-reported type of child abuse.
> (Campbell, 1987, p. 11)

These doctors, working in Leeds, influenced policy and practice in the area of child sexual abuse resulting in 900 referrals and 274 confirmed cases in 1986, with the total of confirmed cases around 500 in 1987 (ibid., p. 11). These cases have involved many more younger children than has traditionally been the case. Doctors working in Worcester have produced similar increases in confirmed cases. In Cleveland in the whole of 1986 there were two confirmed cases of child sexual abuse. From March to July 1987 there were 104 referrals of child sexual abuse with 90 of those referrals occurring in May and June of that year (*Northern Echo*, 12 August 1987). In May 52 children from 17 families were examined for child sexual abuse with 41 showing signs of abuse using this medical diagnostic technique (Butler-Sloss, 1988, p. 5). A significant number of these children were under 5. (See the Butler-Sloss report, 1988.)

The occurrences in Cleveland not only involved a new medical technique, identifying younger children as possible victims of sexual abuse, but also became an issue because the system was rapidly overburdened, not being used to dealing with such high numbers of referrals. In addition there was a dispute between the professionals involved concerning the legitimacy of the diagnoses. These factors may well account, in part, for why Cleveland hit the headlines and other parts of the country using similar techniques did not. The figures for children being taken into care dropped in Cleveland when a 'second opinion' system was introduced; in July 1987 (*Northern Echo*, 30 July 1987) the number was 10, adding fuel to the view which disputed the validity of the diagnoses, with barrister Simon Hawkesworth QC suggesting that wrongful diagnoses had been made in the case of over 20 families during the previous months (*Northern Echo*, 12 August 1987).

In discussing the impending inquiry report on Cleveland, The *Independent* reports:

> Lord Justice Butler-Sloss is expected to find that the two doctors did uncover large-scale child sexual abuse, leading to a rise in numbers in the area last year. At the same time, the judge is expected to make criticisms of the way the cases were handled once suspicion came to light. (*Independent*, 27 June 1988)

The paper further reports that 'practically all' the children involved in the Cleveland affair have now returned home (*Independent*, 27 June 1988). It is worth quoting the report at length concerning what happened to the children involved in the crisis.

> Most of the 121 children diagnosed by Drs Higgs and Wyatt as sexually abused were separated from their parents and their home, 70% or so by place of safety orders. Sixty-seven of the children became wards of court. In the wardship cases 27 were dewarded and went home with the proceedings dismissed; 24 went home to both parents, there were conditions which included supervision orders and conditions as to medical examination of the children, and 2 of them went home on interim care orders. Of those children not made wards of court, a further 26 were the subject of place of safety orders. Of these 17 are at home, 6 still with a social worker allocated. In all 21 children remain

in care. We understand that out of the 121 children, 98 are now
at home. (Butler-Sloss, 1988, p. 11)

These figures seem to suggest that of the 121 children, around half
at the time of the report were still subject to the attention of the
social services in some way, even though the majority were at home.
It is not clear how many families this involved. Butler-Sloss is indeed
critical of the way in which the cases were handled, drawing attention
to a number of failings including the over-reliance on one piece of
diagnostic evidence. Laurance (1988) states that even in cases of anal
abuse only half show dilatation and that in itself constitutes only
one of ten physical indicators (ibid., p. 14). Butler-Sloss also makes
recommendations for future practice including the recommendation
for the establishment of an Office of Child Protection (Butler-Sloss,
1988, p. 21). What the Butler-Sloss report does not do is tackle the
causes of child sexual abuse.

There are a range of questions raised by these events which are
interesting, contentious, but not of direct relevance here. The relevance of Cleveland for an understanding of children as victims is that
it highlights and emphasizes that, despite the difficulties of measuring
child sexual abuse, usually done retrospectively, those prevalence figures cited earlier seem to be confirmed by the events in Cleveland.
The events also emphasized the need to broaden our understanding of
child sexual abuse to include other types of sexual behaviour, buggery
in particular, and to include its possible occurrence among very young
children. Campbell (1987) expresses it this way: an anus is 'easier to
penetrate than an immature vagina'.

It is interesting to note that the impetus for taking abuse of this kind
seriously has come not so much from listening to survivors of incest
but from the medical profession. What Kempe did for child physical
abuse in the 1960s paediatricians seem to be in the process of doing
for child sexual abuse in the 1980s. As in the case of the 'battered
baby syndrome', the issue has become medicalized. It has also turned
full circle. Child sexual abuse, especially when including buggery, is
also child physical abuse, particularly when involving young children.
In this way the strands of this chapter come together.

Whilst a whole range of questions was raised by the Cleveland affair
and a range of answers proffered, no one really wanted to examine
the possible explanations which underpin the statistics of this affair.
Returning to the original theme of this section, which was concerned

to examine the perpetrators of child abuse, it has been indicated that both males and females are perpetrators of child physical abuse, but that males are most likely to be the perpetrators of child sexual abuse. The reaction which the diagnoses in Cleveland received amongst the press and politicians reveals that a 'wall of denial' (Campbell, 1987) faces those who seemingly exposed the possible extent of this abuse; in other words, when the dominant ideology of the patriarchal family structure is challenged. Within this ideology children do not have rights. The accused parents were seen to have rights in so far as they were championed in their claims of innocence. Their potential as voters, at least, was recognized (ibid.). There is a problem, however, with viewing the response to Cleveland solely in these terms; that is, in terms of the challenge it makes to the ideology of the patriarchal family. This overlooks the complexities of the issues surrounding child abuse both physical and sexual. It has been shown clearly here that the dynamics of child physical abuse and the dynamics of child sexual abuse typically involve different actors. It is necessary to examine the ideological argument, therefore, a little more closely. This will be done by examining the notion of 'childhood innocence'.

Childhood innocence

Cleveland illustrates, it might be argued, that children constitute the quintessential victims; they are structurally powerless as well as physically powerless. Three related questions remain, however: does the notion of childhood innocence inform an understanding and explanation of this powerlessness, how does an understanding of the patriarchal family contribute to this and are children victims or survivors of these processes.

Ennew (1986) highlights the changing historical scene in which current notions of childhood have been constructed. These notions emphasize a strict demarcation between adults and children and a concern to make childhood 'the happiest days of your life'. Childhood was not always so conceived. This is not the place to reiterate the evidence and arguments which highlight the late nineteenth century as being a significant time of change for women and children alike in their removal from the workforce and in the creation of housework as women's work and school work as children's work. But it is the place to emphasize that it was during this time that the notion of childhood innocence was also constructed, though this notion also had its converse, 'beating out the devil'. This dual-edged concept is the overarching framework in which the more current demands of the parenting role are constructed. It is a framework which permeates explanations of child sexual abuse.

Morris (1987) offers four ways in which child sexual abuse has been explained, three of which highlight the way in which the notion of innocence permeates explanations in this area. First is sexual abuse as fantasy. Children are often not believed when they recount everyday events. Because they are children, it is argued, they fantasize. This tendency to disbelieve children is transferred to the recounting of events of sexual abuse. (It is a tendency also reflected in the legal context; see below.) Whilst it is difficult to imagine how very young children might make up stories of sexual abuse without having experienced such abuse, there has been a strong tendency not to believe the child. The child is seen as either being malevolent (possessed by the devil!) or as having a vivid imagination. In some respects this tendency to disbelieve the child is changing. Childline, the telephone service for children, for example, starts from the premise that children need someone to listen to them who will believe them.

The second explanation of child abuse discussed by Morris (1987) is the explanation which focuses on the child as seducer. In this explanation the child is seen as precipitator of its own victimization; a willing and knowing participant and certainly not innocent. Again whilst some adolescents might be more sexually mature and provocative than others, this does not necessarily mean that they knowingly precipitate their own victimization, and would certainly seem an inappropriate explanation in cases involving very young children. Kitzinger argues:

> A precocious child who appears flirtatious and sexually aware may forfeit her claims to protection because, if the violation of innocence is the criterion by which the act of sexual abuse is judged, violating a 'knowing' child is a lesser offence than violating an innocent child. (Kitzinger, 1988, p. 82)

The third way does not really constitute an explanation but is more of a mechanism of excusing the behaviour. This line of thinking argues that in general no harm is caused by the child being victimized. This is presumably because of the view that the child is innocent and therefore unlikely to judge what is happening to it. This view suggests that the main problems are posed for the child by the reaction of others when the behaviours are discovered; the removal of the father from the family home, for example. Morris (1987) states that this contrasts strongly with the experiences of incest survivors who talk of 'fear, revulsion, shame and guilt' (ibid., p. 191) at the events which happened to them. Finkelhor (1986) also reports long-term effects of child sexual abuse.

The final explanation for child abuse referred to by Morris (1987) lays the responsibility for what happens to the child at the foot of the mother. The mother colludes, knowingly or unknowingly, with the father in the treatment of the child. Whilst there is some empirical evidence for this – the recent case dealt with in Chester Crown Court, for example, which involved the mother holding down the 5-year old daughter whilst the father abused her – it is difficult to embrace this as a total explanation for the picture of child sexual abuse which appears to be emerging. The ultimate explanation for child abuse, along with rape and wife abuse, for Morris lies in understanding what links the three together; namely men's domination over women. Does this stance constitute a sufficient explanation of all the available evidence on child abuse?

Focusing on the concept of 'childhood innocence' and the way in which it permeates explanations of child sexual abuse also focuses our attention on the child, but what about the perpetrator? Do perpetrators have any specific characteristics which explain why, within the patriarchal framework of the family, some children get abused but not others? After all, statistically, more survive childhood not having been sexually abused than having been abused.

In reviewing the evidence on paedophile offenders, West (1987) states that the most frequently reported characteristics of such offenders are social shyness, timidity, unassertiveness, low self-esteem, and feelings of inadequacy, insecurity and alienation (ibid., p. 50). 'Paedophiles are gentle and tentative in their interactions with children, persuasive and seductive rather than coercive' (ibid.). Hence the validity of the 'Just Say No' campaign for children. Most stranger incidents, it seems, would easily be dissuaded once there was resistance from the child. The characteristics outlined above have been derived from those who have been caught in sexual activity with children and are therefore problematic. West (1987) suggests that those who have not been caught are probably more self-confident, more circumspect and skilled in seduction but does not suggest that they are necessarily more aggressive or insistent. Men who engage in sexual acts with their own children, West argues, are different than other paedophiles. West states:

> As family men they are perhaps less isolated and socially alienated than molesters of strange children, but they may be using their families as a refuge from an outside world in which they feel ill at ease. Typically their emotional life revolves around an intense commitment to family relationships even though these may be unhappy or untypical. (ibid., p. 57)

West also reports that men who sexually abuse their male and female children are more often violent both inside and outside the home. And whilst these typifications may not account for every case, West also cites the domineering, patriarchal father as a type of offender which most usually fits with the feminist position.

This overall picture of paedophiles poses some problems for the ideological argument. It seems that there must be some other motivational factors involved which encourage some rather than others to take advantage of the 'innocent child'. Additionally the ideological argument faces some difficulties in embracing the question of child physical abuse.

It has already been stated that explanations of child physical abuse have been dominated by what Parton (1985) has called the 'disease model'. This approach has a number of elements. Explanations are offered either in terms of the disordered personality of the parent, or by being able to identify factors of 'danger' to the child (heavy drinking within the family, young parenthood, inadequate bonding at birth between parent and child) or more general environmental factors (poor housing, overcrowding, low socioeconomic status, etc.). All these factors are discussed as factors which impinge upon the individual's ability to handle the parenting role. They crystallize in an explanation which Parton argues blames the victim (the victim in this case being the parent). Parton states:

> Essentially parents are studied in terms of what is wrong with them, so that abuse is seen as a problem with certain parents who are unusual, or different to the normal. Abuse results from some individual or family defect and so must be remedied by particular means or exceptionalist solutions which are tailored

71

to the individual case. In the process other parents are seen as normal and the wider society is not seen as problematic. (ibid., p. 149)

Parton is clearly suggesting that there is an ideological dimension to these explanations which serves to maintain some sort of notion, not of childhood innocence *per se* but of the nature of family life. But again the question must be asked, what is then to be made of the evidence which suggests that child physical abuse is perpetrated in some circumstances rather than others by some kinds of actors rather than others? (See the evidence discussed above.) Is it simply the case that if the social deprivation were removed then so would be the physical abuse? Despite the practical difficulties in achieving this goal the evidence would suggest that, whilst some of the known child physical abuse might be removed in this way, not all cases would disappear.

This discussion is clearly suggesting that there are layers within the explanation of child victimization which need to be unwrapped. The processes which culminate in actions perpetrated on a child, in which the child is essentially seen as an innocent pawn, are part of a game structured in society's favour. The frameworks offered by both Morris (1987) and Parton (1985) taken together suggest that part of an explanation of child abuse lies outside of the individual participants. However, the evidence cited by West (1987) and elsewhere concerning the characteristics of known perpetrators of child abuse suggests that some individuals are more likely to participate in this behaviour than others; part of the explanation must also, therefore, lie with them.

Towards an explanation of child abuse

The evidence reviewed in this chapter has highlighted some of the problems associated with measuring child abuse, with defining child abuse and with identifying who is likely to be responsible for abusing a child. In that review it has been shown that child abuse is difficult to measure but that it is probably fair to say that there is considerably more physically and sexually abusive behaviour perpetrated on children than any official figures or surveys reveal. (There is also probably considerably more psychological abuse; even less is known about this type of victimization of children.) The events in Cleveland clearly highlight the response likely to be received if there appears to be a large-scale attack on the family. Yet it is within that structure and the ideologies which surround it, as the previous section suggests, that part of an explanation of child abuse must lie. These ideologies are not only concerned with patriarchy, they are also concerned with ageism; the strict demarcation of adults from children as epitomized in the notion of childhood innocence. Ageist strategies marginalize old and young alike; but the young additionally so, in so far as they have few rights. Kitzinger suggests:

> If we are to tackle the roots of child sexual abuse we have to think about the position of children in society. Perhaps the first step is to change the terms of the debate by replacing the concept of 'vulnerability' with terms such as 'oppression' or 'powerlessness' and by replacing restrictive notions of 'protecting' with liberating notions of 'empowering'. (Kitzinger, 1988, p. 83)

Such a movement would not only entail tackling child abuse, it would require a re-examination of fundamental assumptions concerning adult relationships with children; they would no longer be there to do as they were told but would be demanding a more equal status in a whole range of relationships including those within the family. Thus children's physical powerlessness – they are smaller, and in the case of the very young physically dependent on adults – is compounded by their personal and structural powerlessness. The concept of childhood innocence reflects the ageists' strategies which are used to deny the child personal power. This, when employed as one strategy to legitimize the modern nuclear family, in which the child theoretically receives care and protection, culminates in the child's structural powerlessness. It is only by embracing an appreciation of the personal and structural powerlessness of children in their relation to adults that we can begin to offer a framework for child abuse which encompasses an understanding of the features of both physical and sexual abuse. This framework permits an explanation which includes an understanding of children as property over which adult caretakers, both male and female, have unquestionable rights, which for female children are compounded by the rights of men to control women's sexuality. Thus structurally children are victims of a social system with particular characteristics and particular ideologies.

This type of explanation alone, however, does not fit with all the evidence we have of child abuse. The evidence we have concerning known perpetrators of child abuse, both physical and sexual, clearly suggests that some individuals, both male and female, are more prone to succumb to the pressures inherent in these ideological frameworks of family life. Whilst there does appear to be a considerably greater prevalence of child abuse than comes to official notice, and particularly child sexual abuse, most children survive childhood without such scars. The evidence from the Cleveland affair, though unclear, would suggest that whilst 121 children were the centre of that affair, it involved somewhere in the region of 40 to 50 families. The allegations, on a number of occasions, points to several children in one family being abused by one abuser. It is necessary not to be misled, therefore, into thinking that abusers are as widespread as the abused. Our explanation, consequently, needs also to be cognisant of the social and psychological factors which lead some to abuse children but not others. In any event children are not only victims, they are also survivors. Survivors, not only of family life but also of the legal system should their particular case be proceeded with for prosecution. The legal context of handling cases of child sexual abuse, in particular, interestingly highlights the way in which a number of the processes discussed in this chapter come together.

Child victims in the criminal justice process

Much is made by practitioners of the way in which the discovery of child sexual abuse and its subsequent hardling may lead to further victimization of the child. Ultimately the child fears that the object of both its love and its hate, normally the father or father-figure, will be removed and that somehow all this is its own fault. Much is made, again by practitioners, of the belief that, if at all possible, it is in the best interests of all parties, including the child, not to proceed with prosecution in cases of this sort but to engage in some form of family therapy. Adler (1988) presents an interesting argument posing the alternative position. She states:

> It is not implausible – although more research is needed to support the contention – that the traumatic experience of children in court is in large measure an artefact of the adversarial system, of

inadequate and insensitive procedures, and of an appallingly low level of understanding of children and sexual abuse that prevails among judges and lawyers. (Adler, 1988, p. 140)

She highlights two ways in which this system works to undermine the child sexual abuse case.

In the first way the criminal justice system overlooks the normal process of adaptation to child sexual abuse. This culminates after disclosure of the abuse in the child denying that the events took place. This is normal given the trauma which then unfolds for the child. The criminal justice system deals with evidence and views retraction as evidence of telling lies. This obviously works against the interests of the child if the system fails to recognize the processes involved in normal adaptation to abuse. The image of the malevolent child appears again. (See above.) This is compounded by the way in which the child is treated as a witness. On the one hand children are put on a par with adults; they enter the awesome formal surroundings of the court and all that that entails. On the other hand their evidence is undermined particularly if it is deemed inappropriate for the child to take the oath. When children are considered too young to do this, their evidence cannot subsequently stand as corroborative evidence. Adler states:

the corroboration rule makes a dubious distinction between most adults on the one hand and children on the other. It is assumed in at least two ways that children's evidence is inherently less reliable than that of adults. First, children may lie, and this is assumed to be particularly common with regard to sexual matters. The effect of this is compounded by a general belief that allegations of sexual crimes are more likely to be untruthful than those of other offences, whether they are made by adults or children. Secondly, there is an assumption that children are more likely than adults to be mistaken or inaccurate in their description of events, or indeed of the alleged offender. (Adler, 1988, pp. 144–5)

There is no evidence to support either of these assumptions but the way in which they work to undermine the position of the child and the wider cultural assumptions they reflect is clear. Recently, the Home Office has indicated that the rules regarding the giving of evidence will be relaxed to allow children's evidence to be given via video. This moves the criminal justice process in the right direction. Much more would need to be done to address the general assumption that prosecution is inappropriate in cases of this sort.

There is one further dimension to the criminal justice process which remains relatively unexplored for the victim of child abuse. This is the avenue of compensation. Very few claims are made to the Criminal Injuries Compensation Board on behalf of children who have been taken into care as a result of child abuse. In 1985 Macrae reports that only twelve such claims were made (*Observer*, 31 July 1988, p. 5). He also reports a recent case in which a stepfather was convicted of 'lewd and libidinous behaviour' and the two girls involved received £3,000 and the younger brother who witnessed the events received £1,000. Why more claims are not made is not exactly clear. It is possible to speculate that this has resulted from our inability to see children as victims in the same way as we see adults as victims simply because they do not have the same status. A claim for criminal injuries has to be made on behalf of a child; it requires adults to know that a claim is allowable and to make it. Very few seem to be aware of their general rights in this respect and even fewer seem to be aware of the rights of children. (For a more general discussion of criminal injuries compensation, see Chapter 5.) The financial benefits from such a claim to a child when leaving local authority care may ease that transition into the adult world. The fact that such claims are not made more often confirms the hidden dimension of much child victimization.

Implications for victimology

The question remains: what relevance does the issue of child abuse have for victimology? At one level it can be seen that if victimology is concerned with victims of crime, then actions perpetrated against children are a fertile ground in which to pursue that concern. And whilst some of the early papers reported in the series edited by Drapkin and Viano (1974) do reflect a concern with children as victims, little it appears has been done to pursue these issues in the forum of victimology. More attention has been focused on the care and protection of children in the arena of social work practice. Recent years have seen growth in the work done by feminist researchers in respect of child sexual abuse, but again little of this has yet penetrated victimology. Yet when the concepts which underpin work in this area are examined, there are remarkable parallels between the understandings offered of child abuse and victimology. This is particularly the case with the concept of victim precipitation.

Children may precipitate actions by adults either because they break the disciplinary rules laid down by adults which results in physical punishment which may be defined as excessive, or because they seduce adults which results in sexual relationships. The evidence cited here clearly indicates the limited nature of such a concept not only for understanding child abuse, but for victimology in general. It is a concept which disguises the power relationships which underpin the behaviour under discussion. This disguise hides the way in which age and gender vitally structure any understanding which is framed by the notion of victim precipitation. It also has a tendency to focus our attention on the victim, perhaps at the expense, sometimes, of paying attention to what is known about the offender. Particularly relevant in the context of children.

The concept of lifestyle as used within victimology can also be re-evaluated as a result of considering the victimization of children. This notion is often used implicitly in social work practice when developing a framework for highlighting families in which there might be a risk of child abuse; usually families lower down the social hierarchy. These assumptions reflect an ideology of family life which needs to be questioned. Questioned because it too readily individualizes processes which might be better understood if they were put in a structural framework first of all. This is not to deny the relevance of individual actors or actions but states that they should be structurally located. In this way it is clear that victimology's use of the notion of lifestyle needs to be examined carefully and critically for such bias.

The examination of the evidence concerning children as victims, however, raises more fundamental questions for victimology than simply to re-examine the nature of its concepts. These fundamental questions arise when one examines the parallels between children as victims, the elderly as victims and women as victims.

It has already been suggested that the elderly, like children, are significantly marginalized in modern society. The old, like the young, are subjected to stereotypical expectations which derive from assumptions made as to their capabilities because of their age. It is not uncommon to observe people speaking more loudly or in more basic terms to elderly people simply because they are elderly, not because of their capabilities. Like children, the elderly too are often treated as if they had no rights and are in need of care and protection; being incapable of caring for and protecting themselves. Whilst this may be the case for those who are elderly and also infirm it is certainly not the case for many of those over 60. These assumptions, however, pervade the way in which the elderly's experiences with respect to crime are handled. Chapter 2 clearly illustrates that whilst the elderly are least at risk from being assaulted in the street, they are most afraid of this happening to them. The media report child abuse and assaults on the elderly in an equally graphic fashion. Both are seen as an indicator of the moral decline of society. The elderly then become victims of a moral panic which in reality bears little relation to their actual risk from crime. In this way the elderly become victims, not only of crime from time to time, but of media reporting. This reflects a social system structured with age as a key variable in that process. If ageist assumptions were challenged with respect to children, they would also require challenging with respect to the elderly. If the elderly were reconstituted as full members of society rather than marginal to it there would, of course, be consequences in the way that they were viewed as victims. Full members of society are for the most part male, socioeconomically independent and powerful. If the elderly were no longer marginalized they would no longer fit the idealized view of the victim.

Taking ageism seriously requires locating victimizing processes in particular structural contexts. It is possible to draw similar parallels between that context and women as victims. These parallels have been usefully drawn out by Morris (1987). The intention is not to repeat the detail here but merely to sketch out the possibilities.

The notion of victim precipitation is a useful starting-point for drawing out the parallels between the victimization of children and women as victims. It has been seen that this concept has been used in the context of child sexual abuse. It has been employed in a similar fashion in studies of rape. This parallel highlights the way in which the dual-edged notion of childhood innocence is in many ways similar to the dual-edged way in which women have been viewed; the virgin–whore dichotomy. Rather like the way in which the image of the child as seducer has been used to explain incest, the woman as 'asking for it' has been used to explain rape. Children are innocent but are also in need of control. Women are virgins but their sexuality also requires controlling and keeping in its place. Just as children have been denied full status in society by the nature of their relationships to adults in the context of the family, so women have been denied status because of their position in relation to men in the context of the family. Children are the property of their parents; women are the property of men. Female children frequently learn this in a very real way in the context of those who are deemed to care for and protect them. Thus it is not only ageist assumptions which structure the extent of victimization; it is also sexist assumptions. It is in an effort to take these latter assumptions seriously that Lea, Matthews and Young (1987) were led to state that:

> Women bear the brunt of crime. For a long time it was supposed that they were irrational about crime having, according to official statistics, a high fear of crime compared to men, but in reality a much lower chance of being victims ... For women are, in fact, more likely to be victims of crime than men. (ibid., p. 15)

Whether the work they have done to date actually meets the feminist challenge as this statement is designed to do has been discussed in Chapter 2. It is nevertheless a statement which victimology needs to take seriously and again looking to children enables us to do this. Elsewhere Jones, MaClean and Young state:

> While there are undoubtedly restrictions on women's activity which stem from gender roles and family structure, and which in turn contribute to heightened fear for personal safety, the survey did not investigate this aspect of women's experience. (Jones, MaClean and Young, 1986, p. 183)

The parallels to be drawn from incorporating an understanding of the victimization of children into victimology is one route, which would begin to flesh out those questions of gender roles and family structure to which Jones, MaClean and Young refer.

Conclusion

This chapter has attempted to weave together a range of difficult issues which pertain to the question of child victimization. It is hoped that the reader now has a feel for some of those difficulties. It is also hoped that the reader has a feel for the different issues involved in the questions of child physical abuse and child sexual abuse and the way in which addressing these questions and offering answers to them leads to a more critical examination of the relationship between the individual and the structure of the patriarchal family.

The implications for victimology are substantial. Incorporating an understanding of child victimization into victimology requires that victimology develops a more critical edge. This not only means taking seriously the way in which people see themselves as being victimized and through which they construct strategies of survival. It also means that attention be focused on the structuring of that victimization within the institutions of society underpinned by an ageist and sexist framework; the two variables discussed in this chapter. (There may also be racist frameworks within which to locate child victimization. This is as yet relatively under-researched.)

Whilst this chapter has focused on the relatively powerless in society, children, if victimology is to develop fully a critical framework for analysis it is also necessary to consider the way in which the relatively powerful create patterns of victimization. In this sense whilst child abuse might be understood as a product of the structure of society it is nevertheless perpetrated, experienced and survived by individuals. One of the problems here has been the uncovering and explaining of that victimization. Once this is achieved, recognizing children as victims is not so difficult. There are, however, processes of victimization which are never recognized as such by either the offenders or the victims. These features of victimization are the concern of Chapter 4.

4

Corporate victimization

Introduction

Chapter 3 introduced us to some of the questions and potential explanations of the nature of victimization of arguably the least powerful in a modern Western society: children. This chapter will be concerned to address some of the issues pertaining to victimization by, arguably, one of the most powerful: the business corporation. In order to understand the processes involved in victimization of this sort it will be necessary, first of all, to develop some understanding of the nature of the power possessed by such organizations. Secondly, this chapter will address some of the difficulties involved in trying to measure such victimization. Thirdly, this chapter will review what is known about victimization of this sort and will contextualize that knowledge by examining three specific examples of corporate victimization. Finally some attention will be paid to the implications these issues have for victimology.

What kind of power do business corporations have?

At one level the previous chapter has clearly indicated that there are certain classes of individuals who have more power than others. In order to understand the position of children it is clearly necessary to refer to them as a class of individuals who have less power than adults because of their age and the social expectations associated with age. It has been observed in the previous chapter that this lack of power is compounded by the variable of sex. Female children seem to suffer a disproportionate amount of victimization at the hands of male adults, more than might be expected if age alone was considered. This, it was suggested in Chapter 3, might be understood not only by reference to the way in which expectations associated with gender attribute different personal qualities to individuals, but also by the way in which such expectations are compounded within the institution of the family. This results in the differential power of males over females. This analysis moves away from seeing power merely as a quality which one person possesses over another into an analysis which sees that power as being inextricably constructed within the institutions of a particular society. This power exists over and above any individuals who may occupy particular positions in those institutions. In other words, individuals may construct for themselves the way they relate to other individuals but that relationship is ultimately framed by features of social institutions which set limits on the choices such individuals might make. An understanding of power which is institutionally based as opposed to individually based is a useful starting-point for understanding features of the power possessed by business corporations and the potential victimizing processes which flow from this power.

Institutionally based power permits an examination of relationships between the powerful and the powerless which have not so far been considered; for example, the relationship between the police and the policed. The police constitute an institution in which the power relationship is more than obvious at one level but less than obvious at another.

An individual police officer, by virtue of the position he or she occupies in a modern Western society, is invested by law with discretionary power. How an individual police officer divests himself or herself of that power is related to a number of factors: the dynamics of a particular situation, how that officer has learned to understand and interpret those dynamics (the cop culture), how historical and structural processes have resulted in some classes of individuals being defined as 'police property' – that is, more likely to be subjected to the processes of policing. (See Brogden, Jefferson and Walklate, 1988, for a fuller exposition of this argument.) The cumulative effect of these factors, but particularly the historical and structural ones, results in some groups in society being subjected to policing more than others. In this sense these groups are victimized (an observation made in Chapter 5 in the context of the historical emergence of the current status of the victim in the criminal justice process).

Such differential policing raises serious questions for those communities subjected to such practices in their relationship with the police. Jones, MacLean and Young (1986) attempted to measure this relationship using the local crime survey method, by reference to individuals' experiences of harassment and violence by the police. One feature of that relationship has been analysed in the context of deaths in custody by Scraton and Chadwick (1987).

The individual acts of police officers, then, need to be understood by reference not only to the individual police officers themselves, but also to the institutional framework in which they operate. This framework informs them that the variables of age, race and sex are key variables in determining the nature of their work. Being young, black and male, or any combination of these variables, spells trouble to the police officer. The legal framework provides the context for the emergence of discriminatory practices such as these.

> These discriminatory perceptions have served effectively to remove certain groups from the police province altogether. Much criminal activity, and the individuals who carry out these offences, therefore fall outside conventional policework. These are typically the white-collar or corporate crimes – ranging from municipal corruption to business fraud. (Brogden, Jefferson and Walklate, 1988, p. 146)

This is not to say that there are organizations which are above the law, though some might behave as if they were, it is intended to highlight the way in which institutional practices of the police, for example, pay much more time and attention to the young, black male, and see it as their job to be so doing, than to the marketing of fraudulently described goods. Indeed in that example the police may not be involved until enough evidence has been gathered clearly to identify that there is a case to answer. Work of that sort is more usually in the remit of the Office of Fair Trading.

It can be seen, then, that not only are the activities of business organizations not seen to be the real problem for the police and frequently not their concern, but also that the activities of business corporations are more usually monitored by regulatory agencies other than the police; the Factories Inspectorate, the Inland Revenue, etc. This regulatory process contributes to the way in which the activities of business corporations are not seen as criminal, since they frequently do not come before the criminal courts. The regulatory agencies, for the most part, do just that. They attempt to maintain some common code of practice within the framework of the law in a range of different business and industrial settings by encouraging the acceptance of such a code through the use of warnings, fines, or reaching some other sort of agreement or settlement with the offender. For the most part these processes are hidden from public view. When the activities of a business organization come to public attention it is usually in a dramatic fashion. They are generally referred to as disasters particularly if they involve the loss of life. In this sense, a number of incidents may share a common feature. It is possible to offer an explanation of these happenings not by referring to them as disasters, accidents, or the result of unforeseen circumstances, but by referring to them as the likely consequences of corporate activity. This argument will be developed more fully in the discussion to follow. Suffice it to say at this stage that this does not diminish their status as disasters for those immediately involved and closely related to the events, but does encourage a rethinking of how such events might occur. In this rethinking the victims are not victims of accidents but victims of an economic and legal system which positions corporations in a different regulative and motivational environment than the young, black male who is subjected to differential policing priorities and behaviours of the police force.

It is the victimizing activities of business corporations, who are, in this sense, powerful, not only as a result of their economic power, or the power they possess as institutions, but also as a result of the hidden powers they possess stemming from the way in which their activities are regulated, which will be the focus of this chapter.

Victims of white collar or corporate crime: conceptual issues

Sutherland (1949) first coined the term 'white collar crime'. According to Bequai he was primarily concerned with the criminal of the 'suites'; that is, those who misrepresented the nature of corporate assets in the interests of business and those who used their business power to become involved in political manipulation (Bequai, 1978, p. 2). Sutherland was also concerned that such activities were not subjected to the same regulatory system as other forms of criminal activity. (See above.) They were more usually handled by administrative bodies who imposed relatively minor fines as a way of trying to control such activities.

Since Sutherland first drew attention to this feature of criminal behaviour as a focus of concern for criminology, the conceptual framework has become a little more sophisticated. Levi referencing

Smith (1982) informs us that 'There is a growing tendency among "white-collar crime" academics to differentiate between crimes by business and crimes against business: the former are labelled "corporate crime"; the latter "white-collar crime" ' (Levi, 1987, xix). There are also distinctions to be made between crime for corporations and criminal corporations. In this latter case Levi (1981) suggests the victims tend to be other large companies (ibid., p. 128). Levi (1987), though, finds these distinctions rather simplistic. And, as will be seen below, in the case of fraud it is difficult to draw a clear line between these different sorts of activities. It is, however, the simplicity of the distinction which is valuable for the purposes here. Attention will be paid to corporate crime, as defined above, rather than white collar crime even though this distinction may be a little fuzzy around the edges.

One of the main consequences of employing this distinction is that attention will not be paid to criminal activity which falls into the area of 'fiddling' at work. This is not to say that this kind of behaviour does not have consequences and that, in some part, those consequences may well result in victimization. The primary purpose of this chapter is to draw attention to the way in which the corporate organization promotes certain kinds of activity or inactivity resulting in victimization rather than to consider the way in which individuals negotiate their own activities within an organizational framework (fiddling at work). Whilst recognizing that this is a rather arbitrary distinction to make, it serves the purpose of painting a broad picture of patterns of victimization of this sort.

Geis, focusing on trying to establish patterns of victimization in 'crimes incidental to but in the furtherance of business operations' (Geis, 1973, pp. 89–90), introduces the notion of 'victim responsiveness'. This term is employed to refer to a collection of features pertinent to understanding the victim of corporate crime. (Geis uses the term white collar crime, but in a similar sense to the use of corporate crime here.) Geis argues: 'It is particularly notable, first of all, that people generally do not react vigorously, with deep outrage, to most forms of white collar crimes' (ibid., p. 99). It is arguable that people do not react vigorously since for the most part they are also unaware of their victimization. Bequai (1978) refers to the 'modus operandi' of the white collar criminals playing on the naivety of the victim (ibid., p. 3). Levi states of fraud: 'Fraud, then, is an unusual type of crime because the fraudster gets the victim to part with his property voluntarily, albeit

85

(by definition) under false assumptions about the transaction' (Levi, 1987, p. 1). Thus the notion of victim responsiveness appears to relate to the victims' state of mind: a willingness to assume that the behaviours they are either directly or indirectly involved with are legitimate. In addition, this state of mind appears to include an unwillingness on the part of victims, if they become aware of their victimization, to report such incidents to the relevant regulatory authority. Why this seems to be the case is unclear. It may be, in part, a result of not defining the police as the appropriate agency but not quite knowing who the appropriate agency might be; as well as a general unwillingness to become involved in what can prove to be rather lengthy legal proceedings. What is clear is that this 'state of mind' is hardly ever questioned. As Levi states: 'Business people start with a built-in advantage of the positive stereotype attached to business people generally' (Levi, 1987, p. 209). When campaigns are launched around particular issues, such as the thalidomide drug campaign of the 1960s or the more recent campaign focused on the drug Opren, for example, they constitute rare examples of consumers working in concert. Bequai (1978) argues that, in the American context, the legal system is so cumbersome and easily manipulated that the ordinary consumer might be forgiven for becoming cynical when it is observed that offenders are often let off relatively lightly. Such cynicism is underwritten in the English context by the observation that much of the behaviour of concern here is subject to the control of regulatory agencies rather than the police (see above). Geis (1973) argues that these features combine to create a general public responsive to victimization of this sort.

In this wide sense all members of the general public may be victims of corporate crime whether it involves price fixing in the United States or doctoring consumer goods within the EEC. However, it is necessary, and fruitful, to become somewhat more specific than this. Before turning attention to specific features of corporate victimization, it is enlightening to discuss the difficulties involved in offering any accurate measurement of victimization of this sort.

Measuring corporate victimization

One obvious place to start in trying to assess the extent of corporate crime is the official agencies responsible for regulating such business activity. This, however, is not as straightforward as it seems. The official statistics which are available in this area may not portray an accurate picture of law-breaking business activity which has come to the attention of the official agencies let alone tap the range of activities which have not. A number of difficulties may be involved.

At one level there is the task of collating and comparing statistical information gathered by a number of different sources. Bequai (1978) points out that there are more than 2,000 federal agencies, commissions and departments which may carry information of this sort (ibid., p. 9). Levi points out that the police are not the only agency who might be involved in the policing of commercial frauds:

> Consumer frauds (including restrictive trade practices) may be dealt with by Trading Standards officers or by the Office of Fair Trading; bankruptcy, liquidation, banking, and investment frauds are within the remit of the Department of Trade and Industry; and tax frauds are dealt with by the Inland Revenue or Customs and Excise departments. (Levi, 1987, p. 118)

There may, then, at least be technical problems in collating information from a number of different sources. There is an additional difficulty, however, concerning what these official statistics actually represent. Bequai (1978), again in the context of the United States, points to the secrecy which surrounds the activities of some of the regulative agencies. Their decisions may never be made public. Whilst the making of 'administrative decisions' of this sort is not apparently as widespread in the United Kingdom, this does not mean that the official statistics here can be read with impunity. Carson (1970) found it necessary to examine the actual files relating to particular firms covered by the factory inspectorate since the reports of the chief inspector referred only to the number of prosecutions made and did not include the total number of offences identified or how sanctions other than prosecution had been employed by the inspectorate. A problem of a slightly different sort may arise when examining tax records. A process of negotiation may occur between tax inspectors and those accused of tax frauds. In this case, again, the final number prosecuted reveals little about the number who reached a 'settlement' with the tax authorities. None of these statistical sources is likely to reveal anything concerning the victims of such business activities. So, whilst there are difficulties associated in using official data sources to construct a measure of corporate crime, there are even more difficulties in using these sources as indicators of levels of victimization.

The criminal victimization survey has been used increasingly in the United States and the United Kingdom to overcome some of the difficulties associated with official statistical sources in the incidence of conventional crime. Is this an appropriate method to uncover the incidence of criminal victimization by corporations? Given some of the features of corporate crime and victimization already discussed in this chapter the answer to this question is, as presently constructed, no. Hough and Mayhew clearly state that

> They (crime surveys) can only uncover crimes which have clearly identifiable people as victims – they cannot easily count crimes against organisations (such as company fraud, shoplifting or fare evasion) and 'victimless crimes' involving, for example, drug abuse or some sexual offences. (Hough and Mayhew, 1983, pp. 3–4)

Here they are not excluding the possibility that criminal victimization surveys might be used to cover a range of criminal activities, just that it is likely to become a complex procedure. They are, however, emphasizing the idea that this survey method relies ultimately on clearly identifiable people as victims. Now it may be that some people would clearly identify themselves as being victims of corporate crime. Such individuals may certainly respond to appropriately phrased questions. The intrinsic nature of victimization of this sort suggests that such individuals are likely to be few and far between. The extent to which people clearly identify themselves as victims of conventional crime is problematic. Even more so in the case of corporate crime. People, on the whole, fail to recognize the activities of business corporations as criminal; indeed only the perpetrators of much corporate criminal activity are in a position to know that what is going on is criminal. (See Bottomley and Pease, 1986, pp. 19–20.) This essential characteristic of corporate victimization rules out the criminal victimization survey as an appropriate means for uncovering victimization of this sort. Researchers of corporate crime have, more often than not, used a more imaginative range of research techniques in their efforts to explore particular features of corporate crime.

Detailed information on corporate crime in this country is in short supply. Those studies which have been done have looked at a specific type of corporate criminal activity or activities in a particular industry. In looking at 'long-firm fraud' Levi (1981) employed a range of research techniques: court records, observation and open-ended interviews. In his study of victims of commercial fraud, officials of almost all the investigative agencies likely to be employed by victims were interviewed. In addition a sample of victims from the court records was interviewed; other victims involved in court cases were sent a postal questionnaire. Court records were examined for the two-year period of the investigation and various journalists and media people were interviewed, in depth, concerning the way in which programmes on fraud were constructed. (See Levi and Pithouse, 1988.) Braithwaite (1984) used a fairly open interviewing strategy in exploring the pharmaceutical industry and subsequently recommended the use of two interviewers when exploring corporate crime given the tendency for informants to deny, at a later date, what was said (Braithwaite, 1985). Carson (1970), as already indicated, made extensive use of secondary data sources. These examples illustrate that research on corporate crime is not impossible. Neither must the role of investigative journalism be forgotten in drawing attention to particular issues in this area.

From these examples it can be seen that there is only one study, of which the author is aware, which is directly focused on the victim. The remaining studies, do, however, permit inferences to be made concerning the likely impact of criminal activities of this kind. Both Reiman (1979) and Box (1983) draw together a range of statistical material in an attempt to map a general picture of the impact of corporate activities, into which the more specific studies mentioned above can be located.

Thus, it can be seen that measuring corporate victimization is not impossible but has largely been neglected by both criminologists and victimologists. To offer some picture of the range and extent of corporate victimization it is necessary to make a number of inferences from incomplete statistical sources and specialized studies which for the most part have not been directly concerned with the victims of such activities. The following discussion will attempt to paint a broad picture of the possible incidence of corporate victimization and will then look more closely at three areas of that pattern of victimization, namely fraud, the North Sea oil industry and the pharmaceutical industry. Each of these more detailed analyses may cast some light on the more general problems to be addressed by those working in the area of victimology.

The impact of corporate victimization

There are two ways in which attempts have been made to assess the impact of corporate victimization. In the first instance the evidence concerning the incidence of death and illness related to the workplace will be considered. Secondly, the evidence relating to the economic cost of corporate criminal activity will be assessed.

Reiman (1979) and Box (1983) both offer a review of the United States and United Kingdom evidence respectively concerning the likely incidence of death and illness which may be related to the activities, or, perhaps more specifically, inactivities of business corporations. These reviews focus on, amongst other factors, the violation of health and safety regulations in the workplace. As Box (1983) states, it is difficult to quantify precisely the nature and extent of illness and death which are a direct result of such violations. At one end of the spectrum coroners do not always specify causes of death as being specifically industry-related. Someone might have had asbestosis, and yet died of pneumonia. This works for the most part to the benefit of the industry since, without such evidence of cause of death, payment of compensation may be avoided. Indeed, in general terms it is the medical resistance to establishing causes of illness and death which works in favour of business interests in the industrial environment. Despite this problem there is a good deal of correlational evidence which strongly suggests that some working conditions contribute significantly to the health record of the employees. (Working with carcinogenic substances would be an example.) The fundamental point about considering these correlations is that, in many instances, they are working conditions which could be avoided if the business concerned chose to prioritize the issue of health and safety.

Using the Health and Safety Executive's own statistics, Box (1983) suggests that between 1973 and 1979 there were 3,291 deaths recorded as homicide by the police and a total of 11,436 deaths resulting from occupational accident or disease (ibid., p. 28). It must be emphasized that these figures refer to those deaths officially recorded; that is, all parties agreed on the cause of death. Given the difficulties associated with the construction of these statistics suggested above, it seems fair to agree with Box that the real incidence of such deaths is probably higher. During that same period Box relates that there were 330,000 non-fatal accidents at work. Box states 'The vast bulk of these were not caused by employees' carelessness or stupidity but by the conditions under which they are obliged to work' (ibid., p. 29). If the number of people diagnosed as suffering from occupationally induced disease is added to this figure and compared with those victimized by conventional crime then Box calculates this as being in a ratio of 7 to 1 in favour of 'work-induced' avoidable suffering (ibid., p. 29).

This picture is not peculiar to the United Kingdom. Reiman's (1979) figures for the United States in 1974 paint a similar picture. The total 'murdered' for that year was 168,600; 114,000 deaths occurred as a result of occupational hazard, 200,000 from inadequate emergency medical care, 15,625 were a result of a knife or other cutting instrument including a scalpel, 13,987 resulted from the use of firearms, 2,000 from hypodermics or prescriptions, the remainder included a range of different weapons (ibid., p. 75). Reiman's figures obviously incorporate a broader range of contexts in which the general public is at risk from criminal behaviour or malpractices.

The argument presented by both Box (1983) and Reiman (1979) does not stop there. Corporations are also involved in marketing products, some of which may not have been adequately tested. They may also be involved in polluting the environment and this pollution takes its toll on local residents. Reiman states:

> based on the knowledge we do have, there can be no doubt that air pollution, tobacco, and food additives amount to a chemical war that makes the crime wave look like a football scrimmage. Quite conservatively, I think we can estimate the death toll in this war as at least a quarter of a million lives a year – more than twelve times the number killed by criminal homicide. (ibid., p. 82).

It is interesting to note that in the context of tobacco it was recently reported that the tobacco industry resisted and excluded work which suggested that a non-carcinogenic cigarette could be produced (*World In Action*, 4 July 1988). All things considered this evidence strongly suggests that we are at far more physical risk of being victimized as a result of the activities and inactivities of business and industry than by street crime or burglary.

Physical risk, however, is not the only price paid for the activities of corporations. A number of attempts have been made to try to assess the economic costs of corporate criminal activity. Bequai (1978) suggests that white collar crime costs the United States in excess of $40 billion a year. Many calculations of this sort are, by their nature, speculative. Levi (1987) has perhaps produced the most precise figures of this sort referring specifically to commercial fraud. He indicates that in 1985 the cost of burglary in a dwelling could be calculated as £221,338 million. The cost of police-recorded fraud was £2,113 million and income tax fraud for 1984–5 was estimated at £5,000 million (ibid., p. 52). How these costs are passed on to members of the general public is difficult to permutate. Vanick (1977) does suggest that corporate tax evasion and avoidance may result in higher taxes paid by individuals. Price-fixing strategies, particularly in the United States, but not unknown in Europe especially in the pharmaceutical industry (see below), also take their toll on consumers whether those consumers be individual people or governments. Box concludes:

> Whether we are consumers or citizens, we stand more chance of being robbed by persons who roam corporate suites than we do by those who roam public streets. Furthermore, in the aggregate we stand to be robbed of far more by these fine gentlemen acting in the good name of their corporation than by the common rogues apparently acting from some morally worthless motive. (Box, 1983, p. 31)

This general picture of the extent of victimization as a result of corporate criminal activity indicates quite clearly that it is a level of victimization that necessarily demands serious consideration. All members of society are potentially exposed to victimization of this sort, dependent upon the kind of workplace they work in (some obviously carry more risks than others), and how economic costs are calculated. There are problems, perhaps, in resting the case on such general statistical calculations, open to interpretation as they are. It is therefore useful to examine a little more closely the internal dynamics of particular issues within the context of corporate crime as a way of enhancing our understanding of these general statistics.

Fraud

Levi and Pithouse (1988) have conducted a study which was specifically geared to researching the victims of fraud in a systematic fashion. Their study constituted an analysis of fraud crimes which reached the court, drawing from court records at the London Central Criminal Court (1984–5) and Cardiff Crown Court (1983–4). The general pattern of their research findings suggests that most of the fraud crimes taken to court were committed by people of 'modest social origin' (Levi and Pithouse, 1988, p. 3). Most victims involved in the prosecution process were organizations. Only 15 per cent were private individuals (ibid.). These private individuals were in the minority both in London and Cardiff; and of these those who lost most did so 'at the hands of family and friends' (ibid., p. 4). Of the commercial organizations whose cases reached the courts, the banks fared worst losing £3.2 million (mostly through white collar fraud but including some 'blue collar' fraudsters), with insurance companies coming at the bottom of the list losing £230,000 to nine white collar fraudsters and £60,000 to sixteen blue collar ones (ibid., p. 5). The impact of such losses on the victim is difficult to determine; but arguably a multimillion-pound organization like a bank is going to fare better than the individual whose house has been fraudulently remortgaged. The fraud was reported to the police by 88 per cent of the victims themselves (ibid., p. 6) and whilst, of those who applied for compensation, only 11 per cent of the commercial and 20 per cent of the private individuals actually received it (ibid., p. 8), Levi and Pithouse state that: 'Our data support what has become conventional criminological wisdom regarding the critical role played by victims in managing their victimisation and in activating the criminal justice system' (ibid., p. 9). The unusual nature of this study does provide a useful taste of the kinds of fraud cases which reach the attention of the courts and the likely experiences victims of fraud have within the criminal justice process. (A fuller report of these findings is anticipated.) One striking feature of these findings is the absence of any people 'who could be reasonably regarded as disgraced members of the commercial or industrial elite' (ibid., p. 13). Indeed, one might argue that this study emphasizes the way in which the regulatory agencies might control the white collar or blue collar criminal but not the corporate criminal. Since the time this data was gathered there have been the Boesky and Guinness affairs, neither of which could be argued to be marginal incidents in the financial world.

In the case of Boesky, Levi states: 'Despite the resources of the SEC and the hi-tech of the New York Stock Exchange, it is far from certain than Dennis Levine and Ivan Boesky would have been exposed had it not been for an anonymous tip-off from Venezuela!' (Levi, 1987, p. 334). The Boesky affair had repercussions in the United Kingdom in the form of the Guinness affair. As a result of governments exchanging information the Department of Trade and Industry inspectors raided Guinness offices in December 1986 (Levi, 1987, p. 218). The Guinness affair produced a scandal in the City since the scale of transactions said to be involved was £270 million (ibid.). Whilst this incident also had political repercussions raising again the question of how activities in the City should be regulated, the two affairs are inserted here as a way of contextualizing the findings of Levi and Pithouse (1988).

Whilst the work of Levi and Pithouse might act considerably to modify the fairly simplistic views that all commercial fraud is perpetrated by white collar criminals and that all victims of fraud are businesses rather than individuals, it is a study which is concerned with those fraudulent activities which come to the attention of the courts. The Boesky and Guinness affairs are arguably oddities, not because that scale of fraudulent activity rarely takes place, but because that scale of fraudulent activity involving actors central to the City rarely comes to the attention of the courts. And this did so only as a result of an anonymous tip-off! Reiman (1979) would observe that this serves as a specific illustration of the way in which the system operates to 'weed out the wealthy'. One of the significant features of this specific example is of course its impact in general economic terms, an impact which was dispersed to affect the general public as well as participants closer to the centre of the affair.

It appears that whilst fraud in its entirety is obviously a complex process involving a spohisticated range of actors, and whilst it is also an activity the impact of which is difficult to measure, it is an area in which the fraudsters themselves are not seen to be particularly threatening. Levi and Pithouse point out that 'Though *frauds* may be seen as serious, few fraudsters are seen as evil, and many victims are considered to have precipitated their victimization by greed and/or carelessness' (Levi and Pithouse, 1988, p. 1). Such images fit nicely with the concepts of victimology discussed in Chapter 1 and contribute to an understanding of the implications a study of fraud might have for victimology. (See below.) The study of Levi and Pithouse also emphasizes the way in which the activities of corporations seem, for the most part, to evade the criminal justice process and thus contribute to what is understood as criminal.

The next example of corporate criminal activity to be considered in this way focuses on a different area of potential corporate crime;

the violation of health and safety regulations at work. The particular example to be considered here will be North Sea oil.

Victims at work: North Sea oil

A pall of grey smoke and the still burning stumps of a wrecked oil platform bore grim testimony last night to the world's worst oil disaster.

Dozens of ships and aircraft spent yesterday scouring the calm waters of the North Sea, their crews knowing there was almost no hope for the about 160 men still missing from the Piper Alpha platform. By nightfall only 17 bodies had been recovered, leading to speculation that many of the missing were trapped in the sections of platform which fell burning into the sea.

The platform passed a government safety inspection on 28 June, eight days before the blast. It was carried out by one safety inspector in a single day. (M. Douglas Home and P. Reeves, *Independent*, 8 July 1988, p. 1)

The loss of life incurred as a result of the events on Piper Alpha in the North Sea is undoubtedly sad and regrettable. At the time of writing, the cause of the loss of life is yet to be established. As the extracts from the newspaper article above suggest, the question of safety in the North Sea oil industry very quickly emerged as an issue to be considered when the search for causes is undertaken. What the events on Piper Alpha illustrate and confirm is a longer history of questions pertaining to the operation of and safety within the North Sea oil industry.

Carson (1982), whilst counselling caution in how the statistics pertaining to safety in the North Sea are read, reports that, up to the end of 1980, there had been 106 fatalities in the British sector of the North Sea. There were additionally 450 serious accidents recorded and 528 'dangerous occurrences' (ibid. pp. 17–18). He also states that

by the mid-1970's, the likelihood of being killed in the course of employment on offshore installations operating in the British sector of the North Sea had risen to around eleven times that of accidental death in the construction industry, to nearly nine times that of becoming a fatal casualty in mining, and to nearly six times that of being killed as a quarryman. (ibid., p. 21)

The caution associated with these statistics lies in appreciating that they refer only to offshore installations and the 500 metres surrounding them, thus excluding a range of other North Sea oil working situations. In addition, they may not reflect complete coverage within this boundary. (See ibid., p. 31.) What they do illustrate is the dangerous nature of this kind of occupation. A danger which Carson convincingly argues is not a result of any inherent danger involved in breaking through new exploratory frontiers but a result of workers being exposed to dangerous working conditions which were avoidable and preventable.

In discussing the case of the Alexander Kielland, March 1980, when 123 died, Carson states:

> Clearly, then, we must be careful not to be misled by the sheer scale of disaster or by the apparent complexities of its provenance. The factors leading to the Alexander Kielland disaster were knowable; their remedy lay within the range of existent technology; and no less important, they were almost certainly avoidable if a properly constructed, efficiently administered and faithfully adhered to system of legal regulations had been applicable. Moreover, I remain unrepentantly of the view that the British authorities' complacent belief in the superiority of their own regulatory approach will retain even the semblance of credibility only as long as a similar tragedy does not overtake an installation operating in the British sector of the North Sea. (ibid., p. 289)

It is not only the difficulties of ensuring that a suitably rigorous regulatory structure is in force which Carson draws attention to. He is also at pains to draw attention to the tensions between the demands for profits and the adherence to existing safety regulations, which when infringed are met with 'derisory' fines. (ibid., p. 301). The tension has not diminished since the study made by Carson. In commenting on the economic cost of the events at Piper Alpha, Prest and Donovan state:

> Output of 285,000 barrels is some 12 per cent of North Sea productions of more than 2 million barrels a day. At present prices, 285,000 barrels is worth $4.5m (£2.6m). Britain is broadly self-sufficient in oil, so should all six fields be closed for

six months, the cost of importing oil to make up the difference could be £500m. City analysts are already forecasting a balance of payments deficit of £10bn this year. (M. Prest and P. Donovan, *Independent*, 8 July 1988, p. 1)

Piper Alpha, then, is likely to have a far-reaching impact.

Thus the tension between health and safety and the maintenance of profit margins when involving a significant source of income in this particular example, may need to be taken into account when attempting to construct an understanding of the events which happened.

Whilst the North Sea oil industry highlights the dangers inherent in such working conditions and the human and economic costs involved in working in those conditions, such costs are not peculiar to North Sea oil. As the general statistics concerning health and safety at work illustrate, North Sea oil stands out because of the pioneering spirit which supported the innovations required for such work to take place and the particular harshness of the environment. As has been seen, variables such as these do not constitute sufficient causes for the number of accidents or fatalities which occur. The need to make profit, and the capitalist framework which demands that profits be made, play an important part across a whole range of working environments including North Sea oil. (See the discussion above.)

Additionally, considering the implications of risks involved in the workplace has drawn implicitly on the way in which such dangers are handled before the public. They are seen as disasters. The victims are victims of disasters. They are victims of circumstances which were beyond human control. However, as Carson (1982) points out in his discussion of the Alexander Kielland 'disaster', these circumstances may not always be beyond human control. It is true that for the individuals involved, and their families, the events themselves are personal tragedies and as such may have disastrous consequences. But the ideology of the 'disaster' encourages a lack of recognition of the avoidable nature of such events. It encourages a failure to recognize that criminal activity may have been a contributory factor. This masking is an important mechanism in the subsequent handling of such events, as Carson says:

I have long been struck by the extent to which the issue of deterrence, a standard item in the repertoire of law-and-order

97

debates, so often becomes elided when it comes to the illegalities of corporations, which, par excellence, embody a penchant for calculation in terms of economic gain and loss. (Carson, 1982, p. 301)

Part of understanding this process of elision lies in understanding the view of the victim implied by the 'ideology of disaster'.

The last example to be used here to highlight the range and impact of corporate victimization, focuses on the pharmaceutical industry.

Victims of the pharmaceutical industry

One of the most compelling examples of victimization which resulted from the activities of the pharmaceutical industry occurred in the early 1960s in the use of the drugs containing thalidomide. Braithwaite (1984) reveals that there are 8,000 thalidomide children currently alive in 46 countries around the world (ibid., p. 65). There was, however, a considerable time-lag and repression of information before the drug was finally withdrawn. In some instances this did not happen without the persistence of investigative journalism. (See Braithwaite, 1984, pp. 65–75.) Some would argue that another thalidomide 'tragedy' could not happen again because information networks amongst the various regulatory agencies of different countries are now much improved. I believe that such a conclusion would be premature.

Braithwaite (1984) documents a whole range of activities employed within the pharmaceutical industry in the production and marketing of its products which are clearly criminal. These activities range from bribing local health officials to ensure the acceptance of a product, through negligent and/or fraudulent tactics in testing drugs, to the use of strong and misleading advertising mechanisms in ensuring that doctors prescribe certain drugs, and rather more unsavoury tactics in the marketing and testing of drugs in the 'Third World'.

All of these strategies may have subsequent human costs. They may involve ultimately a doctor's prescribing drugs whose side-effects have been ignored and not communicated to the doctor or whose advertising power has nevertheless convinced the GP of the validity of their use. The victims are those who receive, on an individual basis, a prescription from a professional whom, it is believed, knows best. It is this relationship which the pharmaceutical industry has, over the years, successfully exploited. In this sense Braithwaite (1984) refers to the drug companies as 'pushers'; but pushers of licit rather than illicit drugs. Drugs like Valium and Librium, widely prescribed, particularly to women for 'anxiety', and whose addictive power has only more recently been exposed, are a good example of this exploitation. The ultimate consumer of the drug, the patient, is heavily dependent on the professional knowledge and expertise of the doctor. In the United States, freedom of information has, arguably, made it easier for the development of consumer revolts concerning the use of particular drugs. The campaign for the removal of the drug Opren in the United Kingdom has the status of a 'victim campaign' (Levi and Pithouse, 1988, p. 1.), but does not necessarily suggest that there is any main consumer revolt in the pipeline. Consumers are, for the most part, relatively powerless individuals and such campaigns stand out because they are unusual. In the 'Third World' their status is even less likely to result in concerted action of this sort. The economic and political power of such transnational corporations is probably too great. (See Braithwaite, 1984, Chapter 7.)

The victims of the pharmaceutical industry's activities are not only individuals. There are a number of strategies, through the patents system, which permit companies to maximize their profits. Pearce states:

> Roche, for example, in 1971 claimed that it had made no profits in Britain and therefore paid no tax whereas the Monopoly Commission estimated that it made £4.8 million on two drugs alone. Their British subsidiary claimed to pay another £370 per kilo for the ingredients for Librium and £922 per kilo for Valium – the source of both of which they had monopolised in Britain whereas the free market price (as in Italy) was £9 and £20 a kilo respectively. (Pearce, 1987. p. 118)

The impact that strategies which avoid tax payments and maintain prices for the pharmaceutical industry has had on the National Health Service in the United Kingdom has been and is a source of considerable debate.

This illustration serves to emphasize the wide-reaching impact which can be wielded by large transnational corporations like those in the pharmaceutical industry. As with the two other case studies discussed here, these activities are rarely defined as criminal and have rarely been considered in terms of their victimizing potential by those being victimized. Even in the 'Third World' there might be a certain ambivalence in the way in which the activities of these corporations are viewed given the shortage of drugs and the necessity to combat diseases less prevalent in the 'First World'.

Having established the extent and the variety of corporate criminal activity through these three case studies, the question remains to establish what light these studies have thrown on understanding the nature of criminal victimization. It is to that question we now turn.

Understanding corporate victimization

To reiterate: a key condition for the perpetuation of corporate crime is that

> the majority of those suffering from corporate crime remain unaware of their victimization – either not knowing it has happened to them or viewing their 'misfortune' as an accident or 'no one's fault'. (Box, 1983, p. 17)

Such 'victim responsiveness' (Geis, 1973) is a common thread running through the three case study examples discussed here. However, merely to state the necessary condition does not necessarily complete an understanding of the phenomena described. The case studies highlight a number of ideological strategies which result in not only a lack of awareness of victimization but also a lack of awareness of what constitutes criminality. This requires a closer examination.

The discussion of fraud, whilst indicating that the fraud picture is probably quite a complex one, did raise two issues. First the imagery of fraud: this suggests that victims of fraud might be said to have precipitated their own demise through greed. Secondly, the effectiveness of the regulatory framework: this suggests that it seems to work more effectively on some types of cases than others. The inferences to be drawn from this are, on the one hand, if you are duped by a fraudster then it is more than likely your own fault and, on the other hand, if you are higher up the business world be careful over who has access to a telephone! The main point here being that regulatory agencies are not so constituted to monitor and control all business activities; those who end up before the courts are those who have made mistakes. The clever and powerful frequently remain unscathed. Reiman expresses it this way:

> Their faces rarely appear in the criminal justice mirror, although the danger they pose is at least as great and often greater than those who do.
>
> The inescapable conclusion is that the criminal justice system does not simply reflect the reality of crime; it has a hand in creating the reality we see. (Reiman, 1979, p. 51)

Such a creation of reality contributes to the masking of victimization. It is a reality which is compounded in the example of North Sea oil; compounded by what has been referred to above as the 'ideology of disaster'.

The notion of the disaster or the accident is frequently invoked when events occur which, at the time of their occurrence, are difficult to understand. Carson's (1982) work, however, clearly redresses the tendency to use these notions as if they constituted explanations of events within the North Sea oil industry. These events, are arguably, better understood by reference to, amongst other factors, the prioritization of profit margins or the demand to work within a specified economic framework, as compared with the prioritization of health and safety regulations. The concept of the disaster encourages the masking of such priorities. The disaster is seen as an unfortunate hiccup in an otherwise successful organizational or business enterprise. To examine events in any other way might not only be economically and legally painful for the enterprise concerned but might also paradoxically be more painful for the victims of such events and the victims' families. To know that something was avoidable is perhaps more difficult to bear than to accept an event as an accident. It is clear that individuals are persuaded that accidents do happen and for the most part settle for that and, hopefully, compensation.

The third example discussed here perhaps drew out a further characteristic of this process of victimization. This characteristic builds upon the relationship between doctor and patient, which is for the most part a deferential relationship (doctor knows best), and which exploits that characteristic. Patients rarely question the treatment they receive. Doctors choose the appropriate treatment. This means that patients unquestioningly receive treatment, often involving the use of drugs about which the doctor may have only partial information. This process requires more than a degree of trust between doctor and patient and doctor and drug company which Braithwaite's (1984) analysis suggests is not always founded. The strongly competitive pharmaceutical market is the setting for such potential exploitation. It is a competitive process which may have costs for particular services, like the National Health Service, costs for the individual, as well as political and economic costs for particular societies.

So added to the masking of criminal activity in the form of the ideology of disaster and the lack of power of the regulatory agencies, there is the profit-making motivation of the capitalist enterprise. Our understanding of corporate victimization and the lack of awareness of that victimization lies between these processes. It is necessary to appreciate how the criminal justice system encourages a particular view of what constitutes the criminal; real criminals are caught by the police and appear in the courts, the activities of the regulatory agencies do not involve real crime. Add to this the belief that there are some events which are beyond our control – they are disasters or accidents – and the way in which the profit motive and the drive for capital accumulation may be achieved by fair means or foul, and a particular recipe for action emerges. This recipe results in our rarely recognizing the foul means.

An analysis of this sort has more implicitly than explicitly drawn upon a Marxist framework of analysis, much in the same way as the previous chapter drew upon a feminist framework. However, as with the feminist position with respect to child sexual abuse, the Marxist framework in the context of corporate crime has some limitations. The major limitations to be addressed here are its inability to explain why all business enterprises or industrial settings are not involved in criminal activity and how it is that some people recognize that they have been victimized.

The logic of the framework suggested above would lead to the conclusion that the tendency would be for all corporations, whatever they were involved in, to be engaged in some criminal activities. The ideological and motivational forces of capitalism dictate this. It is clear, however, that the picture is not quite so simple. Let us take the question of health and safety regulations, the focus of one of our case studies here.

Whilst the North Sea oil industry might have a case to answer in this context, other employers work hard at trying to get employees to adhere to the health and safety legislation. The various water authorities would be one example of this. Various inducements are offered to encourage employees to wear appropriate safety clothing and much in-house publicity is made of cases where safety wear has prevented a more serious accident. The argument might be, of course, that still being, to date (1988), a public authority rather than a private one, such concerns should be prioritized. But in an economic climate where public authorities have to be efficient and offer value for money, this argument is not a complete answer to the interest in health and safety taken by this kind of large-scale employer. In another context air traffic controllers, in taking industrial action, not only to better their working conditions, but also to maintain working conditions, in the interests of their health and safety, and consequently in the interests of air travel safety, frequently fly in the face of the profit motivation of travel companies. So, workers and employers, in different settings, can and do prioritize health and safety. Finally, it can be observed that in some settings workers and employers collude in overlooking health and safety regulations in order to maximize output. This is perhaps most likely to happen when the workers' pay is on a 'piece rate'. In order to maintain wages and profit margins health and safety regulations may be put to one side.

The framework employed here also leads to the view that somehow both workers and consumers are unthinking pliable pawns in the process of capital accumulation. This is obviously not the case. It has already been seen that 'consumer revolts' have occurred in response to the way in which some drugs have been prescribed without adequate knowledge being made available as to their side-effects. The case involving the drug Opren would be a good example of this. In addition, it occasionally happens that workers themselves expose the hazardous working operations of companies. A recent example of this occurred in the United States when an ex-employee and current anonymous employees revealed to the press that Eastern Airlines were operating to maintain profit margins at the expense of safety margins (April 1988). Such exposés resulted in the company being investigated, thus suggesting that not everyone fails to 'see' some of the potential victimizing processes.

These examples suggest a number of things: that not all corporations disregard their legal obligations, some may do so more than others; that not all corporations will get away with disregarding their legal obligations, workers may prevent this, individuals may expose them; and that not all criminal corporate activity is conducted without the knowledge of the employees, collusion may occur. Thus whilst our general framework contributes to our understanding of why and how some corporate criminal activity occurs, it is necessary to appreciate that this framework does not have all the answers. Other variables, like the nature of the work setting, the nature of the employer and the corporation, the extent to which the workforce colludes knowingly or unknowingly with such criminal activity, will all have a bearing on the likelihood of a particular employee or a particular consumer being victimized by the activities of a particular corporation. Additionally, of course, employees may, through their own activities, put themselves at risk of injury. Apart from the general picture presented here, therefore, much more needs to be uncovered about the variations in the processes of victimization by corporate organizations.

Conclusion; the implications of corporate victimization for victimology

Like the previous chapter, this chapter has drawn attention to features of the process of victimization which are structurally based rather than individually based. In this chapter, the structural feature invoked both implicitly and explicitly is the nature of capitalism. This assumes a certain motivational framework which encourages corporations to make decisions being reckless as to the consequences of those decisions. Though as noted above, this structural feature does not necessarily constitute a total explanation. Neither would capitalism alone fully explain the lack of awareness of victimization as a result of the activities of corporations. It is also necessary to consider the role of the criminal justice system in this process. The criminal justice system contributes, ideologically, to this process by encouraging a particular view of what constitutes the criminal. This excludes the business corporation. The willingness to see events as 'disasters' adds a further dimension to this. Whilst these features have particular implications for criminology in explaining crime in general and corporate crime in particular (see Box, 1983, and Braithwaite, 1984, for particular recommendations along these lines), the focus here is essentially how these features impinge upon victimology.

The concepts employed within victimology are the first source for such considerations. It becomes difficult to envisage, for example, how concepts like 'victim precipitation' or 'lifestyle' can be maintained.

These concepts have been constructed with an individualistic bias. (See Chapter 1.) They need to be reconsidered in a form which locates victimization in a structural setting rather than an individualistic setting. This means that the explanations offered by victimology need to embrace a view that victimization can occur as a result of processes above and beyond particular individual action or personality. The workers on the Piper Alpha oil rig, for example, may well have had risky individual lifestyles but the causes of those risks do not lie in the individuals themselves but in the context of the processes which construct the workplace for them. One might argue, of course, that they chose their particular occupation and therefore chose the risks to which they were willing to be exposed. The problem is that even if workers were able to make such informed decisions (it is doubtful whether all such relevant information would be presented in a form which would appropriately and fully inform workers), the responsibility for the risks themselves lies beyond the control of the individual. A particular individual may behave precipitously by failing to wear appropriate safety clothing at work. It is also necessary to consider the processes which permit this behaviour to take place.

Essentially, it is important to be aware that, despite the limitations of the framework suggested above, there are features of the victimization process which go on behind our backs. Victimology needs to appreciate these processes as much as it appreciates the more conventionally recognized victims of crime. As Box states:

> This conclusion should not be seen to reflect callous indifference to individuals who have suffered miserably or fatally at the hands of persons committing 'conventional' crimes; their agony is real and should never be ignored. But neither should we enable this sympathy to blind us to the greater truth that more persons suffer, many fatally, from corporate crime than 'conventional' crime. (Box, 1983, p. 30)

This reiterates the importance of taking not only what is real for human beings as a cause for concern but also what they might not recognize as being real.

The second implication for victimology in developing an appreciation of corporate victimization is in the consequences this carries for our stereotypical images of the victim. This was a question also raised by the discussion of the victimization of children in the previous chapter.

In that context it drew our attention to, in particular, the variables of age and sex. In this context, however, it draws attention not so much to the variables of sex and age, though it might be argued that in the context of the pharmaceutical industry such variables might be pertinent, but to the wider economic and ideological processes which frame our understanding of the notion of the victim. This refers not so much to the idea that there are legitimate and illegitimate victims of crime (which is real enough; see, for example, Chapter 5), but that being seen to be a victim of crime at all is an ideological process. As we shall see in Chapter 6 some victim support schemes do not offer support to victims of disasters, regarding this work as being somewhat outside of their remit (and also sometimes their competence). Thus, probably unknowingly, contributing to this ideological process.

The ideological construction of crime, and consequently the crime victim, permeates the system. The willingness with which this is accepted is a key problem in controlling corporate crime. As Box again states:

> Clearly a major problem in controlling corporate crime is raising victim and public consciousness to a level where the community desires and supports a policy of more active and effective state control and regulation (Box, 1983, p. 66)

and:

> If employees, consumers, and other corporate victims had their awareness sharpened and supported by trade unionism consumerism, and environmentalism, and if the state and legal institutions could be shamed into closing the gap between lofty principles and tawdry practices ... (ibid., p. 67)

Box does report that some studies conducted in the United States seem to indicate that there has been some hardening of public attitudes to corporate crime. Levi (1987, Chapter 3) reports on the seriousness with which the general public views commercial fraud. One fears that, on the whole, however, the sleep is too deep; but this should not deter victimology being concerned with the way in which people snore. (With apologies to Goffman, 1975, p. 14.)

The structural features raised by the discussion within this chapter raise one further implication for the victim movement as well as for victimology. Elias (1986) argues that the extent to which we are misled concerning the real nature of crime and criminal activity may lead to the support of policies which not only ignore the sources of victimization but may render that victimization worse.

Clearly identifying the sources of victimization is crucial, as far as Elias is concerned, in being able to pose solutions to the victim's dilemma. He argues that the solution to the victim's dilemma does not lie in tougher sentences, more regulation, or 'isolating evil people', but in encouraging victims to demand more services and a greater role in the criminal justice system, as well as adopting some shorter-term strategies, like, for example, neighbourhood watch schemes, and decarceration. He goes on to suggest that by adopting the standards of the human rights movement victimology and the victim movement can more easily identify the sources and causes of victimization:

> If we accept crime theories that blame institutional inefficiency, or offenders, or victims, then victimology may forever be a science of limited possibilities, restricted to providing victims' aid and comfort, and perhaps minor alterations in crime. If we accept theories which blame the American system, then we confront the formidable task of transforming our political economy. By choosing the latter path victimology encompasses the study and promotion of human rights. (ibid., p. 106)

The extent to which the victim support movement is currently proceeding down this path is the concern of Chapter 6. The specific suggestions made by Elias are of a particular concern in that chapter. Whether one is in agreement with Elias or not as to the validity of the adoption of questions associated with the human rights movement, the clear implication is that if victimology is to make progress it certainly needs to adopt a definitively more critical edge in theorizing and measuring the processes of victimization.

A fuller consideration of what such a critical edge might look like for victimology is illustrated by the last chapter of this book. Before moving too quickly into considering those arguments, it will be useful to have a clearer picture of what the criminal justice system looks like through the eyes of the victim (Chapter 5) and what kinds of support and services are available to the victim in the United Kingdom (Chapter 6).

107

5

Victims and the criminal justice process

Introduction

The purpose of this chapter is to consider the status of the victim in the criminal justice process. Attention will be paid to two features of that process: prosecution and compensation. These features will be examined both historically and contemporaneously with a view to offering a fuller appreciation of the current status of the victim. Finally, in the light of this examination, a critical review of the recent initiatives of mediation and reparation will be offered

The victim in history; a critical appreciation

Harding (1982) and Mawby and Gill (1987) relate that the right of the victim to compensation was firmly located in Babylonian law: the *lex talionis*, an eye for an eye, a tooth for a tooth. The implementation of such rights ultimately relied on the threat of the kinship feud. In Saxon England, under the system of composition, which had Germanic origins, an offender could 'buy back the peace he had broken by paying what was called the "wer" which was payment for homicide, or "bot" which was payment for injuries other than death, to the victim or his kin according to a schedule of injury tariffs' (Harding, 1982, p. 7). In addition to these payments, the offender paid what was called the 'wite' to the king or his lord. This payment constituted a fee for having negotiated the settlement between victim and offender. However, as the influence of the king and the court grew so did their share of the payment, and the sums received by the victim steadily declined. This resulted in the total payment being taken by the Crown with the victim's right to restitution being replaced by a fine decided by a tribunal.

Thus as the state became increasingly centralized (around the time of the Middle Ages), the victim's right to compensation diminished. This constituted what Schafer (1968) has called the 'Golden Age of the Victim'. There appears to have been a consensus to date concurring with Schafer which has disregarded the continuing role of the victim in the process of prosecution. This does not mean of course that a whole range of informal mechanisms, which might have included elements of compensation, ceased to exist. It merely emphasizes that in legal terms the victim's right to compensation became virtually non-existent.

Mawby and Gill (1987) highlight the 1870 Forfeiture Act and the 1914 Criminal Justice Administration Act as making provision for offenders to pay compensation to victims; and the 1907 Probation Act and the 1948 Criminal Justice Act as including reparative possibilities. These possibilities have been developed more recently in the Criminal Justice Acts of 1972 and 1982 respectively. Mawby and Gill seem to agree with Schafer in the view that, despite these legal provisions, it is not until the 1950s and the work of Margery Fry that the question of compensation for victims from the state re-emerges as a serious issue. However, whilst the victim's right to compensation may have diminished in the Middle Ages, victims continued to play a vital part in the process of prosecution until the mid-nineteenth century.

Hay and Snyder (forthcoming) tell us that the term 'private prosecution' was not normal in the eighteenth century. What was normal was to note the exceptional cases which were being prosecuted at the expense of the Crown. It seems clear that, up to that time, for most cases, the responsibility for prosecution lay with the victim. This implicated the victim in every stage of the criminal justice process, from bringing the prosecution, choosing the charge, getting witnesses, to being involved in the court proceedings themselves. Victims also had the ultimate right to intercede on the sentence passed if they felt it was too harsh or likely to be subject to royal pardon. It is not too difficult to conclude that prosecution was a time-consuming, expensive and troublesome process. It is interesting to note, however, that this did not necessarily deter victims from participating in the process.

The work of both Phillips (1977) and Rude (1985) reveals some useful information about criminals and victims, and the willingness of the latter to participate in the criminal justice process. Rude's study, drawing on data from Sussex, Gloucestershire and Middlesex in the period 1800 to 1850, describes who the victims and offenders were:

Criminals tended to be overwhelmingly of the labouring and working classes (though not consistently so in London) and victims to be of the 'middling' or upper classes; most often shopkeepers, merchants, or householders and (in the rural counties) farmers, with a fair sprinkling of gentry with the labourers and craftsmen (though always in evidence) playing a generally minor role. (ibid., p. 117)

Thus seeming to suggest some class base to criminal activity. In Phillips's (1977) study of the Black Country from 1835 to 1850, this class-based activity might constitute stealing coal from an employer.

The work of Phillips reveals somewhat more, however, concerning the willingness of the working class to be involved in the prosecution process. His evidence suggests that, when it came to property taken from themselves (and many of the robberies, housebreakings and larcenies recorded in the Black Country, it seems, were by working-class people on other working-class people), the working classes were still willing to prosecute. It appears that only in the case of assaults was there a marked unwillingness to resort to the criminal justice process. Taking the findings of these two studies together they seem to suggest that overall the working classes and the gentry alike both took recourse to the system when it was felt necessary. The gentry, however, because of the cost and difficulties of conducting a private prosecution were more likely to join 'Associations for the Prosecution of Felons'.

Schubert (1981) indicates that the first voluntary association of this sort was established in Maghull in Lancashire in 1699, and Phillips (1984) cites an example of an agreement to prosecute horse thieves at common expense in Stoke-on-Trent in 1693. It appears, however, that the period when these associations were most active was 1780 to 1850, (ibid., p. 8), coinciding with the historical period of the two studies above.

These associations comprised local gentlemen, farmers and tradesmen, who subscribed to the association in order to finance the detection, apprehension and prosecution of offenders. Some associations included provision for conducting these activities on behalf of those who could not afford to do so for themselves, though this was not necessarily utilized; and some associations stressed their 'insurance' provisions. And whilst these associations were an easy and cheap way of enabling people to enter into the prosecution process, overall they did not initiate large numbers of prosecutions. Few associations managed more than one prosecution a year. (For a fuller description of these features of the associations, ibid., pp. 14–28.) It is apparent that some associations went as far as establishing their own patrols or 'police forces', though most associations did not do this. They did, however, often forge working relationships with the parish constables, frequently tying them to their service with money (ibid., p. 30). The emergence of the 'new' police, especially after 1856 when forces were beginning to be established throughout the country, saw the demise of these associations.

The emergence of the 'new' police, as well as contributing to the demise of these associations, resulted ultimately in a fundamental change in the relationship of the victim to the criminal justice process. Other legislative changes, like, for example, the legislation increasing reimbursement to prosecutors in 1818 and 1826, and the elimination of capital punishment for property offences, were designed in part to encourage people to use the prosecution process more frequently. The introduction of the 'new' police, however, had the effect of increasingly removing the victim from that process. The police forces not only took on the role of searching for and apprehending offenders but also took over the victims' role in prosecution.

This change, of course, took place gradually. Davis (1984) suggests that in London by the 1870s the police were involved in not only prosecuting 'victimless crime' (drunk and disorderly offences) but also the majority of theft cases which came to be recorded. An obviously interesting dimension to this changing role of the victim in the criminal justice process is the way in which the emergence of the 'new' police not only superseded that role but also created a process of victimization in itself; the emergence of what Lee (1981) has called 'police property'. The demand for efficiency and 'value for money' from the new police forces resulted in arrest rates for public order offences increasing (Emsley, 1983) constituting an incursion by the police into Victorian working-class life. A reputation for toughness was an asset in this context. The historical seeds were sown for the more current concerns of, for example, assault by the police. (See attempted measurement of this by Jones, MaClean and Young, 1986, discussed in Chapter 2. Fuller introductions to the historical emergence of the police can be found in Reiner, 1985, Chapter 1 and Brogden, Jefferson and Walklate, 1988, Chapters 4 and 5.)

It is also interesting to note the way in which employers as victims of crime were likely to use this legal process. Rude (1985) comments on the reluctance of employers to prosecute. 'Few employers would be willing to send a good workman to jail' (ibid., p. 76). If forced to prosecute, Rude cites examples where the employer would speak on behalf of the offender in court, sometimes resulting in a lesser sentence. Davis (1984) cites Colquhoun who estimated that employee theft cost about '£700,000 ' in London in 1807, 'exclusive of depredations on ships on the River Thames' (ibid., p. 3).

But as Davis (1984) points out, the prosecution of dockworkers for theft was an exceptional occurrence. Prosecution by larger companies tended to be used as an example to the workforce, to try to contain pilferage rather than eliminate it, particularly in the second half of the nineteenth century. As Davis says:

> campaigns against pilferage by large employers such as dock companies were more likely to coincide with periods of prosperity and high employment than with periods of recession ... For it was when the labour market was buoyant that the informal sanction of dismissal lost its deterrent effect and possibly presented the companies with problems of recruitment. (ibid., p. 4)

Davis also cites the way in which the London and General Omnibus Company, in allowing its conductors to engage in widespread fraud, was enabled to pay poor wages. This continued until 1867 when the shareholders objected. A number of prosecutions ensued, but the fraud was finally dealt with effectively only after a long strike, the introduction of the bell punch and the raising of the basic wage. For the smaller employee dismissal still remained the easiest response to theft. Davis suggests that involving customers as witnesses in the process of prosecution might lead to loss of trade and, in addition, the more intimate relationships small employers had with their employees resulted in a reluctance to prosecute. Prosecution for employers as victims of criminal activity was, therefore, only one mechanism available to them in responding to crime. A mechanism which in the nineteenth century was not automatic; echoing current practices of handling 'white collar crime'.

The historical evidence concerning the process of prosecution suggests that prior to the emergence of the 'new' police it required the active participation of the victim at every stage. The introduction of

the 'new' police changed this relationship markedly, particularly for
the role of individual victims. Where a company was the victim, the
emergence of the police had less of a dramatic impact. Employers used
the prosecution process as one alternative in a repertoire of responses
to victimization. This does not mean that because in certain circumstances the police were called upon there was a general acceptance
of them. The police too played their role in creating a further
level of victimization for those lower-class people whose behaviour
became subject to their discretion. Thus the nineteenth century in
particular witnessed the transfer of considerable personal power from
the individual victims to the police officer who ensured prosecution
on their behalf. In this way by the end of the nineteenth century
prosecutions on behalf of the Crown became the rule rather than
the exception. The consequence, in terms of effectively excluding
the victim from the criminal justice process at this level by the end
of the nineteenth century, is clear.

By the beginning of the twentieth century, it can be seen therefore,
that the status of the victim in the criminal justice process was minimal. Victims played a role obviously in reporting crime to the police
and there was some minimal legislative provision for compensation.
They did not, however, have a right to compensation, neither were
they implicated in the process of prosecution. It is not until the middle
of the twentieth century that the interests of victims re-emerge on the
agenda.

The emergence of the Criminal Injuries Compensation Board

The book by Margery Fry, *In the Arms of the Law*, published in 1951,
and her subsequent address to the Howard League in 1953 saw the
opening of the debate concerning state compensation for victims of
crime. And whilst these ideas took some time to be embraced, by 1959
the notion of compensation for victims of violent crime had become
a part of Tory Party policy. However, it was not until 1964 that
the Criminal Injuries Compensation Board (CICB) was established,
not on a statutory basis but as a Home Office quango. This was
considered to be a more flexible situation for what was seen to be
an experimental scheme. The Criminal Justice Bill, 1987, proposes
to make this compensation scheme statutory for the first time. The
terms of reference for the Criminal Injuries Compensation Scheme

provide a useful insight into the status accorded to the victim in its establishment.

Mawby and Gill (1987) quote this passage from the Home Office White Paper, 1964:

> Compensation will be paid *ex gratia*. The government do not accept that the State is liable for injuries caused to people by the acts of others. The public does, however, feel a sense of responsibility for and sympathy with the innocent victim, and it is right that this feeling should find practical expression in the provision of compensation on behalf of the community. (ibid., p. 43)

This statement contains the essence of several important features of the Criminal Injuries Compensation Board. First it denies any notion of victims' rights; payments were to be received and decided upon gratuitously by the board. Secondly it draws on the notions of public responsibility and sympathy for the victim, suggesting that the state is not responsible but feels a sense of responsibility. Thirdly the statement enshrines the notion of the innocent victim. This reflects, in part, a concern to avoid fraudulent claims, but also embraces the traditional welfare distinction between those who are considered to be deserving and those considered undeserving. The opinion was that the most suitable cases for compensation were those in which individuals had suffered hardship through no fault of their own. Indeed the board was directed to reduce payments of compensation if any portion of the claim could be held to be the responsibility of the victim. The final feature of the board terms of reference is not actually reflected in the quote above but is nevertheless crucial to an understanding of the board's operation. It is confined to compensating victims of crimes of violence. This obviously delimits the potential victim population who can make a claim to the board and has of itself posed difficult definitional debates.

It was the concern to embrace 'public sympathy' which constituted a key feature of the process which resulted in the establishment of the CICB. This concern was also used as a justification for focusing the remit of the board on victims of crimes of violence. This was the area in which it was felt public sympathy was greatest. Duff relates that the original definition of eligibility for compensation referred to those 'who suffered personal injury directly attributable to a "criminal offence" without limiting this in any way' (Duff, 1987, p. 221). In 1969 the phrase 'criminal offence' was amended to 'a crime of violence (including arson and poisoning)'. This clarified the position with respect to much of the factories legislation in excluding victims of such offences from eligibility (ibid., p. 222). In placing the scheme on a statutory basis the question of defining its scope arose again. The 1987 legislation defines eligibility in terms of a victim having received personal injuries 'caused by' or 'closely connected with' a 'violent offence'. A violent offence is defined as an offence which was proven to be perpetrated by intent to cause death or injury or being reckless as to those consequences (ibid., p. 229). Whether this definition will result in a similar or different application of the concept of violent offence in the day-to-day workings of the board remains to be seen. Given that the scheme continues to be justified by reference to the notion of public sympathy a radical change of direction in the workings of the board is not anticipated.

The CICB in operation

Mawby and Gill (1987) report that in the year ending March 1984 the CICB, including Scotland, paid out £32,820,772. Of the applications made, 72.2 per cent received full awards, 2.5 per cent received reduced awards and 25.3 per cent received nothing (ibid., p. 44). Whilst this illustrates to some extent the involvement of the CICB in compensating victims of violent crime, it is useful and necessary to establish what kind of victim receives compensation and what their experience of the scheme is. A detailed study of the scheme's operations has been made by Shapland, Willmore and Duff (1985).

One of the first difficulties facing victims of violent crime should they feel some kind of compensation is in order is their own lack of knowledge. The CICB rests on victims making claims to it. As Shapland, Willmore and Duff (1985) in their study of 276 victims of violent crime report:

> over half the sample did not know of any way in which to obtain compensation. They were, in many cases, deprived of compensation not because of their own actions or inactions, but because they had no idea that any such system might exist.

No one in the criminal justice system had told them anything about it. (ibid., 1985, p. 132)

Knowledge of the scheme is a key determinant in whether an application is made for compensation. Only four applicants in this study were ultimately refused an award; which illustrates what a major hurdle knowledge of the scheme appears to be. The general response of these applicants to the board appears to be that, whilst they found the CICB took considerable time to reach its decision, was impersonal and did not indicate how the award had been calculated, they were generally satisfied with the end result.

This study by Shapland, Willmore and Duff seems to highlight features of the operations of the CICB which could be and need to be changed to improve its effectiveness, in particular ensuring that those who were eligible to claim did in fact do so. And additionally it indicates the way in which such a 'service' has been initiated without considering what the needs of such victims might be. In some respects this last comment emphasizes the context in which the CICB emerged. This context was one in which the victim was being 'politicized' (Miers, 1978). This refers us back to the terms of reference of the CICB It was, and still is, useful for political parties of whatever persuasion to respond to issues which provoke public sympathy, however that sympathy might have been constructed. (The role of the media is, of course, important here.) A growing concern with the crime problem was a concern which was also being seen through the eyes of the victim and, in particular, the impact that crime had on the victim. The impact of violent crime, by its very nature, was, and is, all the more provocative and real. To be seen to be responding to the public sympathy that violent crime, in particular, provoked, was politically useful. And whilst the workings of the CICB have obviously benefited those victims who were eligible to make claims on it, and have in fact done so, its remit is unlikely to change because of the symbolism it represents in political terms. Governments can be seen to be caring without the responsibility for the criminal activity itself being placed at their door. This symbolism invoked by the CICB's concern to compensate the 'innocent' victim of crime builds upon stereotypical images of victims which have been dealt with elsewhere in this text. This imagery is much more fundamentally rooted in the structure of society and it is only to be expected that a reflection of it be found in the remit of the CICB.

Its presence does mean, however, that a fundamental change in that remit is unlikely.

The CICB was not the only initiative which re-emerged in the mid-twentieth century concerning the victim. Legislative changes also made possible a stronger role for compensation via the court.

Compensation orders

It is possible to trace the notion that compensation should be paid by the offender to the victim also to the work of Margery Fry. She felt, as did Schafer (1960), that such a system would have benefits for both victims and offenders. And, whilst we have seen that some opportunities were available for such practices in earlier legislation, these were very much connected with probation orders. The 1972 Criminal Justice Act made a compensation order possible as an addition to another penalty. It was not, however, until the Criminal Justice Act 1982 that the courts were permitted to give a compensation order as a sentence in its own right. Indeed, Shapland, Willmore and Duff (1985) report that if the offender had not enough means to pay both a fine and a compensation order, the legislation gives the compensation order priority. In reviewing the evidence from victims concerning the principle of compensation they state that:

> This almost unquestioning acceptance of the appropriateness of the principle of compensation from offenders, its place in the criminal justice system, and, particularly, the preference for it among those who received such orders is striking. It contrasts vividly with the doubts of legal commentators. (ibid., p. 140)

An examination of the workings of the criminal justice process with respect to these orders does, however, reveal a number of difficulties associated with their implementation.

There is, first of all, a legal tension between the inclusion of the compensation order within the criminal justice process and the availability of making a civil claim. Those involved in the prosecution process do not necessarily see it as their job to pursue applications for compensation on behalf of victims whilst this tension exists. In addition the court in taking into account the means of the offender may choose an alternative which seldom includes a compensation

117

order, prison (see Box, 1987). The work of Softley (1978) in the magistrates court and of Tarling and Softley (1976) in the crown courts reveals a reluctance on the part of the court to use the sanction of a compensation order, though their use has increased since the 1950s (see Bottoms, 1983, p. 173). Shapland, Willmore and Duff's study (1985) suggests that the key variable in the decision to make a compensation order was whether or not it has been mentioned in the court proceedings. This could have occurred in the course of the prosecution making its case, as a result of a direct application, or simply as a reminder to the court of its powers. Indeed they point out that the changing of the wording in the legislation of 1972 and the Criminal Courts Act of 1973 meant that the victim did not have to attend the court proceedings in order to apply for compensation, but does not make clear whose responsibility it is to make such an application (ibid., p. 143). As is the case with the CICB, few victims may be aware that it is possible to make such an application and find themselves, therefore, very much in the hands of the professionals.

Thus, whilst victims themselves seem to be keen on compensation from the court, and whilst the use of compensation orders appears to have increased, by far the majority of the victims in the study by Shapland, Willmore and Duff received compensation from the CICB not from the court. Some have argued (see Mawby and Gill, 1987, p. 230) that one way of perhaps making greater use of compensation might be to include victim impact statements after sentence has been passed. These statements could then be used to adjust the sentence one way or the other and this adjustment could include compensation.

It can be argued that the compensation order has become a serious contender in the 'punishment tariff' only as a solution is sought to the problem of the ever-expanding prison population. Not such a cynical suggestion when the final direction which has implicated the victim more recently in the criminal justice process is examined; namely the mediation and reparation movement.

The reparation and mediation movement

At a theoretical level the paper by Christie (1977), 'Conflicts as property', has been influential in developing the notion that the law, in taking disputes out of people's own hands, has not only denied them the right to manage their own disputes but has also denied the development of more constructive and imaginative responses to their disputes. At a practical level the criminal justice system has responded, though not necessarily to Christie, with the introduction of mediation and reparation projects. Marshall (1984) and Marshall and Walpole (1985) offer a description and review of the kinds of mediation and reparation projects which have been established.

These developments gained some considerable impetus in early 1985 with the establishment of four pilot reparation projects by the Home Office. That moves of this sort were likely was indicated in the Parliamentary All-Party Penal Affairs Group's report, 'A new deal for victims', which suggests that 'A range of experiments should be developed which between them employ reparation, (directly to the victim with his agreement or in the form of community service) at a variety of points in the criminal justice process' (ibid., p. 5). The first report of the Home Affairs Committee, 'Compensation and support for victims of crime' (December, 1984), offers a clearer contextualization of these initiatives in highlighting the beneficial effects they would have in easing the criminal justice system and in introducing sentences more understandable to the offender. The benefits for the victim, as we shall see, were not seen to be so clear.

As can be seen, the All-Party Penal Affairs Group had a fairly broad definition of what might constitute reparation. This fairly broad definition seems to have been incorporated into the first British Crime Survey, but it is potentially misleading if part of the consideration is to match victims' attitudes with the development of such projects. (See discussion on the nature of the support for such initiatives below.)

It is useful to make clear the distinction between retribution, restitution and reparation. That some victims, and other members of the general public, feel the need for retribution, to inflict harm on those who have harmed them, is a dimension of punitive attitudes not infrequently put back on the agenda by what seems to be a vociferous minority, as the debates concerning capital punishment and birching indicate. A minority which seems to be having some success in some of the states in the United States at least, as long-term 'death row' prisoners face a greater likelihood that their sentences will be carried out.

Distinguishing between restitution and reparation is perhaps a little more complex. Restitution is defined as the return of stolen goods by the offender to the victim by Marshall and Walpole and overlaps with their definition of reparation:

the making of amends by an offender, either to his/her own victim ('direct' reparation) or to the victims of other offenders ('indirect' reparation). Reparation may take the form of compensation, atonement, restitution, or the performance of a service for the victim. (Marshall and Walpole, 1985, p.65)

This definition is then added to by stating that

It may be achieved by means of mediating an agreed settlement between victim and offender (by a face-to-face meeting or by a go-between) or by the decision of a third party (e.g. court-ordered compensation). (ibid.)

There are a number of implicit problems here. The suggestion that reparation may be achieved by mediation misses the connotations attached to these concepts. Wright states perhaps more clearly that

Reparation is what the offender gives back to the victim in the form of money service or apology. It is not necessarily agreed; it may merely be ordered by the court. Reconciliation is the removal (or reduction) of hostility between two people when one has caused harm to the other, and this is brought about by a mediation process. It usually includes some sort of reparation, but this need not be tangible. (Wright, 1985, pp. 642–3)

Given the nature of the foregoing discussion, it is in some ways hardly surprising that the BCS questions reflect some of the confusion concerning what exactly victims are being asked to participate in.

Public support for compensation, mediation and reparation

Despite the limited way in which the victim has been embraced at a practical level within the legal process, research suggests that there is some support by the public for the idea of compensation, as indicated by Shapland, Willmore and Duff (1985) above. Attempts have been made recently to explore more fully the attitudes that victims in particular, and the public in general, have towards the wider question of the treatment of offenders, and it is from this evidence that support for the mediation and reparation movement has been constructed.

The reports of the first and second British Crime Surveys have begun to shed some light on the nature of the relationship between victims and offenders. In particular, attention has been paid to the attitude that victims have towards the treatment of offenders. One of the conclusions of the first British Crime Survey states that

> Criminal justice policy might also take into account the fact that people are less punitive towards law breakers than imagined. Asked how 'their' offender should be treated, victims showed awareness of and support for court sentences involving community service and compensation, and frequently favoured informal warnings and reparation. There may, therefore, be scope for diverting offenders from the courts to the non-judicial arbitration and mediation schemes of the type now being developed in the United States. (Hough and Mayhew, 1985, p. 35)

This conclusion demands closer examination. The first BCS report further comments that 'those incidents which go unreported usually do so for a very good reason; victims judge them too trivial to justify calling in the police'. Taking these two conclusions together suggests that it might be important to examine victims' attitudes in the light of their definition of the seriousness of the offence. The second British Crime Survey attempted to do this. In general terms it again concludes that victims' attitudes do not compare unfavourably with current sentencing practice and also suggests that there is a clear demand amongst victims for some sort of 'reparation' from offenders.

The data from the second British Crime Survey on these issues has been examined more closely by Hough and Moxon (1985), Mawby and Gill (1987) and Maguire and Corbett (1987). Hough and Moxon summarize the main findings of the second BCS and add that

> the principle of reparation by offenders, either to individual victims or to the wider community, has some public support and the support of victims in particular. The older people are, the more tough-minded they are about punishment and manual workers are generally more punitive than non-manual workers; those who are the most fearful of crime advocate heavier sentences than others; victims of crime are no more punitive than others. (Hough and Moxon, 1985, p. 7)

Whilst filling out the picture on the variables related to ideas on sentencing, some of which are echoed by Walklate (1986), they add to this by analysing the data on victims of burglary and car theft. They comment on the preparedness of these victims to see offenders warned (10 per cent of burglary victims and 12 per cent of victims of car theft) and their 'enthusiasm for reparation' (7 per cent of burglary victims, 4 per cent of car theft victims). In addition 15 per cent of burglary victims and 25 per cent of victims of car theft specified community service as an appropriate way of handling 'their' offender. They additionally suggest that a further third of victims of both burglary and car theft wanted compensation and some other punishment. They do not comment on the 19 per cent of burglary victims and the 8 per cent of car theft victims who specified a year plus in prison for 'their' offender, neither do they compare the small percentages cited earlier with these equally small percentages. The study by Maguire on burglary suggests that for the victims in his survey

> Even among those who chose custody there was a strong feeling that prison was unlikely to bring about any reform, and in many cases they chose it because of the lack of an effective alternative. If a general 'message' came through, it was that (a) the offender should repay his 'debt' in a useful way, either by straightforward restitution or by working for the community, and (b) if he could be reformed, other households would be spared the same experience. (Maguire, 1982, p. 139)

Pursuing this theme all victims of crime identified in the second BCS were asked a rather more hypothetical question posed in the following way:

> The Government is considering schemes in which victims and offenders would meet out of court in the presence of an officially appointed person to agree a way in which the offender could make a repayment to the victim for what he had done. Would you have accepted a chance of such a meeting after this crime? (Quoted in Mawby and Gill, 1987, p. 59)

Mawby and Gill (1987) and Maguire and Corbett (1987) offer analyses of the responses to this. (The statement itself seems to reflect the definitional problem discussed earlier.)

122

Mawby and Gill document 49 per cent of victims responding to the above question by saying yes. Of those who said no, a further 40 per cent said they would have agreed to the proposal if they did not have to meet the offender. Also, 20 per cent said that they would agree to some form of reparation if the offender was to be prosecuted/punished as well. Mawby and Gill report that if these respondents were excluded from the analysis, 55 per cent of victims 'saw some form of reparation/mediation as a sufficient and appropriate means to resolve their particular crime' (ibid., p. 59). It appears that in responding to this idea victims of household crime are more willing to consider it than victims of personal crime; 56 per cent and 30 per cent respectively (ibid.). As far as household crimes were concerned, victims of such crimes committed by strangers were least likely to favour reparation; and personal crimes involving one offender, females, and offenders aged over 26 were considered least suitable for reparation (ibid., pp. 60–1). They conclude by saying that

> There is certainly no evidence that reparation initiatives should focus exclusively on young offenders, impersonal crimes, or crimes by strangers, although there is an indication that personal crimes between neighbours may present a challenge to neighbourhood mediation initiatives. (ibid., p. 60)

The analysis by Maguire and Corbett (1987) reveals a little more detail about the likelihood of accepting the idea of the statement above by type of victimization. Theft of a bicycle heads this list with 64 per cent of all victims saying yes to the idea, theft of a car is next at 59 per cent, burglary 57 per cent, with wounding at 33 per cent and common assault at 26 per cent. Of those who reported the event to the police 58 per cent wanted the offender to be punished or prosecuted as well (ibid., p. 229). Maguire and Corbett's study also included some in-depth work with victims of crime contacted through victim support schemes. In this context they appear to recognize a problem with the way in which the BCS data explores this issue. They say: 'Our first question was slightly different, referring not to "repayment", but to "making personal amends", the aim being to get closer to the idea of mediation rather than simply financial restitution' (ibid., p. 230). From this data they found that the number of burglary victims prepared to meet their offender was lower than the BCS data, 44 per cent as compared with 57 per cent, but the response for victims of assault was almost identical, 32 per cent as compared with 31 per cent (ibid.). The reason for this difference may be attributable to the question asked or possibly that the offences in their in-depth sample were more serious.

Whatever the explanation, it is important to develop some clarity as to what might be understood by reparation and mediation, since these two analyses have failed to unwrap the ambiguities posed by the question itself. It may therefore be possible that victims of burglary are responding to the repayment element of the question, which would explain the difference between the findings of the BCS data and Maguire and Corbett's in-depth data; and it may be that respondents who knew the offender are responding to the mediation elements of the question. The discussions of the data do not explore these possibilities; care must therefore be taken in how the findings are interpreted. The writers themselves seem to assume that there is some logic to the views of victims and in assuming this seem more than willing to interpret these findings optimistically in favour of mediation and reparation initiatives.

Why should caution be exerted? Initially this stems from two concerns. First, as will be seen, whilst reparation and mediation projects are still fairly young and outside most victims' experiences, they come in a range of shapes and sizes. Some accurate knowledge as to what kind of projects victims and the general public might respond to would at least inform such projects. The second reason for caution stems from developing an appreciation of the wider political context in which such schemes have emerged. Each of these features of the reparation/mediation movement will be discussed in turn.

Many of the schemes described by Marshall (1984) and Marshall and Walpole (1985) are still in their early days; and whilst some of the initiatives have been subjected to separate examination – Blagg (1985), Launay (1985) and Walklate (1986) – little is known about the overall picture of how these schemes are operating and their effectiveness. Many of them have, it seems, particularly focused on young offenders. The emergence of the Forum for Initiatives in Reparation and Mediation (FIRM) as the umbrella organization for these projects is likely to develop into a useful information bank on them. Marshall himself expresses some doubts about reparation projects:

> The offender may not be the most appropriately skilled person, or the most reliable to carry out the repairs, if heavily supervised

or directed the offender's personal involvement with the act of atonement may be reduced to a trivial extent ... What, however, are the implications for any insurance claim the victim might have? And is the immediate aftermath of victimization the best of times for a person to encounter his/her offender or other offenders? Many of the schemes described above offering the offender's services suffer from a very low take-up, which may be indicative of victims' feelings. (Marshall, 1984, p. 37)

Marshall, whilst indicating what might be termed administrative difficulties of such projects, also draws attention to the broader question of whose interests are being served by such projects, the victim's or the offender's (or indeed, the state's), and the question of whether one set of interests should be paramount rather than another.

Marshall and Walpole (1985) discuss in greater detail implications of the development of mediation. Amongst other issues, they highlight the difficulties which may arise when a commitment to mediation signs away the participant's rights to legal access (p. 43); when the offender may be put under pressure to make unrealistic promises in order to be diverted from prosecution (p. 44); and in the context of making reparation to a corporation, ensuring that it is appropriate and that the offender is not being exploited as cheap labour (p. 48). In the context of this discussion it is important to assess what these developments mean with respect to the status of the victim.

Implications of reparation and mediation

At one level it can be cogently argued that the initiatives discussed above can only be of benefit to victims of crime. They are initiatives which depend upon the involvement of the victim in some form or another in order for them to operate. Indeed, despite the confusions implicit in the evidence which indicates public support for such opportunities, this evidence has been read optimistically. It has been seen that, given the political mood supporting such moves, and given the increasing concern about the 'offending population', such a reading of the data might not be unexpected. These initiatives have developed despite not knowing precisely what victims want, or expect, or desire from the criminal justice process in this respect. Shapland (1986) argues that the system of compensation ignores the expressed needs of the victim. Nevertheless the CICB manages to go about its work to the ultimate satisfaction of those victims who apply to it. Reparation and mediation projects would find it very difficult to engage in their day-to-day operations without embracing the needs of some victims at some level. However, the low take-up of many of the victim assistance schemes commented on by Marshall (1984) must be noted, as must the possibility that offenders are, at this stage in the development of these projects, more likely to gain in either some constructive work experience and/or a reduced or diverted sentence. Thus whilst some individual victims may have derived some benefit, as a consequence of being involved in such a project, and whilst there may be some public support for such opportunities, the broader implications for the victim movement need to be considered. These broader implications stem from appreciating the wider debate concerning the 'rhetoric' of decarceration. Before turning to that debate it is important to clarify what so far has not been addressed: the victim's role in and experience of the court.

The victim in the court

It is important to remind ourselves at this point of the relevance of the historical discussion with which this chapter began. From that discussion it was learned that by the beginning of the twentieth century the majority of prosecutions were undertaken by the police on behalf of the Crown (more currently referred to as the state) not by victims on their own behalf and that this change was significant. It is important, therefore, to develop an appreciation of the current status of the victim in the criminal court setting.

Much has been written and commented on concerning the treatment of the rape victim in the court setting; particularly concerning the way in which such victims are cross-examined and subsequently frequently degraded. McBarnett (1983) clearly suggests that this experience is not peculiar to the rape victim but is a direct consequence of the legal framework in which victims as a whole find themselves. There are two features of this legal framework which McBarnett examines: the structure of the trial and the function of the trial. A brief appreciation of the issues she raises will be of value to our discussion.

In the structure of the trial the victim shares much in common with the offender; indeed, in legal terms they are complainant and defendant. They are frequently both witnesses and it is that status which contributes particularly to the victim's experiences of the court. As a witness the victim is in some ways more vulnerable than the defendant. Victims can be asked about their history and character, which defendants cannot, and once called as witnesses they have to stand; a defendant may choose not to. Once on the witness stand a victim is subjected to questioning by both counsels.

The questioning by the defence counsel is intended to establish any provocation or culpability on the part of the victim; however, the questioning by the prosecution can be equally problematic for the victim as McBarnett clearly illustrates. Prosecuting counsel in trying to secure a conviction will often cut witnesses short or confine them to very specific answers which victims find difficult to relate to since such a process does not match with their actual experiences of events. Indeed, McBarnett offers several examples where victims who were not strictly controlled in this way have implicated their own culpability in the events which happened. Thus victims often experience the court process as frustrating and difficult to understand. This derives from their quite vulnerable legal status in the adversarial system. A vulnerability which victim support has recognized and made recommendations on; there is at least one support scheme established in the court setting to help victims through this legal process. (See the next chapter.)

The second feature of this legal process, the function of the trial, emphasizes our original historical point. McBarnett expresses it this way:

> The civil trial takes the form of victim v offender, but the criminal trial takes the form of state v offender. The offence is not just against the victimised person, the offence is against the state. The state is not just the arbiter in a trial between victim and offender; the state is the victim ... If victims feel that nobody cares about their suffering, it is in part because institutionally nobody does. (McBarnett, 1983, p. 300)

Thus those who withhold evidence, or refuse to give evidence, or in any way try to subvert the course of justice may be prosecuted. The court's legal powers must be seen to be upheld in spite of the wishes of victims. In this way victim and defendant, structurally, share much in common. Their roles in the court are determined ultimately by the overriding interests of the state (ibid., p. 302).

McBarnett goes on to argue that the way in which victimology has focused on the manner in which victims are treated by defence lawyers, particularly in cases of rape, has masked the importance of the legal structures outlined here – legal structures which remain intact even in the context of mediation and reparation projects as currently conceived. Thus whilst victims' experiences of the court may be better handled by the development of victim support in the court as described in the next chapter, and some victims may feel better after having engaged in mediation and reparation, the feature of the criminal justice system which remains intact in both these sets of circumstances is the feature which relates these processes to the process of social control.

Victims, criminal justice and social control

There are a number of ways in which one might begin a discussion of social control in this context. It is sufficient at this stage to introduce some ideas. At one level there are a number of key agents of social control, the police being one, social workers another. The overarching framework for both of these is the legal one in which the victim also figures (see above). In another way the legal framework disposes of offenders as a means of engaging in control of behaviours regarded as unacceptable to society. It was suggested earlier that the rising prison population has, in recent years, been seen, increasingly, as a problem. Much debate has surrounded the viability of alternatives to custody as a way of disposing of offenders. Such alternatives are often referred to as part of the 'decarceration' debate.

The academic debate surrounding the question of decarceration has focused in recent years on the work of Scull (1977), Foucault (1977) and Cohen (1985). Scull's initial critique originally addressed the community imagery invoked in the care of the mentally ill and he himself admits this does not translate easily to the criminal justice process. (See Scull, 1983, p. 158.) Bottoms (1983) has argued for the importance of the image of the victim in contemporary society which he suggests does not sit easily with the social control theorizing of Scull and Cohen (see ibid., p. 192). This image has been powerful, as we have seen with the notion of the innocent victim which underpins the compensation system. It has not, however, been powerful enough, to date, to initiate the notion of victim's rights nor has it questioned in any way the fundamental structuring of the role of the victim in the criminal justice process. It has been an imagery which has grown in momentum in the voluntary sector in the form of victim support schemes in particular (to be discussed in the next chapter). And it is within that movement and its necessary implication in mediation and reparation projects that the question of social control re-emerges.

Reparation and mediation schemes, it has been seen to date, have been demonstrated to have little general value for the structural position of the victim. Whilst it is true that individual victims may have felt some benefit, the motivation for the generation of such schemes has largely come from the general problem with the rising prison population. There has been no demonstrable desire to promote these schemes in terms of their benefits to victims. The benefits for offenders seem clearer but the benefits to the state seem clearer still. Whether in a detention centre or entering into mediation, the offender is being offered some kind of supervision and/or training. The mechanisms for controlling offenders are being extended. In extending the mechanisms of social control in this way it matters little whether victims' interests are being met. What matters is that victims participate in them, for the imagery to work. At the same time the state can be seen to be doing something for the victim; an unintended consequence of a much needed further avenue for controlling the offending population. In some respects this imagery builds on the assumptions which underpin the status of the victim in the court commented on by McBarnett (1983).

Mediation and reparation acknowledge that there is a relationship between the victim and the offender similar to the relationship between them in the court. They share much in common in the two contexts. They are both implicated in maintaining law and order. An examination of the nature of the voluntary movement which has grown around the victim will enhance our understanding of this implication.

Summary and conclusion

This chapter has charted the changing status of the victim within the criminal justice process since the beginning of the nineteenth century. It has been seen how the introduction of the 'new' police effectively removed the victim from the process of prosecution. Whilst possibilities remained for offenders to pay compensation to victims it was a very much under-used facility. The mid-twentieth century saw a renewed interest in the image of the victim at which point impetus was given to the idea of compensation, and in particular to state compensation, for the innocent victim of violent crime. This, it has been suggested, constituted a politicization of the victim which has continued in the initiatives designed to bring victims and offenders together. These initiatives, whilst still in their infancy, look to continue so long as the motif of the victim has political value and carries with it mechanisms for maintaining social control. In this discussion three important themes in understanding the societal response to victims have been highlighted.

First, there is the question of the notion of the 'innocent victim'. This notion has significantly underpinned the state response to criminal victimization. When the evidence on victimization, which was discussed in Chapter 2, is put alongside this notion, there emerges a conflict. The notion of innocence is a problematic one. Victims of violent crime in particular have many of the same characteristics as their offenders. Thus the image of the innocent victim constitutes an idealized image. This idealization is very important for understanding not only society's response to the victim but also the response of victimology to the study of victims. The intermeshing of such idealizations in legislation, in academic thinking and in everyday thinking, needs to be addressed critically if a full appreciation of the connection between the victim and social control is to be made.

Secondly, there has been the question of social control itself. This chapter has highlighted not only a politicized response to the victim but one which, in policy terms, can be seen to have more connections with the concern to maintain law and order than a genuine commitment to victims of crime in general. It will be seen later in the text that this concern with victims is in many ways an oblique one. It is not expressed directly within the criminal justice process; such a concern is left to the voluntary sector.

Thirdly, this chapter has highlighted the minimal and limited response that the criminal justice process has made to the victim in more recent times. It has been largely through the voluntary sector that the needs of victims have been met. Whilst this chapter has indicated that the state and the voluntary sector may be becoming increasingly intertwined as some victim support schemes become implicated in reparation and mediation projects, a more detailed examination of the voluntary sector remains to be developed.

6
Voluntary organizations and victim support

Introduction

The previous chapter was concerned to outline the way in which the state has historically responded to the victim of crime. Two main themes emerged from this: first that by the beginning of the twentieth century increasing state involvement in the relationship between victim and criminal led to a diminished role for the victim of crime in the criminal justice system; and secondly, when a concern for victims of crime re-emerged it did so as a political response rather than a response based on a real consideration of victims' needs or victims' rights. These questions have been more seriously embraced in the context of a range of voluntary organizations. This chapter will consider several features of that response within the voluntary sector. It will first of all consider the question of victims' needs and the difficulties there might be in matching response to need. Secondly it will trace the development of two strands within the voluntary sector which attempted to respond to victims' needs; that which emerged largely from the feminist movement and that which came from the victim support movement. This chapter will also consider the changing nature of the victim support movement and will outline the way in which the question of victims' rights might be addressed within the present victim support and criminal justice context.

The voluntary response and the question of need

The concept of need, as researchers and workers in the field of social policy well know, is very difficult to define. Typologies of need abound. The only general agreement seems to be that there is a distinction to

132

be made between absolute needs and relative needs, but the criteria on which this distinction is drawn and how needs might subsequently be measured are far from clear. In the context of victims of crime Maguire suggests that despite these difficulties

> Ultimately, victims are in competition with many other groups which have a claim to attention and resources, and while it is vital to argue their case on the grounds of entitlement, it is equally important to present their claim in a more concrete way by making some attempt, however crude, to assess levels of need and to determine what kinds of services are particularly appropriate. (Maguire, 1985, p. 540)

However, how are these needs and services to be assessed? Maguire and Corbett (1987) rightly point out that using general statistical data as an indicator of need can result in an overstatement of needs if the data base is primarily drawn from victims of serious crime, and an understatement of those needs if that data base is largely drawn from victims of petty offences. (This is a similar problem to that of trying to assess the impact of crime, see Chapter 2.)

Maguire (1985) identifies three approaches which have been adopted in the attempt to measure victims' needs: the survey approach which focuses on the effects of crime, the more direct approach which asks victims to assess their own needs and finally the approach which examines the response to and demand for services. Drawing the findings from these different approaches together he identifies a range of needs which have become associated with victim services.

A need commonly identified by many victims of crime is the need for information. This may range from the need for information on insurance and crime prevention, through a desire to know how a case is proceeding. It may culminate in a need for information on court proceedings if required, for example, to attend as a witness. Lack of information has been a source of criticism of the police by victims of crime highlighted in Maguire's study of burglary (1982) and in Shapland's observations on victims of crimes of violence (1984). This need for information is reiterated by the findings discussed in Chapter 5 concerning victims' knowledge of the Criminal Injuries Compensation Board. Maguire argues that

> There is a strong case, indeed, for it to be a statutory duty of the police to provide *every* victim with a card or information sheet

about available services, and to officially inform every victim of the outcome of investigations. (Maguire, 1985, p. 546)

This suggestion appears to translate a 'need' into a 'right'. The question of the relationship between needs and rights will be returned to. (See below.)

A second need often identified by victims of crime is the need for practical help. This can include repairing property, fitting new locks, help with form-filling and short-term financial support. Such needs are most likely to occur in the immediate aftermath of an event. (Help with transportation for hospital visits for victims of violent crime is a longer-term need of the practical sort identified by Shapland, 1984.) The incidence of such needs is difficult to identify since many victims of crime can manage such practicalities for themselves or will receive such help from family and friends. With respect to service provision the problem lies in identifying those who need help of this sort. Whilst there may be some difficulty in identifying those who need this kind of practical help, the last type of need identified by Maguire (1985), emotional need, is probably the most difficult area of all to assess.

The question of emotional need is difficult in the first instance since simply asking people whether they have suffered any emotional problems as a result of an event does not always elicit relevant information. Human beings are not necessarily very good at identifying the links between their feelings and events which they have experienced. The difficulty of identifying the actual impact of crime was discussed in Chapter 2. There, differences were observed between the findings of the 1984 British Crime Survey and the findings of the more in-depth study conducted by Maguire and Corbett (1987). Maguire and Corbett were recording, on the whole, a higher incidence of impact. A similar discrepancy arises when asking respondents about their emotional needs. The greater the depth to which this question is probed the more need is uncovered. Whilst this might be a difficult need to identify and measure there is some evidence to suggest that victims of crime suffer emotional and psychological distress in not insignificant numbers.

Maguire's (1982) study of victims of burglary reports that 60 per cent of that sample of victims experienced emotional upset. A finding not out of line with Friedman *et al.*'s (1982) study of, again, predominantly burglary victims. Emotional problems are also reported in response to vandalism and threatening telephone calls (Hough and Mayhew, 1985, and Pease, 1986). Even if the most conservative figures recording emotional distress as a result of a criminal offence are considered, Maguire (1985) argues that this grosses up to several hundred thousand people in England and Wales each year suffering some sort of emotional disturbance as a result of crime. This is of course only a general picture. It is well documented that a high proportion of victims of rape suffer lasting psychological damage, in clinical terms referred to as 'post-traumatic stress disorders', as do victims of hijacking, kidnapping and other serious criminal events. It is also suggested that some victims of burglary suffer emotional distress equal to the distress felt in those obviously more traumatic circumstances. Maguire and Corbett, in attempting to assess victims' emotional needs based on the victims' understanding of the impact of the event and the availability of support from family and friends, conclude:

> about 1 in 4 victims of the crimes (excluding rape) found to have the greatest emotional impact – i.e. burglary, robbery, 'snatch' thefts and serious assault – and 1 in 10 of all recorded offences against individuals, can be shown to 'need' a visit from a volunteer to provide some form of psychological support or reassurance. (Maguire and Corbett, 1987, pp. 76–7)

Maguire and Corbett are here attempting to make some sense of their findings and in the process match them with service delivery; the question of who needs what kind of support, when and for how long. It is this kind of question for which the research conducted to date cannot provide adequate answers.

There are clear indications that victims of rape suffer severe long-term effects and therefore may have long-term needs, and Shapland, Willmore and Duff (1985) suggest there are psychological effects for many victims of violent crime up to two years after the event. How such findings could be or need to be matched with service remains unclear. Mayhew suggests that the victim movement may be in danger of overstating its case.

> Past victimisations often do not seem memorable enough to be recalled for survey interviewers, and even those which are remembered are frequently trivial and of little import; they are

part of life's vicissitudes, not ineffectively coped with by victims with help from family, friends and insurance premiums. (Mayhew, 1984, p. 30)

This conclusion may be reached on the basis of generalizing from crime survey data and is perhaps a plea not to assume that all victims of crime need interventionist crisis support. The evidence is, however, clear on the question of need for information and on the needs of some victims for practical support. The question of emotional need is more complex and a little less clear but the evidence suggests that emotional needs exist for a substantial number of victims of crime.

The discussion so far has focused on what is known, empirically, about the needs of victims. Somewhat independently of this knowledge, responses to the perceived needs of victims have been constructed. These responses have occurred largely in the arena of the voluntary organization. Before examining these responses it is necessary to develop an understanding of why victims' needs were primarily responded to in this way.

Why the voluntary sector?

Mawby and Gill (1987) observe that the increasing involvement of the state in welfare provision has seen the gradual decline of voluntary organizations. Major voluntary organizations, like, for example, the NSPCC, have taken on increasingly the characteristics of statutory agencies. By the 1970s voluntary organizations were for the most part increasingly interdependent with the statutory social services. (See Clayton and Walklate, 1979, on the role of voluntary organizations during the social workers' strike, 1978–9.) However, as Mawby and Gill state:

Then, as government spending became identified as a key issue, anti-collectivist governments in Britain and the United States promised to roll back the boundary of state intervention. Voluntary bodies, alluringly a more independent and apparently cheaper alternative, were back in fashion, allowing governments to demonstrate concern without financial obligations. (Mawby and Gill, 1987, p. 69)

This changing political climate was likely to endorse initiatives within the voluntary sector. It was also coupled with a distinct lack of official policy with respect to crime victims.

The emergence of the CICB, discussed in the previous chapter, illustrates the rather piecemeal approach adopted in official policy-making circles. This piecemeal approach is characterized by a number of themes. Rock (1988a) suggests these include: a desire not to inhibit community initiatives, not to spend more money, not to pre-empt government policy, a concern with the rising costs of criminal injuries compensation and a feeling that to focus on victims of crime is not the 'proper business' of the criminal justice system. (See ibid., p. 55.)

Recently there has been demonstrated considerable will to support the National Association of Victim Support Schemes (NAVSS) crytallizing, in 1986, in the form of some financial support. This official support for NAVSS is self-evidently in contrast with the kind of support available for its 'less attractive rivals' (ibid., p. 55). Amongst those 'less attractive rivals' have, arguably, been those initiatives which have emanated from the feminist movement. This is in contrast to the way in which Rock (1986) views the progress of the Canadian initiative of justice for victims of crime.

In discussing the development of the victims of crime initiative in Canada, Rock relates the importance of the women's movement in spurring the victims' initiative forward: 'Women were politically consequential in a setting which contained no other corporate representatives of the victim' (ibid., p. 210). And, whilst Rock goes on to observe that the groups consulted were never really designed to support the interests of victims as a whole, and neither did they necessarily see the criminal justice system as a forum for their activities, their existence as a 'victims lobby' was significant. (See ibid., Chapter 8, for a fuller discussion of their influence on the victims initiative in Canada.) In contrast, Rock (1988a) argues that the formulation of victim policies in England and Wales has been marked by a 'sexual neutrality'. In addition to the absence of what Rock terms the 'attentive feminist official' (ibid., p. 57), the style of the British feminist movement he suggests has militated against its likely inclusion within official decision-making. This style, which Mawby and Gill (1987) characterize as being one which stands as a critique of conventional social provision, is self-supporting, is concerned with social movement and mutual aid, and has not resulted in government aid:

137

When rape and battering received Government attention in England and Wales, it was chiefly as a result of the intervention of men and women who did not call themselves radical separatists or feminists ... Rape crisis centres and refuges for battered women have not been the beneficiaries of new Government spending on victims. (Rock, 1988a, p. 58)

This does not mean that the feminist movement has not been influential in its concern with women as victims of crime. But its influence has remained local and specific. This has resulted in the formation of official policy on crime victims being focused on the somewhat less politically contentious NAVSS.

Thus, within the voluntary sector, it is possible to identify two strands of support which have been constructed as a response to the perceived needs of victims of crime; one which stems from the feminist movement, and one which stems from the more general victim support movement. In terms of official policy formation the latter has gained greater credence and support; however, in formulating an understanding of the nature of the victim movement as a whole, it is important to develop a more detailed appreciation of each of these strands, beginning with, first of all, the concerns addressed by the feminist movement.

The feminist response to criminal victimization

Rock in describing his experiences of interviewing members of the women's movement in Canada in the context of the Justice for Victims of Crime Initiative recalls: 'If they *did* talk about victims, it was not in the language of the victims movement or the criminal justice system. They preferred to speak of violence against women' (Rock, 1986, p. 211). As Rock goes on to explain, this is not surprising. The women's movement exists to promote issues pertaining to women, which may include some issues of criminal victimization, but does not mean that such organizations are concerned with or for victims of crime at large. In the context of crime victims this has meant that the feminist movement has focused its attention on violence against women, namely, domestic violence, incest and rape. This concern has been the impetus for the development of the refuge movement, Rape Crisis centres and incest survivor groups. Each of these will be examined in turn.

The refuge movement

The first women's refuge was set up in Chiswick in 1972, the Chiswick Women's Aid, founded by Erin Pizzey. Pizzey later split with the feminist movement. This was a result of a difference of opinion in understanding the nature of domestic violence. Pizzey became more concerned with understanding why women were attracted to violent relationships rather than seeing domestic violence as a product of a sexist society. Since 1972, however, the refuge movement had grown considerably in strength. Binney, Harkell and Nixon (1985) report an estimated 11,400 women and 20,850 children had been accommodated in the 150 refuges they traced between September 1977 and September 1978 (ibid., p. 167).

The need for such refuges is demonstrated not only by the response to the refuge movement but also more recently by the scale of the problem. (See, for example, on the Islington Crime Survey, Jones MaClean and Young, 1986, and Chapter 2.) In addition the response to the refuge movement is also an indicator of the dissatisfaction felt with the way in which domestic violence is handled by the statutory services, the police in particular. Johnson highlights the police view in the following statement by The Association of Chief Police Officers, ACPO:

> We are after all dealing with persons bound in marriage, and it is important, for a host of reasons, to maintain the unity of the spouses. (Johnson, 1985, p. 112)

In addition this is not seen to be real police work (Faragher, 1981) and when all the conditions are met for the police to make an arrest, this is rarely done (Edwards, 1986). The dissatisfaction this results in is not only felt towards the police. Other agencies are equally reluctant to get involved. (See the collection of papers edited by Pahl, 1985.) The refuge movement, in particular those refuges attached to the National Federation of Women's Aid, in the light of this general lack of willingness on behalf of the statutory services to embrace this problem, have constructed their own approach to domestic violence.

The refuges offer a situation of mutual support, power-sharing and self-help. Men are excluded from refuges and their management since the point which brings women together is the violence perpetrated by men on women in a sexist society. Mawby and Gill argue that this

139

has resulted in a situation where 'the refuge movement in Britain has balanced somewhat precariously between an oppositional relationship with conventional statutory services and a dependence on state grants for funding' (Mawby and Gill, 1987, p. 77). Such funding has largely emanated from the Manpower Services Commission (MSC) [now Training Agency], Urban Aid, or local housing departments, and has been for the most part short-term. And whilst Gill (1986) has identified a refuge model which has close relationships with statutory services (and government grant funding), that model locates domestic violence within the family rather than within a sexist society. Little is known, as yet, about the nature and extent of such alternative models of provision. Despite such possible alternatives and its precarious funding base, the refuge movement does seem to meet a considerable need for women and children who are victims and survivors of domestic violence.

Rape Crisis centres

As with the refuge movement the response by feminists to the question of rape emerged not only from a critical awareness of the scale of the problem – the failure of women to report sex offences to the police is well documented (for recent evidence, see Chapter 2) – but also from an awareness that when they do so they are subjected to a further process of victimization (see Chambers and Millar, 1983). This process is firmly rooted in a victim precipitation view of rape. Women are interrogated as if they were the offender. This has been translated in the courts as 'contributory negligence' (see Jeffreys and Radford, 1984; Edwards, 1987). Given this general framework for the handling of rape, it is not surprising that women's organizations run by women for women should develop.

The first Rape Crisis centre opened in Britain in London in 1976 and by May 1983 there were six such centres across the country. Anna T. (1988) reports that there are currently forty such centres. Each of these centres operates autonomously and offers some form of 24-hour service for any woman who calls it. The London Rape Crisis Centre describes its work in the following way:

> Our primary aim is to provide a place where women and girls who have been raped or sexually assaulted can talk with other women, at any time of the day or night.

Unlike most agencies that women come into contact with we always believe any woman who calls us. We also offer emotional support and/or legal and medical information according to what each woman wishes. We are also committed to educating and informing the public about the reality of rape, to refute many myths and misconceptions which distort and deny women's experiences. (London Rape Crisis Centre, 1984, ix)

This reflects a very similar model of help to that of the refuge movement. Thus the concern is not only to fill a gap in the provision for victims of rape, it is to educate and to change attitudes. Illustrating this, the report of the London Rape Crisis Centre does not use the term victim: 'Using the word 'victim' to describe women takes away our power and contributes to the idea that it is right and natural for men to 'prey' on us' (ibid., p. x). Whilst the Metropolitan Police have been involved in establishing special centres for the handling of complaints of rape by non-police counsellors with no imperative to report such incidents to the police, this, Rock (1988a) suggests, has largely been in response to the much-publicized handling of such a complaint by the Thames Valley Police (BBC1, January 1982) rather than to the feminist movement. In any event such changes are seen by many feminists as mere window-dressing since the fundamental question of the patriarchal nature of society still remains. It is in this context that many feminists working in the area of sexual violence prefer the term survivor rather than victim. 'This term draws attention to the many ways women resist violence and to the coping strategies they use in dealing with the effects of sexual violence on them over time' (Kelly and Radford, 1987, p. 247). This draws the line very clearly between the traditional responses of the statutory services to the question of rape and the feminist movement. It is a line also clearly drawn in the feminist approach to incest.

Incest survivor groups

Chapter 3 clearly highlighted the difficulties involved in documenting child abuse in general and indicated the current increasing awareness of child sexual abuse and of incest in particular. One of the difficulties in responding to incest is the guilt and anger that the child who has survived incest is likely to feel. The guilt derives not necessarily from the behaviour itself but from the consequences of the behaviour being discovered. The child frequently sees itself as responsible for the break-up of the family if the father's behaviour is reported. In this way the child is not only a victim and survivor of the incest but is also victimized by the likely response of the statutory services, and ultimately the courts, whose actions may result in the removal of the father from the home.

Dominelli (1986) in a critical evaluation of the traditional social work interventionist and family therapy approach argues that these strategies can be employed to hold the male abuser as responsible for his actions rather than focusing on the traditional dynamics of the family unit. In this context incest survivor groups (ISGs) have evolved, in which Dominelli suggests: 'The exploration of options ... is more likely in the supportive environment of the ISG where, being amongst equals sharing similar predicaments, girls can offer one another solidarity and comfort' (Dominelli, 1986, p. 14). In this way the incest survivor can work through problems away from the authority structure of the family. Such groups display the same co-operative characteristics as the other movements discussed here. This co-operation and willingness to listen have in part been translated into the work of the telephone service for children, Childline. Whilst a contentious approach to helping children (see Seaton, 1987), it certainly caused a response. There were some 50,000 attempted calls to Childline during the programme in which it was launched, *Childwatch*, 30 October 1986 (Rantzen, 1987). Additionally, Adler (1988), discussed in Chapter 3, suggests that a greater use of prosecution might also be considered as appropriate.

As a result of this characteristically different approach of the initiatives which emanate from the feminist movement, it is clear that, as Mawby and Gill (1987) predicted, 'Rape crisis centres and refuges for battered women have not been the beneficiaries of new government spending on victims' (Rock, 1988a, p. 58). The victim support schemes have benefited from such funding and have also begun in some areas to include rape cases within their remit as the following discussion will highlight.

The victim support movement

The first victim support scheme was established in Bristol in 1974. The seventh annual report of NAVSS (1986–7) states that there were 305 schemes which dealt with more than a quarter of a million new victims of crime in that year. The aim of these schemes is to help people cope with the crime they have experienced. Reeves (1985) outlines the model of victim support in the UK and emphasizes the community base of the schemes, both in the structure of their management committees and their use of volunteers. The aim, she argues, is to offer short-term help, to offer that help on a 'good neighbour' basis so that people do not have to ask for it and not to duplicate the services of other agencies which exist in the community. This model has proved to be remarkably successful. 'These early Victim Support Schemes (VSS) had no political aims or 'hidden agendas'. They took little interest in the offender, the court process, or the sentences passed' (Maguire and Corbett, 1987, p. 2). In this way they managed to secure the co-operation of the police in referring victims to such schemes. (Mawby and Gill (1987) refer to the 'crucial' role of the police as 'gatekeepers to victims'.) By mid-1984 some 57 per cent of all schemes were operating a direct referral policy, a system in which the police refer all cases whether or not the victim wants support and whether or not their consent had been obtained, except for certain types of offence; around 80 per cent of all victims referred to schemes are victims of residential burglary (Maguire and Corbett, 1987, p. 26). In asking senior officers what kinds of cases are considered to be inappropriate for victim support, Maguire and Corbett found that incidents of racial harassment and domestic violence were mentioned most often as being inappropriate. There may also be local agreements concerning the referral of cases of rape known to the police. On Merseyside, for example, the official policy to date has been to refer such cases to Rape Crisis. Maguire and Corbett also comment on this referral process being subject to 'individual whim, prejudice, or predilection' (ibid., p. 97) whereby cases undergo a further filtering process. Such a filtering process may reflect a police view of the 'archetypal victim' (Jefferson and Grimshaw, 1987, p. 152) or may reflect the views of a particular co-ordinator with respect to victims' needs. The evidence suggests that at the end of the day many victims 'slip through the net' (Maguire and Corbett, 1987, p. 118). Indeed, Hough and Mayhew (1985) estimate that only about 1 per cent of all those who report a crime to the police are ever referred to a victim support scheme.

Despite what might be referred to as a significant level of 'unmet need' suggested by this figure, victim support is currently one of the fastest-growing organizations in the voluntary sector. This growth has not confined itself to simply increasing numbers of support organizations. Victim support has been the spawning ground for FIRM (Forum for Initiatives in Reparation and Mediation, mentioned in the previous chapter), as well as some organizations having reached out into areas of victim support not initially felt to be within the scope of the movement, namely the areas of non-crime victims, rape and victim support in the court. It is useful to examine this growth a little more closely.

The relationship between NAVSS and FIRM is an interesting one. Just as in the early years NAVSS received sponsorship and initial impetus from the National Association for the Care and Resettlement of Offenders (NACRO), and has subsequently retained important informal if not formal links with that organization, so as NAVSS became better established as the representative of victims it was soon faced with requests concerning victim/offender schemes. Initially NAVSS acted as host for discussions on such schemes but it was recognized that victims and offenders might have interests which were irreconcilable and so the separate organisation of FIRM was established. But as Rock (1988a) observes, these organizations occupy a very small world and continuities remain between them.

> Indeed, it does appear as if the orchestration of criminal justice policy-making has been entrusted to a very small intimate social world with few people and multiple affiliations. The same persons may be encountered in very different settings, settings that may seem functionally or ideologically incompatible with one another. They are present precisely because they have stocks of practical knowledge ... And the result is they knit the criminal justice system together. (ibid., p. 64)

Whilst this small group of people may be entrusted at this moment in time with maintaining positions and loyalties, there are dangers inherent in knitting together the criminal justice system in this way. Not only do the persons occupying such positions change, the system itself, inevitably, takes on a life of its own. Interests for victims may currently be sustained in their present form. The question is whether the reliance on, and trust in, individuals, is sufficient to maintain that position in the future, as the progress towards reparation and mediation schemes, suggested in the previous chapter, gains momentum.

The next three areas of growth are not so much instances of giving birth as they are instances of adoption. Offering support to non-crime victims is not approached with any consistency between schemes (Maguire and Corbett, 1987, p. 90). The rationale for reaching out to victims of accidents, fire, etc., seems for the most part to be humanitarian, though some schemes appear actively to seek out such cases to make use of under-used volunteers (ibid.). Others feel, however, that there are specialist skills required in this area and have consequently not become involved. However, Maguire and Corbett do report that some schemes find themselves under increasing pressure to accept such referrals either because the police do not want to refer such cases to the statutory services, or because the statutory services do not want to refer such cases to the police! More recently further initiatives have sprung from NAVSS which are concerned to monitor, for example, the viability of moving into the support of the families of victims of murder. Whatever the circumstances of such referrals it is clear that not all victim support work is always the short-term 'good neighbour' ideal of the model, since much of this work often involves a longer-term commitment.

A further area of work which conflicts with the short-term help implied by the Reeves model, is the increasing involvement of victim support with cases of rape. The seventh annual report of NAVSS indicates that for 1984–5, there were 220 rape referrals to victim support schemes; by 1986–7 this had risen to 673 (p. 24). A similar rise is recorded for referrals of other sexual offences. Given the growth in number of schemes, the gatekeeping role of the police in referring victims, and the reputedly poor relationship between some Rape Crisis centres and the police, this increase is perhaps not surprising. Given the nature of the support rape victims (victims in this context not survivors) more often than not need, the involvement of victim support in this kind of work is.

Corbett's (1987) specific study of victim support work in this area shows that victims frequently received between two and twenty visits. She argues that the outreach philosophy of victim support, offering immediate, frequent, long-term help, is suited to some people (Maguire and Corbett, 1987, p. 186). Maguire and Corbett seem to suggest that there is a place for both victim support and Rape Crisis but go on to conclude that

145

In similar vein, there is no reason, too, why some volunteers could not be permanently deployed assisting rape victims. We believe that this is essential work, of the highest priority for VSS, and deserving, above all else, of financial and other assistance from central and local government. (ibid., p. 208)

It is true that there is room for both types of organization: victim support and Rape Crisis. They do draw upon potentially different populations of rape victims. Victim support gets referrals from the police. Rape Crisis relies on women getting in touch with it. There is, however, an increasing tendency within some victim support schemes, particularly if they are well known locally, to take 'self-referrals'; that is, people who have referred themselves. (This is an issue currently on the agenda for victim support.) There is a likelihood that given the increasing reliance of victim support on state funding and the continuing lack of state funding for the feminist-inspired organizations, victim support work in this area will continue to increase.

Victim support in the court is yet another new avenue for the victim support network. The lack of consideration given to the needs of victims in the court setting is well documented. The first report of the Home Affairs Committee *Compensation and Support for Victims of Crime*, (December 1984) states: 'We feel that much more could be done by court authorities both to provide reasonable waiting facilities within their premises and to ensure that victims of crime are treated with courtesy and humanity.' (ibid., para. 27) Cohen and Shapland in reviewing facilities for victims offered by the police and the courts conclude: 'The courts' awareness and initiative in respect of victims has not progressed very far' (Cohen and Shapland, 1987, p. 31). NAVSS established a working party, chaired by Lady Ralphs, to examine the victim in the court. This working party produced a detailed report in 1988 of the ways in which victim support and the Crown Prosecution Service might respond to the victim in the court setting. And whilst one scheme has already been established in the local crown courts at Guildford, with others likely to follow, this initiative poses some problems for victim support.

The intention, presented in the working party report, is for victim support to provide a sensitive caring service for the (technically speaking) complainant in the court setting. This may involve advising on court procedures, explaining why cases might be deferred, explaining the problems associated with being a witness, providing a place for coffee away from the defendants. These intentions fit well with the caring ideology of victim support in the United Kingdom; but the question remains: whose responsibility is it to provide such information and services? Some would say the Crown Prosecution Service not victim support. In addition, whilst victim support seems willing to move into this arena, the implication arises as to whether the criminal justice system is getting a service 'on the cheap' which ought to be provided other than from within the voluntary sector. These questions lead into the debate of whether the key issue is victims' needs or victims' rights, more fully explored below.

Mawby and Gill (1987) characterize victim support schemes typically as having close relationships with the statutory services, as being state-financed, as being concerned with social provision, and as making a clear distinction between helper and helped. On the other hand, they suggest, Rape Crisis often has no relationship with the statutory services, has a lesser dependence on state finance, is concerned with social movements, and has a fellowship relationship between helper and helped (ibid., pp. 113 and 85). Expressed in these terms it is not difficult to see why the more traditional voluntary organization stance of victim support has superseded, and is likely to continue to supersede, other organizations when it comes to official policy and funding. That funding has so far been used, primarily, to provide most schemes with a full-time, paid co-ordinator. This may ultimately result in additional demands and expectations of victim support, expectations associated with 'professionalism'; a tension already being felt in some schemes on Merseyside, for example. In this way victim support may now be on a road away from its original community-based ideal.

The question of victims' needs reconsidered

In attempting to evaluate the performance of victim support schemes, the task which faced them, Maguire and Corbett (1987) met a number of difficulties. First, whilst NAVSS offers schemes a framework for practice, each scheme may operate in its own way and consequently establishing common criteria for evaluation is a problem. There were, however, more fundamental questions to resolve: what were victims of crime entitled to expect and how far was the state responsible for meeting their expectations (ibid., p. 209)? The answers to these

147

questions, they argue, depend upon whether the support of victims is seen purely as an act of charity, whether it is seen as a response to a social need (the underlying assumption of the discussion to date, and the overall way in which Mawby and Gill, 1987, discuss crime victims), or, finally, whether it is felt that victims have rights which form the basis of the response regardless of need (ibid., pp. 209–10).

Arguably, underpinning the two strands within the voluntary sector which address victims' needs in different ways is the way in which they use the concept of need. This difference is highlighted in the concern within the feminist movement to address the question of women's need for support in an educative manner; that is, to encourage a view within women in which they are seen, not to be victims, but to be survivors. Put another way this enshrines a view of women's rights. (Mawby, 1988b, also makes this point.) On the other hand victim support addresses itself to the notion in terms of responding to an unmet need within the community; being the 'good neighbour' for those who require that kind of support. The tension which exists between these two frameworks becomes tighter when an examination is made of the ways in which the criminal justice system might be changed in order to enhance the status of the victim and whether these changes incorporate a notion of need or right. It is that question to which we now turn.

The victims' rights movement

The question of victims' rights can be approached both at a specific and a general level. Specifically, a particular criminal justice system can be examined and found wanting in the status it accords to individual victims. At a general level, victims can be placed in a broader framework of 'oppression'. In this context, the question to be addressed is interlinked with the question of human rights. In some ways the distinction between the specific and the general is an arbitrary one; but is a useful one to follow in drawing out some of the questions which appear to be on the current agenda for victimology.

In 1985 the United Nations adopted a charter of victims' rights: the Declaration on the Basic Principles of Justice for Victims and Abuse of Power. Waller (1988) details from this resolution four principles of justice which specify basic standards of treatment for crime victims. They are: access to administrative and judicial procedures, restitution, compensation (from governments) and assistance (ibid., p. 196). He goes on to argue that four countries have blazed the trail in providing assistance to victims some of which involve changes within the criminal justice process. A brief overview of these comparative changes will be informative.

Waller suggests that two main pieces of legislation have advanced the victims' cause in the United States: the Federal Victim Witness Protection Act, 1982 and the Federal Victims of Crime Act, 1984. The first of these introduced strong penalties for those who interfered with witnesses and also introduced the notion of restitution. The second introduced taxes on federal offenders and the use of fines. This second initiative now apparently raises $60 million annually (ibid., p. 198). Most states have also established 'crime victim commissions' whose responsibility it is to improve the services for victims of crime.

Canada has developed a co-ordinated 'needs assessment' approach to crime victims through official agencies working together in the form of victim assistance programmes. Waller reports that the police have been significantly involved in such programmes. In France victims have always had the right to be heard and to claim restitution but since 1981 moves have been made to widen the support offered to victims of crime usually on a professional basis. Waller also includes England and Wales in his list of those setting the trail for victim support, highlighting the early establishment of the Criminal Injuries Compensation Board and the voluntary tradition for victim support.

These examples highlight the way in which other responses are possible to meet the needs of victims, in which victims' needs can be met by addressing those needs in the context of rights; see France and the United States, for example. In discussing the thorny problem of the relationship between needs and rights, Mawby (1988b) argues that for a justice approach to victims of crime, the question of needs can be only a starting-point. The evidence reviewed here illustrates the nature and extent of victims' needs, how they might be met by different services, but also how those services probably fail to meet the needs of the majority of victims. The answer does not necessarily lie in more volunteers or more schemes or a better matching of resources to needs. It is clear that some of those needs, highlighted here and in the previous chapter, are unmet because the needs approach is inappropriate. The general view of the forgotten victim, in terms of the victims' status in the criminal justice process, can only really be tackled fundamentally by the justice approach recommended by Mawby. Mawby (1988b) states that:

> The fact that we accept that certain needs exist and warrant concern does not entail any obligation by the State to meet those needs. Thus, one view of the role of welfare in society (readily identified with the creation of the CICB) is that which sees statutory welfare provisions as a generous and humane gesture, but involving no obligation on behalf of society to provide help. In contrast, under a rights-based model citizens have moral claims to state help, and conversely the State is obliged to acknowledge the rights of citizens with regard to welfare. (ibid., p. 133)

He goes on to suggest that three principles stem from this for victims of crime: that victims have rights irrespective of needs, that such rights should be substantive and, thirdly, that in constructing these rights attention should be paid to public opinion to ensure that regard is given to what is considered important.

One aspect of these movements towards a rights-based initiative for victims of crime has been the movement towards crime prevention. NAVSS, in fact, withdrew from membership of the World Society of Victimology partly as a result of that society's acceptance of this kind of move (Mawby and Gill, 1987, p. 104) and partly in response to the call for greater involvement of victims in the sentencing process. NAVSS was concerned with the possible injustices which might result from embracing the implications of such a declaration. Others would argue that crime prevention in general is not the concern of victims. Indeed this appears rather like blaming the victims for their own victimization; a victim precipitation model of victimization in another guise. (See Chapter 7.) However, this text, and others, have highlighted features of the criminal justice process which undermine the position of the victim, so the question of specific rights for crime victims demands closer scrutiny.

Mawby and Gill (1987) argue that there are four areas in which victims' rights need strengthening: the right to an active role in the criminal justice process, the right to information, the right to financial help and the right to support (ibid., p. 229). An examination of Mawby and Gill's proposals in each of these areas will enable a number of issues to be addressed.

In considering the role of the victim in the criminal justice process, Mawby and Gill reject victim impact statements which go alongside a recommendation for sentence favoured in some parts of North America. They favour increasing the power of victims through mediation and reparation and the use of victim impact statements after sentence has been passed as a way of making greater use of the present disposition of compensation.

The right to knowledge or information builds on the available research concerning victims' experiences of the criminal justice system. Consequently Mawby and Gill highlight the way in which making it an obligation for the police to inform the victim of the progress of a case, of rights with respect to compensation and of the availability of support, and also making it an obligation on the Crown Prosecution Service to keep the victim informed should proceedings reach this stage, would improve victims' experiences of the criminal justice process considerably. These proposals overlap to a degree with the proposals concerning victims' rights to financial help.

Greater knowledge of the availability of the system of compensation as it is presently organized would certainly entail more claims being made on the system. However, a stronger claim is made by Mawby and Gill who call for a 'comprehensive system of crime insurance' (p. 231) financed either through taxation or national insurance contributions. This they suggest would establish criminal injuries compensation as a right (at present it constitutes 'ex gratia' payments; see previous chapter) and would also incorporate rights for property losses. Finally they argue that victims should have the right to specialist help and support, in which they include the availability of women's refuges and Rape Crisis centres as well as victim support.

Whilst it may be possible to make a range of observations about the likely drawbacks and impact of each of these particular proposals there are a number of general comments to be made. Shapland (1988b) in her analysis of how change might be accomplished within the criminal justice system for victims argues that you can introduce changes but you cannot necessarily ensure that participants within the criminal justice process adopt the required courses of action. She calls for not only legislative changes but also a 'package of directives, codes of practice or circulars' and the 'promotion of training and different attitudes' (ibid. p. 193). Constituting rights within the English criminal justice system would, it seems, not necessarily achieve the goals which Mawby and Gill (1987) might hope for. Their suggestions are, however, a move in the right direction towards reconstituting formal recognition of the victim. Waller (1988) argues that the answer lies in 'crime commissions' to implement the principles of the UN declaration. Reeves is less convinced by the validity of moving in the direction of rights at all:

> The issue of victims' 'rights' raises similar difficulties, not least the problem of definition. To take an example, the provision of personal services, absolute rights could only be given in the United Kingdom through legislation, and responsibility for service delivery would normally pass to statutory bodies such as Local Authorities, Police, or Probation Services. The benefits of voluntary commitment and inter-agency work would be a high price to pay. (Reeves, 1988, p. 206)

Such reservations from the current director of NAVSS are to be expected. There are, however, some difficulties associated with the victims' rights movement which, as yet, have not been articulated.

To take the suggestions of Mawby and Gill (1987) as an example. First, Mawby and Gill focus attention on improving the experiences of victims within the criminal justice system. This implies that these mechanisms come into play when the victims recognize that they have been criminally victimised and have called upon the official agencies within the criminal justice process to 'do something about' that criminal victimization. In this way they constitute a series of proposals which may or may not improve those victims' experiences. They are proposals which are curtailed implicitly by the official parameters within which they have been constructed. This construction assumes a sexually and racially neutral view of the victim.

It has been highlighted elsewhere in this text that for some groups who are routinely subjected to law-breaking behaviour, sexual violence, racial violence and harassment, for example, one of the problems lies in getting these experiences to be recognized as criminal victimization. Such cases are more often than not the cases which never become a part of the formal criminal justice process to which Mawby and Gill relate. This neutral view fails to recognize that the question of victims' rights examined within the narrow orbit of a particular criminal justice system cannot propose to empower the victim without recognizing that such power is structurally constrained.

The empowerment of victims requires embracing an understanding of the structural base of that victimization. This in the first instance requires that the currently available and popular stereotypical images of the legitimate victim be questioned. This involves unpacking the ageist, sexist and racist assumptions on which these images are constructed. This unpacking is not necessarily at odds with Mawby and Gill's suggestions or the victims' rights movement as a whole. It is an issue raised to emphasize that what goes on within the criminal justice process, for victims and offenders alike incidentally, does not necessarily tackle the issues of victimization which go on outside the criminal justice process. It might be said that very little could tackle these processes. However, it is possible that Waller's (1988) commitment to 'crime commissions', if part of their role was educative, could go some way in this direction. Waller's priorities are first of all to improve the responses of the police, secondly to allow victims greater participation in the criminal justice process and thirdly to reduce victimization through crime prevention. In this way victimology and the victim movement become concerned with questions of oppression.

It has perhaps been more usual for such questions to be concerned with politically oppressed minorities. However, as Elias points out,

> The study of victims of crime and oppression cannot be separated from understanding political and economic systems. Thus we must consider political and economic solutions and probably not those that merely tinker with institutions and processes, but those that go to the heart of our political economy. (Elias, 1986, p. 242)

The consideration given to children as victims and corporate victimization in this text adds weight to this position. This avoids hoping, as Fattah (1986) appears to, that 'in the long run humanity and compassion', 'tolerance and forgiveness' (ibid., p. 13) will result in caring communities recognizing and sharing the responsibility for the process of victimization. It also supersedes the relativism of Weisstraub (1986) who states that 'Anyone who has experienced political or emotional conflict knows the extent to which victimisation, even more than beauty, is in the eye of the beholder' (Weisstraub, 1986, p. 318). Much of the material of this text has been concerned to point out

153

that there are objective dimensions to victimization. Whether those being victimized recognize and define themselves in these terms is analytically another matter.

This view is not necessarily intended to undermine those suggestions which are designed to improve the way in which victims are able to handle their experiences. It is merely intended to emphasize that whilst this is a useful and positive achievement in itself, it can never be anything more than a partial tinkering with the system whilst the fundamental assumptions on which that process is built remain unchallenged.

Conclusion

This chapter has attempted to outline the way in which the question of victims' needs has been addressed and the way in which organizations within the voluntary sector have responded to this. It has been suggested that the two strands within the voluntary sector with which we have been concerned, namely the feminist movement and the victim support movement, reflect different assumptions on the question of victims' needs, the initiatives emanating from the feminist movement showing a concern with women's rights, and the victim support movement concerning itself more with what might be called a social need. It has also been observed that the victim support movement has been considerably more successful in securing official sponsorship, particularly in the form of government funding. Rock (1988) has argued that the victim movement in the United Kingdom has been characterized by a sexual neutrality. The importance of this characteristic, from the analysis offered here, lies not only in the observation that the initiatives which have emanated from the feminist movement have been largely overlooked by official policy initiatives, but also in the way in which the neutrality of the victim support movement has been an essential feature of its successful growth and development. This latter point requires further development.

The success of the victim support movement in securing the initial co-operation of the police in referring victims to it is largely attributable to its political neutrality. It is a movement which values its neutrality at this level. It can be seen from the way in which the movement conceptualizes the notion of victims' needs that this neutrality also pervades the way in which victim support conducts the work that it does. Victims may be anyone in the community. Whilst there might be some variation in the way in which individual workers within victim support identify the kind of support needed by a particular kind of victim, the movement as a whole makes no statements which indicate that a victim of crime might have particular characteristics. Neither does it necessarily attempt to engage in educating the victim. (The difference between the feminist movement and the victim support movement in the way in which each handles cases of rape illustrate this last statement.) An educative stance would also imply a stance on the question of victims' rights. To date the victim support movement has found this difficult to embrace.

For some sections of the community criminal victimization is a way of life; it is a part of their everyday existence. This is particularly the case for the ethnic minorities and women. A public statement supporting a recognition of this would remove the characteristic neutrality from the victim support movement – the same kind of neutrality which was observed as being characteristic of the criminal justice process as a whole in Chapter 5. The victim support movement gells nicely with the accepted order of the criminal justice process as a whole and can therefore be easily and readily absorbed within it, perhaps ultimately as another 'fief'. (See Shapland, 1988.)

In this way, then, because the victim support movement does not question the accepted image of the victim either in the way it conceptualizes victims' needs or in the way it conducts its business, it has been successful. This analysis also implies that whilst the victim support movement is an initiative outside of the state, it is firmly located in the voluntary sector and its traditions, and the success of its operation has brought it closer to the state. If one of the key features of the state is the way it functions to maintain social control, then in the images it operates with, the victim support movement is implicated in those questions of social control. The reluctance of the movement to develop a framework for conceptualizing victims' rights highlights this. It remains to be seen whether the more recent involvement of victim support in rape cases and the even more recent initiative to develop an involvement in racial harassment will result in the victim support movement developing a more critical position with respect to the victim. On the present evidence it seems unlikely.

We end, therefore, in a rather similar position to the end of Chapter 5. Both the criminal justice process and what appears to be an increasingly important feature of the voluntary sector as far as official policy is concerned, victim support, display similar images of the victim. An image which fails to draw our attention to those features of the victimization process which are structured by the nature of the social system rather than by individual actions. Those features may be uncomfortable to recognize but they are nevertheless real, and real in the consequences that they have for whole sections of society. To question them involves questioning the existing social order; to leave them unquestioned seriously neglects what must be the key considerations for victimology. One issue remains. Towards the end of this discussion, the question of the relationship between the victim and crime prevention emerged. It is to a critical examination of crime prevention from the viewpoint of the victim that we now turn.

7

Victims, crime prevention and the community

Introduction

The last two chapters have addressed the role of the victim in the criminal justice system and the response of the voluntary sector to the victim of crime. In these chapters we began to get a feel for the kind of policy responses in which the victim of crime seems to figure. This chapter will be concerned to draw out further some of the policy issues which relate to victims of crime but within the more general framework of crime prevention. This will facilitate a consideration of a number of processes currently fashionable in the 'fight against crime'. These may be labelled victim blaming, offender blaming and community blaming. These labels are deliberately emotive. They not only facilitate a consideration of different kinds of crime prevention initiatives and their likely success or failure in the fight against crime; but also ensure that we are sensitive to what is assumed by these initiatives and the implications of such assumptions for victims of crime.

Victims and crime prevention; a framework

Elias (1986), preferring to talk about crime reduction rather than crime prevention (a preference not peculiar to Elias; see Hope and Shaw, 1988), states that 'Crime reduction seeks to help victims by devising strategies to reduce crime and victimization, largely by increasing victim participation' (ibid., p. 182). However, as Elias himself goes on to illustrate, not all crime reduction policies necessarily involve greater victim participation. This characteristic most appropriately describes community crime reduction programmes. There are other crime reduction strategies which Elias calls 'victimiza-tion avoidance' and 'enforcement crackdowns' (ibid., p. 182), which we shall call 'victim blaming' and 'offender blaming', in which the principle of victim participation is interpreted somewhat differently. All three strategies, victim blaming, offender blaming and community blaming, claim to tackle the questions of victimization and fear of victimization, and therefore demand closer scrutiny. Each, along with the crime prevention initiative appropriately subsumed by these headings, will be discussed in turn.

Victim blaming

There are two main crime prevention strategies which fall under this heading: those which promote behavioural changes in individuals and those which involve 'target hardening' of properties or environments. Both of these strategies start with the victim; in the first the victim is an individual human being; in the second the victim is a property or an environment. The first strategy assumes that what needs to be changed to prevent crime is the individual victim's behaviour. It assumes that if the individual is made a 'harder target' then the opportunity for him or her to be victimized will diminish. The second strategy assumes that it is necessary to make the property or environment a 'harder target' and in this way reduce the opportunities for crime. These assumptions clearly highlight what both of these strategies assume to be key contributing factors in the aetiology of crime; the criminals makes the most of opportunities presented to them by individuals or the environment and in giving the criminals such opportunities the victims precipitate their victimization. Before examining some of the drawbacks to this view of crime it will be useful to examine the nature of these strategies a little more closely.

It has already been seen that some victims, or potential victims, engage in 'risk management behaviour' as a way of reducing their chances of further victimization or as a way of reducing their own exposure to situations of which they are fearful. So, they avoid going out alone after dark, for example. The mechanisms which provoke such behavioural responses are not altogether clear; certainly fear of crime seems to be important associated particularly with the variables of age and gender. (See Chapter 2 for a fuller discussion of this.) It is obvious then that, fairly spontaneously, individuals may construct their own response to crime or the fear of crime. However, such spontaneous responses can be built on either positively or negatively in policy initiatives and consequently in the implications such initiatives have for individual freedom.

A positive response to fear of assault might be self-defence classes, carrying a small canister of offensive spray or a very loud whistle, or always ensuring that someone knows where you are going and what time you might be expected back. These are positive in so far as they constitute strategies which have a minimal impact on an individual's day-to-day routine activities and lifestyle. They minimally curtail individual freedom. A negative response might be to avoid going out, or to change one's route to or from work regularly, or to change one's style of dress. Responses of this kind maximally curtail individual freedom. The feminist movement, for example, has periodically held 'Reclaim the Night' marches to make the point that women often avoid the dark and that their freedom has been curtailed as a consequence. Taken together, both positive and negative responses clearly encourage the victim and the potential victim to take better precautions against possible victimization. They presume that some feature of the victim's behaviour facilitates or precipitates the occurrence of an offence. Whilst this may be the case in specific instances of victimization, as a general strategy for crime prevention or reduction, this emphasis may in fact increase anxiety and fear of crime rather than reduce it.

The second strategy of victim blaming focuses on property and the environment. The crime prevention initiatives subsumed here cover a wide range and fall into the more traditional remit of the local police force's crime prevention officer. They involve at one level general 'target hardening' advice and include fitting window locks, cancelling the milk when going on holiday and using property-marking schemes. Such tactics have become increasingly more technically sophisticated; infra-red burglar alarms, the development of car radios which require the insertion of a personal code before they will work. It is important to recognize that some of these tactics are useful only in a specific context. Window locks make a house more difficult to break into only provided that the doors are also adequately protected. Hough and Mo (1986) report from British Crime Survey data that attempted burglaries are prevented from becoming successful burglaries by appropriate security strategies. But this suggestion must be tempered by the argument which suggests that it is surveillance which deters burglars (Bennett and Wright, 1984). This led Forrester, Chatterton and Pease (1988) to adopt a total approach towards 'target hardening' which included some community initiative in crime reduction, thus emphasizing the view that 'target hardening' alone does not necessarily achieve the desired effect.

So far we have focused primarily on property 'target hardening'; what about the environment? Victim blaming strategies which focus on the environment stem largely from the work of Newman (1972). Newman's notion of 'defensible space' stood largely as a critique of much of the tower block style of accommodation built particularly in the 1960s. It is a view which implies a form of architectural determinism; that is, that the built environment provides the precipitative framework in which crime occurs. A built environment in which there is little private space but a good deal of public space for which no one takes responsibility and of which there is little surveillance, gives the prime opportunities for crime. This emphasis on the built environment seems to have taken a new lease of life in the United Kingdom in the work of Coleman (1985) who has been involved in, for example, programmes to create private garden space where there was once none and in the disassembling of concrete walkways which she argues permit numerous routes of unsurveyed access and egress within some housing estates. The aim of such programmes is to reduce the opportunities for crime by changing the structure of the environment. Such programmes are known in the United States as Crime Prevention Through Environmental Design. These strategies of victim blaming which focus on property and the environment may also restrict the freedom of individuals.

Target hardening involves a good deal of conscientious effort on the part of the property owner; more informal surveillance means surveillance of all not just of potential offenders. Kinsey, Lea and Young (1986) develop this argument. They suggest that such 'situational crime prevention' is limited by two tendencies. The first they call an inherent 'social behaviourism'. This is a tendency to see behaviour as a product of physical structures and opportunities which are presented within such structures. This leads, they argue, to an over-optimistic view of what crime prevention strategies can achieve:

> Beyond a certain point, increases in such measures as 'target hardening' and 'natural surveillance' will have marginal effects in further reducing crime, yet markedly increase the apprehension of innocent citizens and restrict their free social space. (ibid., p. 121)

The second tendency they call 'the displacement of politics by technology' (ibid., p. 120). This is a tendency to see crime prevention simply as an issue of increasing technological expertise (primarily associated with the police) rather than an issue which involves full community debate and participatory decision-making. As will be seen, not all crime prevention strategies are technically defined, the recent movement towards community crime reduction (Hope and Shaw, 1988) does not rest solely on technical expertise, though it may, nevertheless, still be subject to the same criticism made by Kinsey, Lea and Young (1986) on the question of community debate and participation.

Victim blaming crime prevention strategies, whether focused on individuals or properties, place the responsibility for crime reduction on the individual. Such an allocation of responsibility not only misses the point of the causation of crime, but has the effect of heightening the victimization process. Individuals see themselves not only as potential victims but as potentially responsible for preventing their own victimization. Whilst it has been more commonplace to voice this view of victim blaming in the context of rape, it is a view which is none the less relevant in other, perhaps less traumatic circumstances. This is not to deny that some of the suggestions made for victimization avoidance may constitute sound advice. The problem lies not so much in the soundness of the advice but in the implications which underpin a view of crime prevention which has its origins in a victim precipitation view of crime. Such a view masks the consequences for individual freedom which are entailed in this approach and discourages a deeper examination of the causes of crime.

Offender blaming

Offender blaming correlates with Elias's (1986) category of 'enforcement crackdowns'. This form of crime prevention tries to reduce victimization by increasing the police force and its resources. The Victims Committee of the International Association of Chiefs of Police and Victim Advocates for Law and Order (VALOR) is a good example of a victims group in the United States which adopts the 'enforcement crackdown' style; calling for more prosecutions, convictions and punishment. The United Kingdom has a vociferous 'hang 'em and flog 'em' brigade, and the 'Victims of Violence' organization headed by Joan Jonkers comes closest to representing victims of crime from a viewpoint such as this. Particular campaigns against particular crimes do not necessarily need the blessing of victims of crime to gain legitimacy; the support of the victim may be present (as with police campaigns against drug abuse on the Wirral and the Wirral Parents Against Drug Abuse organization) or such support may be invoked symbolically. This latter strategy has been successful in the more general law and order political campaign of the Tory Party in the 1980s in putting the crime problem on the agenda. This campaign has encouraged a view that the answer to the crime problem is a tougher approach to punishment in the belief that other approaches to crime are either ineffective (soft) or inappropriate. And whilst imprisonment seems to have increased as an option in the sentencing process, in part as a result of this political framework (see Box, 1987), that same framework has not resulted, necessarily, in the allocation of unlimited resources for the police. (It is a political campaign which has also embraced other strategies of crime prevention by invoking the image of the community; see below.) Such offender blaming strategies often only temporarily reduce victimization. There is no evidence to suggest that offender blaming, as a major strategy of crime prevention, has made any inroads into rates of victimization.

Offender blaming, rather like victim blaming, works only in a limited number of cases. There is enough evidence to suggest that factors such as personality, attitude and moral sense predispose some individuals to criminal behaviour. In individual cases, strategies which focus on individual characteristics may prevent that individual from committing further offences. There is a difference between considering such strategies as being relevant for some individuals who are known to have committed particular crimes, and considering their relevance for crime prevention in general. There is a clear difference, for example, between crime known to the police and the incidence of criminal victimization. If crime prevention is to tackle the latter then offender blaming strategies mask, first, the nature and extent of criminal victimization and, secondly, the possibility that there are causes of crime which stretch beyond the offender; that is, are related to the structure of society rather than the individual criminal or types of crime. Once this possibility is raised, in terms of crime prevention, offender blaming is unlikely to bear much fruit.

Community blaming

To argue that certain crimes occur with greater frequency in some areas rather than others is not new. As Reiss (1986) has pointed out, the criminal victimization survey has done much to confirm the overall spatial patterning of crime. However, as Reiss also points out, this evidence is collected from individuals, and it is from these individual responses that a community view of crime is constructed. There is, however, no guarantee that the views of those individuals are necessarily representative of the community. There are also clear problems in defining what is meant by the community. Willmott (1987) calls it a 'seductive word' and suggests it is useful to make a distinction between the 'territorial community', meaning people who live in a particular area, the 'interest community', meaning people who have something more in common than territory alone and the 'attachment community', meaning people having a sense of belonging to a particular area (ibid., p. 2). These different definitions of community have some bearing on the discussion to follow. What is obvious is that this is a concept which is open to interpretation and not always clearly defined.

Despite the difficulties discussed above, Hope and Shaw (1988) argue that in the last ten years there has been an increasing tendency to widen the responsibility for crime prevention to include the community. They suggest two reasons for this. First, there has been an increasing awareness of the fear of crime and the belief that such fear is having a deleterious effect on community life. Secondly, there has been an increasing awareness that many people are affected by crime either as victims or friends of victims. As a result of these two factors, they suggest, two policy responses have emerged. These responses have focused their attention on the role of the community in crime prevention. The first encourages greater participation and involvement of individuals in crime prevention; the second relies on greater co-operation and co-ordination between agencies within the community. Each of these will be examined in turn.

Encouraging greater participation of individuals in the community in crime prevention programmes is not a particularly new idea. The more recent initiatives have, however, promoted a victimization perspective. This development relies on what Hope and Shaw (1988) call 'the mobilisation of informal community controls' which are directed 'in the defence of communities against a perceived predatory threat from outside' (ibid., p. 12). Taking a lead from similar developments in the United States, this defence has emerged in the United Kingdom in the form of neighbourhood watch schemes. Our concern here is the extent to which such schemes can tackle the questions of criminal victimization and the fear of victimization.

There are in essence two different strands of thought which suggest that neighbourhood watch schemes are a positive step to take in the fight against crime. The first strand constitutes an opportunity reduction view of crime. This stresses the importance of having 'eyes on the street' since there is some evidence indicating that surveillance will deter criminals and thus reduce crime. Hence neighbourhood watch schemes are described as the 'eyes and ears of the police'.

The second strand stresses the importance of creating and harnessing community cohesion. Such cohesion may have been undermined in the process of neighbourhood decline (a process which Hope and Hough, 1988, argue involves rising 'incivilities'). Increasing the interaction which takes place between different members of the community in the common purpose of crime prevention through the mechanism of neighbourhood watch may lead to greater civility and trust within the community and reduce the fear of crime. There is a tension between these two strands of thought. This is most obviously displayed when the questions of how and where such schemes seem to be most readily implemented and the extent to which they are effective in achieving these goals are raised.

The development of neighbourhood watch schemes has been very rapid. (In 1987 there were over 29,000 registered schemes, twice as many as in 1986; Hope, 1988, p. 146.) The 1984 British Crime Survey provided an opportunity to explore the extent to which there was support for this development. Hope provides an analysis of those findings. He suggests that

> Where the strongest spontaneous support for Neighbourhood Watch resides is in those communities where people are sufficiently worried about crime, where they feel the need to do something about it, and where they feel positively towards their neighbours and to the community in general. (Hope, 1988, p. 159)

He goes on to add that the social characteristics of those who seem willing to involve themselves in neighbourhood watch are similar to those shared by people willing to involve themselves more generally in voluntary activity: white, middle-aged, lower middle/middle-class. Such general findings on the support for neighbourhood watch concur with the more specific findings concerning the circumstances in which neighbourhood watch is most likely to achieve some of its objectives; amongst white, middle-class home owners. (See Bennion *et al.*, 1985, Donnison, Skola and Thomas, 1986, and Bennett, 1987.) The objective most likely to be achieved seems to be to reduce the fear of crime. (Though Rosenbaum (1988) raises some useful questions as to whether the goal of fear reduction is itself a valid one and whether in fact neighbourhood watch achieves this.) Rosenbaum's discussion raises the question as to whether the answer is to 'try harder' in those areas of high crime rates in which neighbourhood watch is much less popular. This is where the tension between the two strands of thought on neighbourhood watch lies.

Neighbourhood watch seems to be popular in areas where the worry about crime is high but the actual risk of residential crime is relatively low. In other words it seems to build on an already existing network of relationships in which crime is most likely to be seen as an external threat to the community. On the other hand, in areas where the crime rate is high, neighbourhood watch is less popular. It is also likely that people within these areas believe that the offenders are local. They are probably neighbours. In other words the problem here is that crime is not seen to be an external threat to the community against which the community can defend itself, but it is seen to be a problem internal to the community. Neighbourhood watch is not necessarily the mechanism on which trust can be built or fear reduced under these circumstances. Community members may see and hear what is going on in their community but this does not necessarily lead to opportunity reduction, or reduction in fear of crime. People's beliefs about crime do not facilitate strategies which have these goals. Under these circumstances Rosenbaum (1988) suggests that a multiple strategy approach is probably more appropriate. Bright (1987) outlines what might be considered such an approach.

Using the term 'community safety' rather than crime prevention Bright suggests a framework which includes strategies for local councils, for protecting groups most at risk (women, ethnic minorities, children), for services to victims of crime, for responses to offending, for different residential areas and finally for schemes involving the police. (See ibid., pp. 49–50.) This framework embraces a number of critical issues in the context of community initiatives in crime prevention. First it sees the responsibility for tackling victimization and the fear of victimization as being broadly based within the community. It is not solely the responsibility of the police to initiate crime prevention strategies. Secondly, it sees the importance of creating local networks through the local authority to deal with the issue of community safety and crime. Thus the initial responsibility for crime prevention does not necessarily rest with the citizen but with agencies within the community. It recognizes that it is necessary to create the circumstances in which citizen participation might then follow. Thirdly it sees crime as a problem of the community; not as something external to it. And fourthly, it recognizes that specific groups within the community are more vulnerable than others and therefore might benefit from strategies which do not curtail their freedom. This approach clearly moves away from the property and street crime emphasis of neighbourhood watch. Bright's model has some similarities with the multi-agency policing approach to be discussed shortly; but is different in the key respect that the police are not seen to be the leaders of crime prevention. Crime prevention is a co-operative community-led issue. In the context of community crime prevention it is arguable that Bright's model comes closest to embracing all three of Willmott's (1987) definitions of community whereas one of the major limitations to the neighbourhood watch approach is that it is primarily territorial in emphasis. Before considering the extent to which community initiatives such as these can tackle the problem of criminal victimization, it is useful to consider the role of multi-agency policing in dealing with this problem.

Hope and Shaw define multi-agency policing in the following way:

> inasmuch as crime within local communities is likely to be sustained by a broad range of factors – in housing, education, recreation etc. – the agencies and organisations who are in some way responsible for, or capable of, affecting those factors, ought to join in common cause so that they are not working at cross purposes or sustaining crime inadvertently. (Hope and Shaw, 1988, p. 13)

The extent to which such joining together is feasible and likely to be fully democratic is raised by Kinsey, Lea and Young (1986). They suggest that whilst housing authorities, youth workers and social workers might be concerned with preventive issues in the normal course of their work, aligning such work with the police poses dilemmas for such workers. Youth workers, for example, might find their work with young people who have a less positive relationship with the police, compromised. Additionally, agencies coming together with the police might find themselves involved in a less than democratic process. The presence of the police with their 'expert' status may create an atmosphere in which the police consequently take the lead. Kinsey, Lea and Young (1986) argue that such 'soft' approaches to policing are unlikely to supersede the importance of 'hard' approaches, 'pinching collars', which the police, ultimately, take more seriously.

Focusing on the dilemmas and likely relationships between agencies involved in multi-agency policing is similarly developed by Blagg *et al.* (1988). They discuss the problems faced by the probation service in its involvement with multi-agency policing. The question remains, however, what is multi-agency policing likely to achieve for the community with respect to criminal victimization and the fear of criminal victimization?

Some agencies have taken criminal victimization seriously. The probation service, for example, has acknowledged the importance of extending the definition of its role to considering ways in which its knowledge and expertise can be used to help victims of crime in general and victim support schemes in particular. Indeed many local victim support schemes have received initial help, either in accommodation, administration, or mutual use of volunteers, from the probation service. In a similar vein there has been a good deal of co-operation between victim support and the police in the process of victim referral. (See Chapter 6.) These can be seen as examples of inter-agency co-operation which have been of benefit to the victim support movement and consequently victims of crime. They are, however, initiatives which have not had as their main aim the prevention of crime; though subsequent advice offered to victims might have a preventive element. They are initiatives which pick up on criminal victimization after the event. This does not mean that inter-agency co-operation cannot and does not operate in a preventive fashion. Some would argue that the co-operation between social workers, the police, educational welfare officers, and various voluntary agencies in the arena of intermediate treatment for juveniles has this very characteristic. (How and in whose interest this works, however, is open to considerable debate.) Blagg *et al.* (1988), however, suggest that examining the features of inter-agency co-operation which are neglected within the parameters of local multi-agency policing policy and practice highlights the issues which might be usefully handled in a preventive manner by such agencies.

They suggest two arenas in which inter-agency co-operation might be useful: violence against women and racial attacks. They are not very specific concerning the strategies which might be involved in tackling racial attacks but are more specific in the context of domestic violence. Blagg *et al.* state:

> But what is most striking is the contrast between the neglect of domestic violence as a site upon which to enact measures of crime prevention (in other words, to regard such violence as 'crime') or to invoke the concept of inter-agency co-operation, when set against the elaborate liaison apparatus which is arranged around child protection. (ibid., 1988, p. 217)

Blagg *et al.* seem to be suggesting that in theory it is possible in the context of domestic violence, if the appropriate agencies were brought together, including the less (formally) recognized women's and community groups, and if domestice violence was prioritized, to establish a network of agencies concerned with monitoring and preventing domestic violence in the same way that efforts are made to police child abuse. Presumably the question of racial attacks would involve developing similar mechanisms. Whether such mechanisms would work in every case is of course open to question. This, patently, does not occur in every case of child abuse. The suggestion, however, is certainly a more radical view of multi-agency policing than has, for the most part, been implemented to date. These 'neglected issues' of crime prevention raise a number of questions concerning the nature of multi-agency policing and its ability to tackle criminal victimization.

First, multi-agency policing has, for the most part, been implemented in a 'top down' style. The initiative requires the co-operation of agencies within the community which are formally recognized as being appropriate to the issue of crime control. Less formal community groups are frequently neglected. Such neglect is not a requirement of multi-agency policing as defined by Hope and Shaw (1988). A less formal approach might more effectively reach into questions of crime prevention. Secondly, in many ways it appears that multi-agency policing has been more of a rhetoric than a reality when an examination is made of the dilemmas and the willingness of various agencies to become involved in such co-operation. Thirdly, where such multi-agency co-operation has occurred, it has done so very much within a conventional definition of crime prevention, involving emphases on young people and property crimes. Such a conventional framework is of course not peculiar to multi-agency policing, it is also an intrinsic characteristic of neighbourhood watch. (See above.) Ultimately, this vision of crime prevention is an important limiting factor on any success of multi-agency policing.

This section began with the heading 'community blaming', implying that the mechanisms to be discussed largely held the community responsible for its own victimization and that solutions to this problem lay in the community's own hands. It has been seen that neighbourhood watch schemes have been considered an appropriate community-based mechanism by which the problems of victimization and the fear of victimization can be tackled. It has been suggested that this mechanism of 'community blaming' is most likely to work in those communities where a degree of social cohesion already exists and where crime is seen to be a threat to the community from outside. These characteristics align most neatly with the imagery of neighbourhood watch. It has been suggested that for other communities where such characteristics are absent a more complex array of strategies might be more appropriate in creating a 'safe community'. Whilst both these mechanisms move away from making crime prevention the responsibilty of the individual neither of these mechanisms suggests that the cause of crime, and therefore victimization, lies beyond the individual's community. Neighbourhood watch and community safety are both initiatives which attempt to contribute to the kind of informal social control which Shapland (1988b) argues already exists in some communities and in which it is felt a solution to the victimization process lies. The community safety approach was, however, different in one key respect; it highlighted that some sections of the community needed more protection than others. This recognizes a sensitivity to the structural features of victimization which have been a theme in this text, as did the suggestions by Blagg *et. al.* (1988) concerning the neglected features of multi-agency policing. The dominant approach within both frameworks of community blaming, neighbourhood schemes and multi-agency policing, however, is characterized by its emphasis on conventional public crime.

Ultimately, then, whilst 'blaming the community' might make some inroads into criminal victimization by conventional crime and fear of conventional crime, we have yet to establish an approach to crime prevention which recognizes the private nature of much criminal victimization. Is it possible to conceptualize crime prevention in these terms? At one level this is obviously the case since examples have been presented which attempt to embrace the private nature of crime; community safety initiatives and alternative interpretations of multi-agency policing. Additionally, concern with child abuse has fostered numerous recommendations for the promotion of inter-agency relationships and codes of practice; the Butler-Sloss recommendations being the latest in a long line of such initiatives. Whilst it is possible to argue that such recommendations do nothing to penetrate the causes of child abuse (see Chapter 3), where perhaps the real issue of crime prevention lies, they nevertheless constitute real attempts to police the private. Conventional images of crime in crime prevention in the community prevail. The question is, why?

Community rhetoric and social control

First, it is important to state that what follows is not intended to constitute an argument for some kind of 'Big Brother' policing of our private lives. The intention is to unwrap why crimes which occur in the community within people's homes, like rape and physical assault, do not, for the most part, figure in community crime prevention strategies. Secondly, it is important to make quite clear that some of the schemes outlined above do seem to work. They either reduce conventional crime or make the community 'feel better' about crime as a problem in its area. As Rock (1988b) states, in discussing the initiatives led by NACRO (safe neighbourhood units) and the Land Use and Resource Centre (led by Professor Alice Coleman), they both seem to work. What is much more uncertain is why. The same could be said for mediation and reparation projects, (Chapter 5). It is clear that for some victims there are some benefits from being involved in such initiatives. What kind of victim in what kind of circumstances is again less than clear.

Many projects, like examples given, rely ultimately on the participants' interpretation of and commitment to the project's goals. As such the participants become the controlling mechanisms whereby such projects succeed or fail. That some succeed may be because of the participants as much as the validity of the overall community approach. That such successes are used to justify further community developments is, of course, a political manoeuvre rather than one that is necessarily justified by the overall findings from community-based initiatives. There is a continued overwhelming commitment to neighbourhood watch schemes despite the fact that there is little reliable evidence for such whole-hearted support. The motivation and commitment of those involved in particular projects may, therefore, account for the particular successes of the community approach. Given, however, that there is little consistent and reliable evidence that such strategies work on a large canvas we must look elsewhere for an understanding of the persistence of the community imagery.

A second reason for the continuance of community initiatives is, arguably, economic in origin. The economic rationale has two strands. The first relates to an overall economic philosophy which includes 'rolling back the state' and permitting the greater influence of market forces. The second is more specifically fiscal. In the search for a reduction in public expenditure it is implied that community-based initiatives for dealing with offenders, for example, may constitute a relatively cheap alternative to imprisonment. This has been a view expressed across the range of services in which the image of the community has been invoked. The 1980s have seen the emergence of community-based mental health care, community medicine, mediation and reparation as different institutions attempt to respond to the goals of 'value for money' and efficiency'. What this movement frequently overlooks is that to establish effective community medicine, for example, requires locating a whole range of resources in the community. In other words it still costs money. Whether such moves are, on the whole, cheaper is open to debate. However, the rationale for such initiatives is not, of course, solely economic. The expression of such economic ideals is underpinned by a particular set of political ideals which place great emphasis on encouraging individuals and communities to take responsibility for a whole range of activities in order to reconstruct a society bonded together by shared norms in which a traditional view of the family figures prominently. (Likened by Lea, 1987, to Durkheim's conception of mechanical solidarity.)

The political, then, constitutes a third strand in our understanding of the persistence of community-based strategies of crime prevention. But not only the community base of these initiatives, also their emphasis on conventional crime. There are two related processes at work in the context of criminal victimization at this level; the first, political, the second, ideological. The political process has run through a number of the issues addressed in this text, from the way in which criminal victimization surveys have been used (Chapter 2), through the emergence of the Criminal Injuries Compensation Board (Chapter 5), to the financial backing given to the National Association of Victim Support Schemes (Chapter 6). It has been suggested that one of the reasons these particular initiatives have been successful in receiving such 'official' backing is the conventional image of the victim which pervades them. It is clear that there are similar political dimensions to the development of mediation and reparation projects as well as community-based crime prevention initiatives. Political in the sense that they have become further strategies whereby political parties, particularly those on the right, can be seen to be embracing the problem of criminal victimization and to be offering a response to that problem. Individuals or communities are responsible for their own crime prevention; they are 'free' to take that responsibility or ignore it. This of course meshes with the economic philosophy, particularly of those on the right.

This emphasis on crime prevention, however, overlooks a number of difficult implications in the right's own position on the freedom of the individual. Encouraging individuals to make themselves harder targets for criminal victimization might also curtail their individual freedom. (Is the answer to street crime, to avoid going out after dark?) It fails to recognize that some are 'freer' than others to buy sophisticated burglar alarm systems. It fails to recognize that some sections in society are freer than others from criminal victimization and the fear of criminal victimization. (See Chapter 2). It fails to recognize that some of the issues pertaining to criminal victimization and the prevention of that victimization are deeply implicated within a particular economic framework; victimization by corporations, for example. Failing to address questions such as these is not just a case of deliberate political machination. As the previous discussion has illustrated, some of the crime prevention strategies discussed here, for example, seem to have some good effects for some people. The same can be said for the examples cited above in which the political arena has been important in their adoption and subsequent development. Having said this, however, what has, for the most part, remained unquestioned is the structural base of the criminal victimization process. The advances which have been made for victims of crime in general and crime prevention in particular have proceeded with a structurally neutral image of the victim. Such an image serves not only political ends but also ideological.

The ideological mechanisms which run through how criminal victimization is viewed, within which crime prevention mechanisms are one strategy, ultimately serve to maintain a particular social order. This is achieved by a strategy of avoidance which links a range of processes together. This avoidance strategy works to encourage a conventional definition of crime and the crime problem, thus failing to embrace the structural bases to criminal victimization. In the context of crime prevention the individual and the community have been the mechanisms whereby such a conventional understanding of criminal victimization has been maintained. Cohen (1983, 1985) has described how community 'alternatives' can easily become part of widening the network of social control rather than real alternative strategies to the criminal justice process. It must be stressed that in the context of this discussion of crime prevention we have observed the existence of alternative ideas of crime prevention which do embrace an appreciation of the structural bases of criminal victimization. We have also seen that they are the exception rather than the rule. There is a clear tendency within the initiatives discussed not to embrace such questions. The issue of criminal victimization is not peculiar in this respect; there is a continued reluctance to recognize the racist, sexist and ageist biases in our social system as a whole. The processes of criminal victimization relate to that wider reluctance. However, part of the reluctance associated with criminal victimization is also a continued denial, by those on the right in particular, that features of the economic and social system do contribute to crime.

The denial that unemployment is related to crime, for example, pervades the crime prevention initiatives discussed here. It has been observed that the different chances of neighbourhood watch being accepted by different 'communities' are connected to whether those communities see crime as an internal threat or an external threat. It comes as no surprise that those communities for whom crime is an

173

internal threat are also those likely to be suffering disproportionately from other social problems, like unemployment, poorer housing, etc. Crime prevention strategies which fail to embrace these problems add to the belief that something is being done about crime but additionally that the crime problem is not related to such wider structural questions. And as the spectrum of our understanding of what constitutes criminal activities broadens to include racial harassment, domestic violence, sexual harassment, for example, the delimiting focus and narrow tendency of crime prevention strategies in general as well as crime prevention as interpreted by right-wing political strategies in particular becomes even more acute. The question remains, however, whether left-wing strategies would look any different.

In many respects the left faces the same dilemmas on the question of crime prevention as those faced by the right. The feminist movement, for example, has been very effective in uncovering and highlighting much 'invisible' criminal victimization with respect to domestic violence, child sexual abuse, etc. This progress, however, has not necessarily always been associated with a liberal stance towards offenders. There have been strong feminist opinions voiced on the need for more severe punishments for sex offenders, for example. There have been equally strong voices recommending that women carry appropriate instruments with which to defend themselves should they be attacked in the street. The question of crime prevention, then, from a feminist position is not necessarily clear-cut or diametrically opposed to that of the right. This tension between radical and conservative is perhaps most poignant in the case of child sexual abuse. Does a feminist recommend severe punishment of the father and his removal from the home and the further infliction of pain on the child, or does she seek an alternative strategy which does not compromise her position on the nature of patriarchy or inflict further pain on the child? Dominelli (1986), discussed in Chapter 6, gave some insight into how the latter position might be achieved.

In general, then, it can be argued that the left position on crime prevention is characterized, as in the example of child sexual abuse, not necessarily by the novelty of the strategies suggested but by how they are to be employed. This is clearly the case in Bright's (1987) discussion of the 'Safe Neighbourhood Unit'. A strategy in which the concept of community was plainly still important but how that community was to be approached, harnessed and encouraged in its organization towards crime prevention was clearly different from that of neighbourhood watch.

Lea states that: 'The maximization of the democratic participation is ultimately the solution both to the problem of what is crime and to the problem of how to deal with it' (Lea, 1987, p. 369). He further argues that an important element of a realist approach to crime prevention would be a real plurality of agencies to be involved, both formal and informal, centrally organized and locally organized. These would work on the basis of the contradiction of interests that would exist between them and which they would be forced to resolve and re-evaluate on a regular basis. In this way he suggests that the relationship between institutions and communities could be reworked. Matthews (1987), in a similar vein, whilst usefully critical of the concept of community, suggests that radical realism needs to examine the potential of a diverse range of community involvement in crime control from vigilantism to the less retaliative elements of such involvement. He states that

> 'Community' crime control strategies can clearly be double-edged. We cannot assume therefore that greater public participation will necessarily be progressive. Rather we need to explore the range of strategies as well as specific networks which may encourage new forms of social cohesion. (ibid., p. 397)

Young (1988b) also comments on the way in which the findings of the radical victimization surveys will have a real effect on the world of crime prevention. However, little of this indicates what a radical realist crime prevention strategy might look like in specific policy terms.

There is an obvious commitment on the left in general, and radical realism in particular, to increased democratization; to developing strategies which will improve both the representation and participation of all groups within the community. This view is most closely married with the Safe Neighbourhood Unit, but to what extent this meets the requirements of the radical realist is unclear. Whilst the aims of such a radical policy tendency might be laudable, there are inevitably practical difficulties in achieving the goal of increased democratization. Jefferson, McLaughlin and Robertson (1988) usefully highlight the difficulties and dilemmas of implementing policies which are sensitive to the questions of participation, representation and community. Such practical problems need to be more clearly addressed by the left. In theory, however, focusing on the questions of participation, representation and community in a truly democratic spirit should avoid the trap of extending the mechanisms of social control which appear to be so readily a concomitant of current community-based initiatives within crime prevention. This avoidance occurs because of the way in which the discourse which then follows between the various parties is limited not only by the attitudes, values and commitments of the individual participants but also because the framework in which that discourse subsequently takes place has been clearly delimited both politically and ideologically.

It is clear, then, that the left would equally invoke the image of the community, but would interpret and implement that imagery in a different spirit. The question of crime prevention in the widest sense, that is, that which would include the activities of corporations, however, has not been fully attended to by either the left or the right. Chapter 4 drew attention to the possibilities of enhancing the legal framework in controlling such activities. Whether such moves would also facilitate crime prevention is debatable. It is clearly a question which cannot be answered simply by calling for change in the capitalist system. If that were a simple process!

Conclusion

This chapter has been concerned to demonstrate that different crime prevention or crime reduction strategies involve making different assumptions about the nature of criminal victimization. Crime prevention strategies which blame the victim operate for the most part with a victim precipitation view of crime, emphasizing the role of the victim in reducing the opportunities for crime to occur. Such a view marries well with the conventional victimology outlined in Chapter 1. Offender blaming operates within a conventional criminological framework and, whilst perhaps giving expression for more retributive views of crime and crime prevention, will always be limited by its conventional framework.

Community blaming, which has formed the basis of most of the coherent approaches to crime prevention, has been successfully harnessed by the right as both a political and a policy approach to crime control. Such approaches have operated within a fairly narrow definition of crime. They have focused primarily on crime as it is conventionally understood: street crime and burglary. And they have focused on these crimes uncritical of the way in which the initiatives themselves assume a neutral view of the victim. Consequently the right has not only successfully harnessed the crime prevention arena, it has also been able to build upon people's everyday conceptions of crime. The left, on the other hand, would invoke the same imagery, the community, but would want to ensure that crime prevention was not achieved at the expense of appreciating the structural base of the criminal experience; that is, that victimization is not evenly and randomly distributed across the population; some groups suffer more than others from some crimes more than others.

It is not clear, however, how the democratic process can be harnessed in terms of specific policies to take account of this as well as achieve the necessary representation and participation from the appropriate sections of the community. This does not mean to say that it cannot be achieved. Some local authorities are continually striving to achieve these goals in the context of police monitoring groups. There is no reason, other than political will and individual motivation, that the same goals cannot be set for crime prevention.

Most of the discussion within this chapter has been concerned to outline the assumptions underpinning approaches to crime prevention, to suggest why they have been successfully harnessed by the right, and to suggest what the left's approach to crime prevention might look like. This has involved considering the way in which these initiatives focus on conventional crime and proceeded to broaden the basis of our understanding of crime in order to appreciate the limits of those initiatives. None of this has intended to imply that conventionally understood crime prevention initiatives do not work at all. They do in defined circumstances. Writ large they only partially address the issues involved. A key issue which is not addressed is how we place 'non-criminalised problematic situations' (Lea, 1987, p. 362), that is (in part) the activities of large corporations, in the frame. Again for the left we are brought back to resting our hopes on harnessing the democratic process. Lea states:

The development of the categories of criminal law in any free
society requires the maximum public participation in processes of
democratic discourse. The distinction between what is embod-
ied in the criminal law and what are regarded as problematic
situations will always retain an element of arbitrariness outside
such conditions. (ibid., p. 364)

The question remains as to whether it is pious to hope that ensuring
maximum public participation is enough to ensure that the activities
of business corporations, many of which have international connections, are seriously placed on the agenda. The democratic process
may have something to offer the disenfrachised but what does it
have to offer the already powerful?

The Home Secretary and the Chief Commissioner are going
to clean up 'the physical and moral degeneration' of London.
If they really want to do it, they will have to spread their net
wider than the Night-Clubs. Capitalism is the great Criminal.
It starves and degrades thousands by poverty, unemployment,
overcrowding, and disease. (*New Leader*, 8 February 1929: front
page)

The spirit of this quote draws attention to the need to consider not
only the material conditions of capitalism as people understand them
but also the ways in which they fail to understand those conditions.
Only by tackling the latter can the question of corporate victimization
also be tackled. The crime prevention debate has yet to address this
issue meaningfully.

Conclusion

The intention of this text was to introduce the reader to the concepts and data generated within victimology and victim-oriented research. In so doing there have been a number of recurrent themes. We have seen that the notion of the innocent victim and the concept of victim precipitation have been powerful images of victimization both within academic debate and policy formation. The influence of these ideas is still felt particularly in policy formation. We have also seen that these ideas have not gone unchallenged. The feminist movement has done much to encourage a rethinking of both notions in the context of rape and child sexual abuse. In addition, the development of the criminal victimization survey has provided an empirical base from which a further challenge to these ideas has been constructed.

The criminal victimization survey reveals that there is a pattern to victimization. A pattern in which place of residence, age, sex and race play a significant part. It has been the commitment to unfold the detail of this pattern, as well as a commitment to meet the challenge of the feminist movement, which has led to the construction of the radical 'new realism' and the local crime survey. The question remains, perhaps, to consider the extent to which this development contributes to our knowledge and appreciation of criminal victimization.

It has been seen that the 'new realism' has done much to challenge the thinking of radical criminology in particular. It has taken a number of contentious issues, in particular the issues of intra-class and intra-racial crime, and made a serious attempt to tackle these. In so doing it has revealed much empirical information concerning the local patterning of crime on class and racial dimensions. It has also attempted to measure and tackle the question of gender relations and criminal behaviour. Again, the efforts to take this issue seriously have resulted in the local survey approach revealing considerably more incidents of domestic violence and sexual assault than either of the British Crime Surveys. There are, however, three tensions (there may

179

of course be more) deriving from the new realist position, as it relates to the concerns of this text, which fail to convince the author that we should put all our eggs in the new realist basket.

The first is methodological. Whilst the local crime survey approach does seem to have been successful in revealing more incidents of crime as they relate to women, the question still remains as to the appropriateness of the survey method alone in tackling such issues. Used on its own the survey method as employed by the new realists clearly places women and crime on the agenda, but subsequently raises as many questions as it answers (see Chapter 2). How crime and the fear of crime structure women's lives in relation to men, as the new realists themselves recognize, is a fundamental feature of a patriarchal society. To explore this, and to begin to understand the mechanisms of it, demands an in-depth exploration of women's (and perhaps men's) everyday lives. The criminal victimization survey cannot achieve this. Its individual and democratic bias, to paraphrase Galtung (1967), prevents its use in this way. Thus the commitment to feminist issues is subsequently tempered by methodological commitments.

The second tension is theoretical. This tension emerges in two ways: first, from the new realists' conception of material conditions and, secondly, from their conception of consciousness. Or, put another way, from the new realist understanding of objective conditions, subjective evaluation and the relationship between the two. Young states that 'victimization research commonly *trivializes that which is important and makes important that which is trivial*' (Young, 1988, p. 173; italics in original). Here he is drawing our attention to the necessity of embracing what human beings consider to be important as our yardstick for appreciating the impact of crime. At the same time we must recognize that victims are not equal in their experience of crime; some groups experience more criminal victimization than others. So we have to take seriously what people define as real as well as taking seriously the material conditions which frame that reality; the variables of race, class, age, sex. The problem remains: what do we do with those features of criminal victimization which people do not define as real (and yet which still have an impact) and what do we do about the material conditions which frame that process for us? In other words, how are the processes which go on behind our backs to be inserted into the equation? This text has argued that such processes have a real impact, though for the most part we fail to recognize them; in particular, the activities of business corporations. This is not intended to suggest that one level of analysis should be abandoned in favour of another. It is intended to suggest that the narrowly defined subjective material conditions of the new realist should not be explored at the expense of developing some understanding of the relationship between this and those processes which we fail subjectively to see. This theoretical tension connects with the third tension to be mentioned here: the policy implications of this position.

The policy implications which have been derived from the new realist position have been critically assessed by Sim, Scraton and Gordon (1987). They state:

> What has been absent from the new realist analysis and its political pronouncements have been analyses of the processes by which specific groups become economically marginalized and politically targeted on the basis of ideological justifications which equate their struggles with the breakdown in moral values and social discipline. While critical criminology has sought to locate the processes of criminalization within a critique of the advanced capitalist state and its institutions of regulation and control the new realists appear to have faith in the potential of political reform under a Labour government. (ibid., p. 59)

This text has been concerned to indicate the ideological processes which permeate what is seen as victimization and what is not, as well as drawing out the way in which the policy initiatives concerned with victims of crime, from compensation to crime prevention, serve to sustain particular images of victimization and its causation, and in so doing serve a wider process of social order. The focus throughout has been not to deny the real value that this range of policy initiatives might have for some victims of crime, but to call for an understanding of such initiatives as a part of the wider context of social control. Thus rather like Sim, Scraton and Gordon the author finds the new realist faith in the potential of the political process, without a commitment to viewing the whole question of social regulation and control as problematic, somewhat difficult to embrace. Policy initiatives need to be critically assessed in terms of what they imply practically, symbolically and ideologically for victims of crime as well as for offenders. We know a little about the practical implications, we have observed the symbolic value of the crime victim, we have yet to fully theorize the ideological processes involved. Without this level of analysis the political process can make only limited gains, and perhaps some losses, for victims of crime.

Thus the new realist position, like others we have dealt with in this text, is not without its shortcomings. What this text has, it is hoped, achieved in introducing the reader to victimology and challenging the reader's common-sense knowledge of victims of crime, is a development of a critical appreciation of the theoretical, political and policy issues which pertain to victims of crime. It is not expected that the reader will necessarily agree with the analyses and criticisms offered in this text of these issues. Enough will have been achieved if the reader now has more questions to ask about victims of crime than at the beginning of this book.

References

Adler, Z. (1988), 'Prosecuting child sexual abuse: a challenge to the status quo', in M. Maguire and J. Pointing (eds), *Victims of Crime: A New Deal* (Milton Keynes: Open University Press), pp. 138–46.

Amir, M. (1971), *Patterns of Forcible Rape* (Chicago: University of Chicago Press).

Anna T. (1988), 'Feminist responses to sexual abuse: the work of the Birmingham Rape Crisis Centre', in M. Maguire and J. Pointing (eds), *Victims of Crime: A New Deal* (Milton Keynes: Open University Press), pp. 60–5.

Antilla, I. (1974), 'Victimology – a new territory in criminology', in N. Christie (ed.), *Scandinavian Studies in Criminology*, Volume 5 (London: Martin Robertson), pp. 3–7.

Bennett, T. (1987), *An Evaluation of Two Neighbourhood Watch Schemes in London, Executive Summary*, final report to the Home Office Research and Planning Unit (Cambridge: Institute of Criminology).

Bennett, T. and Wright, R. (1984), *Burglars on Burglary* (Aldershot: Gower).

Bennion, C., Davie, A., Hesse, B., Joshua, L., McGloin, P., Munn, G. and Tester, S. (1985), *Neighbourhood Watch: The Eyes and Ears of Urban Policing?*, Occasional Papers in Sociology and Social Policy, no. 6 (Guildford: University of Surrey).

Bequai, A. (1978), *White Collar Crime: A 20th Century Crisis* (Lexington Mass.: Lexington Books).

Binney, V., Harkell, G. and Nixon, J. (1985), 'Refuges and housing for battered women', in J. Pahl (ed.), *Private Violence and Public Policy* (London: Routledge & Kegan Paul), pp. 166–78.

Blagg, H. (1985), 'Reparation and justice for juveniles', *British Journal of Criminology*, vol. 25: pp. 267–79.

Blagg, H., Pearson, G., Sampson, A., Smith, D. and Stubbs, P. (1988), 'Inter-agency co-ordination: rhetoric and reality', in T. Hope and M. Shaw (eds), *Communities and Crime Reduction* (London: HMSO), pp. 204–20.

Block, C. B. and Block, R. L. (1984), 'Crime definition, crime measurement, and victim surveys', *Journal of Social Issues*, 40: pp. 137–60.

Bottomley, K. and Pease, K. (1986), *Crime and Punishment: Interpreting the Data* (Milton Keynes: Open University Press).

Bottoms, A. E. (1983), 'Neglected features of the contemporary penal system', in D. Garland and P. Young (eds), *The Power to Punish* (London: Heinemann), pp. 166–202.

Bourne, R. (1979), 'Child abuse and neglect; an overview', in R. Bourne and E. H. Neuberger (eds), *Critical Perspectives on Child Abuse* (Lexington, Mass.: Lexington Books), pp. 1–14.

Box, S. (1983), *Power, Crime and Mystification* (London: Tavistock).

Box, S. (1987), *Recession, Crime and Punishment* (London: Macmillan).

Braithwaite, J. (1984), *Corporate Crime in the Pharmaceutical Industry* (London: Routledge & Kegan Paul).

Braithwaite, J. (1985), 'Corporate crime research; why two interviewers are needed', *Sociology*, vol. 19, no. 1: pp. 136–8.

Bright, J. (1987), 'Community safety, crime prevention and local authority', in P. Willmott (ed.), *Policing and the Community*, Policy Studies Institute Discussion Paper 16 (London: PSI), pp. 45–53.

Brogden, M., Jefferson, T. and Walklate, S. (1988), *Introducing Policework* (London: Unwin Hyman).

Butler-Sloss, E. (1988), *Report of the Inquiry into Child Abuse in Cleveland 1987 Short Version* (London: HMSO).

Campbell, B. (1987), 'The skeleton in the family's cupboard', *New Statesman*, 31 July, pp. 10–12.

Carson, W. G. (1970), 'White collar crime and the enforcement of the factory legislation', in W. G. Carson and P. Wiles (eds), *Crime and Delinquency in Britain* (Oxford: Martin Robertson), pp. 192–205.

Carson, W. G. (1982), *The Other Price of Britain's Oil* (Oxford: Martin Robertson).

Chambers, G. and Millar, A. (1983), *Investigating Sexual Assault* (Edinburgh: Scottish Office).

Christie, N. (1977), 'Conflicts as property', *British Journal of Criminology*, vol. 17: pp. 1–15.

Clarke, R., Ekblom, P., Hough, M. and Mayhew, P. (1985), 'Elderly victims of crime and exposure to risk', *Howard Journal of Criminal Justice*, vol. 24, no. 1: pp. 1–9.

Clayton P. and Walklate, S. (1979), 'What did you do in the strike, volunteer?', *Community Care*, 7 June: pp. 11–12.

Cohen, L. E. and Felson, M. (1979), 'Social change and crime rate trends: a routine activity approach', *American Sociological Review*, vol. 44, no. 4: pp. 588–608.

Cohen, S. (1983), 'Social control talk: telling stories about correctional change', in D. Garland and P. Young (eds), *The Power to Punish* (London: Heinemann), pp. 101–29.

References

Cohen, S. (1985), *Visions of Social Control* (Cambridge: Polity Press).

Cohen, D. and Shapland, J. (1987), 'Facilities for victims; the role of the police and the courts', *Criminal Law Review*, January: pp. 28–38.

Coleman, A. (1985), *Utopia on Trial* (London: Hilary Shipman).

Conklin, J. E. (1975), *The Impact of Crime* (New York: Macmillan).

Corbett, S. and Maguire, M. (1988), 'The value and limitations of victim support schemes', in M. Maguire and J. Pointing (eds), *Victims of Crime: A New Deal* (Milton Keynes: Open University Press), pp. 26–39.

Creighton, S. (1980), *Child Victims of Physical Abuse, 1976* (London: NSPCC).

Creighton, S. (1984), *Trends in Child Abuse 1977–1982* (London: NSPCC).

Davis, J. (1984), 'Criminal prosecutions and their context in late Victorian England', paper given at the Crime, Law and Society Conference, University of Warwick, April.

Dominelli, L. (1986), 'Father–daughter incest: patriarchy's shameful secret', *Critical Social Policy*, issue 16: pp. 8–22.

Donnison, H., Scola, J. and Thomas, P. (1986), *Neighbourhood Watch: Policing the People* (London: Libertarian Research and Education Trust).

Drapkin, I. and Viano, E. (1974), *Victimology: A New Focus*, Volume IV, *Victims of Violence* (Lexington, Mass.: D. C. Heath & Co.).

Duff, P. (1987), 'Criminal injuries compensation and "violent" crime', *Criminal Law Review*, April: pp. 219–30.

Edwards, S. (1986), *The Police Response to Domestic Violence in London* (London: Polytechnic of Central London).

Edwards, S. (1987), 'Provoking her own demise; from common assault to homicide', in J. Hamner and M. Maynard (eds), *Women, Violence and Social Control* (London: Macmillan), pp. 152–68.

Elias, R. (1986), *The Politics of Victimization* (Oxford: Oxford University Press).

Elias, R. (1986), 'Community control, criminal justice and victim services', in E. A. Fattah (ed.), *From Crime Policy to Victim Policy* (London: Macmillan), pp. 290–316.

Emsley, C. (1983), *Policing and its Context 1750–1870* (London: Macmillan).

Ennew, J. (1986), *The Sexual Exploitation of Children* (Cambridge: Polity Press).

Faragher, T. (1981), 'The police response to violence against women in the home', in J. Pahl (ed.), *Private Violence and Public Policy* (London: Routledge & Kegan Paul), pp. 110–24.

185

Fattah, E. A. (1979), 'Some recent theoretical developments in victimology', *Victimology*, vol. 4, no. 2: pp. 198–213.

Fattah, E. A. (1986), 'Prologue: on some visible and hidden dangers of victims' movements', in E. A. Fattah (ed.), *From Crime Policy to Victim Policy* (London: Macmillan), pp. 1–16.

Finkelhor, D. (1979), *Sexually Victimized Children* (New York: Free Press).

Finkelhor, D. (1986), *A Sourcebook on Child Sexual Abuse* (New York: Sage).

Forrester, D., Chatterton, M. and Pease, K. (1988) *The Kirkholt Burglary Prevention Project, Rochdale*, Crime Prevention Unit Paper 13 (London: HMSO).

Foucault, M. (1977), *Discipline and Punish: The Birth of the Prison* (London: Allen Lane).

Friedman, K., Bischoff, H., Davis, R. and Person, A. (1982), *Victims and Helpers: Reactions to Crime* (New York: Victim Services Agency).

Galtung, J. (1967), *Theory and Method of Social Research* (London: Allen & Unwin).

Garofalo, J. (1986), 'Lifestyle and victimization: an update', in E. A. Fattah (ed.), *From Crime Policy to Victim Policy* (London: Macmillan), pp. 135–55.

Geis, C. (1973), 'Victimization patterns in white collar crime', in I. Drapkin and E. Viano (eds), *Victimology: A New Focus*, Volume V, *Exploiters and Exploited* (Lexington, Mass.: D. C. Heath & Co.), pp. 86–106.

Genn, H. (1988), 'Multiple victimization', in M. Maguire and J. Pointing (eds), *Victims of Crime: A New Deal* (Milton Keynes: Open University Press), pp. 90–100.

Gil, D. G. (1970), 'Violence against children', in C. M. Lee (ed.) (1978), *Child Abuse: A Reader and Sourcebook* (Milton Keynes: Open University Press), pp. 48–53.

Gil, D. G. (1979), 'Unravelling child abuse', in R. Bourne and E. H. Neuberger (eds), *Critical Perspectives in Child Abuse* (Lexington, Mass.: Lexington Books), pp. 69–80.

Gill, M. (1986), 'Wife battering; a case study of a women's refuge', paper presented to Crime Victims Conference, Plymouth.

Goffman, E. (1975), *Frame Analysis* (Harmondsworth: Penguin).

Gottfredson, M. R. (1981), 'On the etiology of criminal victimization', *Journal of Criminal Law and Criminology*, vol. 72, no. 2: pp. 714–26.

Hall, R. (1985), *Ask Any Woman* (London: Falling Wall Press).

Hall, S., Cricher, C., Jefferson, T., Clarke, J. and Roberts, B. (1978), *Policing the Crisis* (London: Macmillan).

References

Harding, J. (1982), *Victims and Offenders*, NCVO Occasional Paper Two (London: Bedford Square Press).

Hay, D. and Snyder, F. (forthcoming), *Using the Criminal Law 1750–1850*.

Hindelang, M. J., Gottfredson, M. R. and Garofalo, J. (1978), *Victims of Personal Crime; An Empirical Foundation for a Theory of Personal Victimization* (Cambridge, Mass.: Ballinger).

Hope, T. (1988), 'Support for neighbourhood watch: a British Crime Survey analysis', in T. Hope and M. Shaw (eds), *Communities and Crime Prevention* (London: HMSO), pp. 146–63.

Hope, T. and Hough, M. (1988), 'Area, crime and incivility: a profile from the British Crime Survey', in T. Hope and M. Shaw (eds), *Communities and Crime Reduction* (London: HMSO), pp. 30–47.

Hope, T. and Shaw, M. (1988), 'Community approaches to reducing crime', in T. Hope and M. Shaw (eds) *Communities and Crime Reduction* (London: HMSO), pp. 1–29.

Hough, M. (1986), 'Victims of violent crime: findings from the British Crime Survey', in E. A. Fattah (ed.), *From Crime Policy to Victim Policy* (London: Macmillan), pp. 117–36.

Hough, M. and Mayhew, P. (1983), The British Crime Survey: First Report, Home Office Research Study no. 76 (London: HMSO).

Hough, M. and Mayhew, P. (1985), *Taking Account of Crime: Key Findings from the Second British Crime Survey*, Home Office Research Study no. 85 (London: HMSO).

Hough, M. and Mo, J. (1986), 'If at first you don't succeed', *Home Office Research Bulletin 21*, pp. 10–13.

Hough, M. and Moxon, D. (1985), 'Dealing with offenders: popular opinion and the view of victims', *Howard Journal of Criminal Justice*, vol. 24: pp. 160–75.

Janoff-Bulman, R. and Hanson-Frieze, I. (1983), 'A theoretical perspective for understanding reactions to victimization', *Journal of Social Issues*, vol. 39, no. 2: pp. 1–17.

Jefferson, T. and Grimshaw, R. (1987), *Interpreting Policework* (London: Unwin Hyman).

Jefferson, T. McLauglin, E. and Robertson, L. (1988), 'Monitoring the monitors: accountability, democracy and policewatching in Britain', *Contemporary Crises 12*: pp. 91–106.

Jeffreys, S. and Radford, J. (1984), 'Contributory negligence or being a woman? The car rapist case', in P. Scraton and P. Gordon (eds), *Causes for Concern* (Harmondsworth: Penguin), pp. 154–83.

Johnson, N. (1985), 'Police, social work, and medical responses to battered women', in N. Johnson (ed.), *Marital Violence*, Sociological Review Monograph 81, pp. 109–23.

Jones, T. (1988), *Corporate Killing: Bhopals Will Happen* (London: Free Association Books).

Jones, T. MaClean, B. and Young, J. (1986), *The Islington Crime Survey* (Aldershot: Gower).

Jones, D. N. Pickett, J., Oates, M. P., and Barbor, P. (1987), *Understanding Child Abuse* (London: Macmillan).

Kelly, L. (1987), 'The continuum of sexual violence', in J. Hamner and M. Maynard (eds), *Women, Violence, and Social Control* (London: Macmillan), pp. 46–60.

Kelly, L. (1988), 'What's in a name? Defining child sexual abuse', *Feminist Review*, no. 28, Spring: pp. 65–73.

Kelly, L. and Radford, J. (1987), 'The problem of men: feminist perspectives on sexual violence', in P. Scraton (ed.), *Law, Order, and the Authoritarian State* (Milton Keynes: Open University Press), pp. 237–53.

Kempe, R. S. and Kempe, C. H. (1978), *Child Abuse* (London: Fontana).

Kinsey, R. (1984), *Merseyside Crime Survey: First Report* (Liverpool: Merseyside County Council).

Kinsey, R. (1985), *Merseyside Crime and Police Surveys: Final Report* (Liverpool: Merseyside County Council).

Kinsey, R., Lea, J. and Young, J. (1986), *Losing the Fight Against Crime* (Oxford: Blackwell).

Kitzinger, J. (1988), 'Defending innocence: ideologies of childhood', *Feminist Review*, no. 28, Spring: pp. 77–86.

Launay, G. (1985), 'Bringing victims and offenders together: a comparison of two models', *Howard Journal of Criminal Justice*, vol. 24, no. 3: pp. 200–12.

Laurance, J. (1988), 'The drama of Cleveland', *New Statesman New Society*, 1 July: pp. 12–15.

Lea, J. (1987), 'Left realism: a defence', *Contemporary Crises* 11, pp. 357–70.

Lea, J., Matthews, R. and Young, J. (1987), *Law and Order Five Years On* (Middlesex Polytechnic: Centre for Criminology).

Lee, J. A. (1981), 'Some structural aspects of police deviance in relation with minority groups', in C. Shearing (ed.), *Organizational Police Deviance* (Toronto: Butterworth), pp. 49–82.

Levi, M. (1981), *The Phantom Capitalists: The Organization and Control of Long-Firm Fraud* (London: Heinemann).

Levi, M. (1987), 'Crisis? What crisis? Reactions to commercial fraud in the United Kingdom', *Contemporary Crises* 11, pp. 207–21.

Levi, M. and Pithouse, A. (1988), *The Victims of Fraud*, Report of the Economic and Social Research Council Project.

London Rape Crisis Centre (1984), *Sexual Violence: The Reality for Women* (London: Women's Press).

References

McBarnett, D. (1988), 'Victim in the witness box – confronting victimology's stereotype', *Contemporary Crises*, 7: pp. 279–303.

McNeil, S. (1987), 'Flashing; its effects on women', in J. Hamner and M. Maynard (eds), *Women, Violence and Social Control* (London: Macmillan), pp. 93–109.

Macrae, C. (1988), 'Child abuse victims miss payout', *Observer*, 31 July: p. 5.

Maguire, M. (1980), 'The impact of burglary upon victims', *British Journal of Criminology*, vol. 20, no. 3: pp. 261–75.

Maguire, M., in collaboration with Bennett, T. (1982), *Burglary in a Dwelling: The Offence, the Offender, and the Victim* (London: Heinemann).

Maguire, M. (1985), 'Victims needs and victims services', *Victimology*, vol. 10: pp. 539–59.

Maguire, M., and Corbett, C. (1987), *The Effects of Crime and the Work of Victim Support Schemes* (Aldershot: Gower).

Maguire, M. and Pointing, J. (1988), *Victims of Crime: A New Deal?* (Milton Keynes: Open University Press).

Mahoney, P. (1985), *Schools for the Boys? Co-education Reassessed* (London: Hutchinson).

Marshall, T. (1984), *Reparation, Conciliation and Mediation: Current Projects in England and Wales*, Home Office Research and Planning Unit Paper 27 (London: HMSO).

Marshall, T. and Walpole, M. (1985), *Bringing People Together: Mediation and Reparation Projects in Great Britain*, Home Office Research and Planning Unit Paper 33 (London: HMSO).

Matthews, R. (1987), 'Taking realist criminology seriously', *Contemporary Crises* 11, pp. 371–402.

Mawby, R. I. (1988a), 'Age, vulnerability, and the impact of crime', in M. Maguire and J. Pointing (eds), *Victims of Crime: A New Deal* (Milton Keynes: Open University Press), pp. 101–14.

Mawby, R. I. (1988b), 'Victims' needs or victims' rights: alternative approaches to policy making', in M. Maguire and J. Pointing (eds), *Victims of Crime: A New Deal* (Milton Keynes: Open University Press), pp. 127–37.

Mawby, R. I. and Firkins, V. (1986), 'The victim/offender relationship and its implications for policies: evidence from the British Crime Survey', paper to the World Congress of Victimology, Orlando, Florida.

Mawby, R. I. and Gill, M. (1987), *Crime Victims: Needs, Services and the Voluntary Sector* (London: Tavistock).

Maxfield, M. G. (1984), *Fear of Crime in England and Wales*, Home Office Research Study no. 78 (London: HMSO).

Mayhew, P. (1984), 'The effects of crime; victims, the public and fear', Council for Europe Sixteenth Criminological Research Conference: Research on Victims, Strasbourg, November.

189

Mayhew, P. and Hough, M. (1988), 'The British Crime Survey: origins and impact', in M. Maguire and J. Pointing (eds), *Victims of Crime: A New Deal* (Milton Keynes: Open University Press), pp. 156–63.

Miers, D. (1978), *Responses to Victimization* (Abingdon: Professional Books).

Miers, D. (1987), 'Compensation and support for victims of crime', *British Journal of Criminology*, vol. 27, no. 2: pp. 382–9.

Morgan, J. (1988), 'Children as victims', in M. Maguire and J. Pointing (eds), *Victims of Crime: A New Deal* (Milton Keynes: Open University Press), pp. 74–82.

Morris, A. (1987), *Women, Crime, and Criminal Justice* (Oxford: Blackwell).

Nash, C. L. and West, D. J. (1985), 'Sexual molestation of young girls', in D. J. West (ed.), *Sexual Victimization* (Aldershot: Gower).

NAVSS (1988), *Victims in the Court: Report of a Working Party* (London: NAVSS).

Newman, O. (1972), *Defensible Space: Crime Prevention Through Urban Design* (New York: Macmillan).

Newsom, J. and Newsom, E. (1965), *Patterns of Infant Care in an Urban Community* (Harmonsworth: Penguin).

Newsom, J. and Newsom, E. (1978), *Seven Years Old in the Home Environment* (Harmonsworth: Penguin).

Nkpa, N. K. U. (1976), 'The practice of restitution to victims of crime in a traditional society', paper presented at the Second International Symposium on Victimology, Boston, Mass.

Normandeau, A. (1968), 'Patterns in robbery', *Criminologica*, 6.

Pahl, J. (1985), *Private Violence and Public Policy* (London: Routledge & Kegan Paul).

Parliamentary All-Party Penal Affairs Group (1984), *A New Deal for Victims* (c/o 169 Clapham Road, London SW9 0PU).

Parton, N. (1985), *The Politics of Child Abuse* (London: Macmillan).

Parton, N. (1986), 'The Beckford Report: a critical appraisal', *British Journal of Social Work*, 16: pp. 511–30.

Pearce, F. (1987), 'Corporate crime; review article', *Critical Social Policy*, 19, Summer: pp. 116–25.

Pease, K. (1986), 'Obscene telephone calls in England and Wales', *Howard Journal of Criminal Justice*, vol. 24: pp. 275–81.

Peckham, C. (1978), 'Problems in methodology', in C. M. Lee (ed.), *Child Abuse: A Reader and Sourcebook* (Milton Keynes: Open University Press), pp. 45–7.

Phillips, D. (1977), *Crime and Authority in Victorian England* (London: Croom Helm).

References

Phillips, D. (1984), 'Good men to associate and bad men to conspire; associations for the prosecution of felons, England 1770–1860', Crime, Law and Society Conference, University of Warwick, April.

Phipps, A. (1988), 'Ideologies, political parties, and victims of crime', in M. Maguire and J. Pointing (eds), Victims of Crime: A New Deal (Milton Keynes: Open University Press), pp. 177–86.

Rantzen, E. (1987), 'Adult response to childhood suffering', The Listener, 16 July: pp. 8–9.

Reeves, H. (1985), 'Victim support schemes: the U.K. model', Victimology, vol. 10: pp. 679–86.

Reeves, H. (1988), 'Afterword', in M. Maguire and J. Pointing (eds), Victims of Crime: A New Deal (Milton Keynes: Open University Press), pp. 204–6.

Reiman, J. H. (1979), The Rich Get Rich and the Poor Get Prison (New York: John Wiley).

Reiner, R. (1985). The Politics of the Police (Brighton: Wheatsheaf).

Reiss, A. (1986), 'Official statistics and survey statistics', in E. A. Fattah (ed.), From Crime Policy to Victim Policy (London: Macmillan), pp. 53–79.

Rock, P. (1986), A View from the Shadows (Oxford: Oxford University Press).

Rock, P. (1988a), 'Governments, victims, and policies in two countries', British Journal of Criminology, vol. 28, no. 1: pp. 44–66.

Rock, P. (1988b), 'Crime reduction initiatives on problem estates', in T. Hope and M. Shaw (eds), Communities and Crime Reduction (London: HMSO), pp. 99–115.

Rosenbaum, D. P. (1988), 'A critical eye on neighbourhood watch: does it reduce crime and fear', in T. Hope and M. Shaw (eds), Communities and Crime Reduction (London: HMSO), pp. 126–45.

Rude, G. (1985), Criminal and Victim (Oxford: Clarendon).

Russell, D. (1984), Sexual Exploitation (Beverly Hills, Calif.: Sage).

Schafer, S. (1960), Restitution to Victims of Crime (London: Stevens & Sons).

Schafer, S. (1968), The Victim and his Criminal (New York: Random House).

Schafer, S. (1976), Introduction to Criminology (Reston, Virginia: Boston Publishing Co.).

Schubert, A. (1981), 'Private initiative in law enforcement: associations for the prosecution of felons', in V. Bailey (ed.), Policing and Punishment in Nineteenth-Century Britain (London: Croom Helm), pp. 25–41.

Scraton, P. and Chadwick, K. (1987), 'Speaking ill of the dead: institutionalized responses to deaths in custody', in P. Scraton (ed.), Law, Order, and the Authoritarian State (Milton Keynes: Open University Press), pp. 212–36.

Scull, A. (1977), Decarceration: Community Treatment and the Deviant – A Radical View (Englewood Cliffs, NJ: PrenticeHall).

Scull, A. (1983), 'Community corrections: panacea, progress or pretence?', in D. Garland and P. Young (eds), *The Power to Punish* (London: Heinemann), pp. 146–65.

Seaton, J. (1987), 'Odious to the conscience of the country', *New Statesman*, 1 May: pp. 16–17.

Shapland, J. (1984), 'The victim, the criminal justice system and compensation', *British Journal of Criminology*, vol. 24: pp. 131–49.

Shapland, J. (1986), 'Victim assistance and the criminal justice system', in E. A. Fattah (ed.), *From Crime Policy to Victim Policy* (London: Macmillan), pp. 118–236.

Shapland, J. (1988a), 'Fiefs and peasants: accomplishing change for victims in the criminal justice system', in M. Maguire and J. Pointing (eds), *Victims of Crime: A New Deal* (Milton Keynes: Open University Press), pp. 187–94.

Shapland, J. (1988b), 'Policing with the public', in T. Hope and M. Shaw (eds), *Communities and Crime Reduction* (London: HMSO), pp. 116–25.

Shapland, J., Willmore, J. and Duff, P. (1985), *Victims in the Criminal Justice System* (Aldershot: Gower).

Sim, J., Scraton, P. and Gordon, P. (1987), 'Introduction: crime, the state, and critical analysis', in P. Scraton (ed.), *Law, Order, and the Authoritarian State* (Milton Keynes: Open University Press), pp. 1–70.

Skogan, W. G. (1986a), 'Methodological issues in the study of victimization', in E. A. Fattah (ed.), *From Crime Policy to Victim Policy* (London: Macmillan), pp. 80–116.

Skogan, W. G. (1986b), 'The fear of crime and its behavioural implications', in E. A. Fattah (ed.), *From Crime Policy to Victim Policy* (London: Macmillan), pp. 167–90.

Smith, D. C. (1982), 'White collar crime, organised crime, and the business establishment: resolving a crisis in criminological theory', in P. Wickham and T. Dailey (eds), *White Collar Crime and Economic Crime* (Lexington Mass.: Lexington Books), pp. 23–38.

Smith, S. (1982), 'Victimization in the inner city', *British Journal of Criminology*, vol. 22: pp. 386–407.

Softley, P. (1978), *Compensation Orders in Magistrates Courts*, Home Office Research Study 43 (London: HMSO).

Sparks, R. F. (1981), 'Surveys of victimization: an optimistic assessment', in M. Tonry and N. Morris (eds), *Crime and Justice: An Annual Review of Research*, Vol. 3 (Chicago: University of Chicago Press), pp. 1–58.

Sparks, R. F. (1982), *Research on Victims of Crime: Accomplishments, Issues, and New Directions* (Rockville, Md: US Dept of Health and Human Services).

Sparks, R. F., Genn, H. and Dodd, D. (1977), *Surveying Victims* (London: John Wiley).

References

Stanko, E. A. (1987), 'Typical violence, normal precautions: men, women, and interpersonal violence in England, Wales, Scotland, and the U.S.A.', in J. Hamner and M. Maynard (eds), *Women, Violence and Social Control* (London: Macmillan), pp. 122–34.

Stanko, E. A. (1988), 'Hidden violence against women', in M. Maguire and J. Pointing (eds), *Victims of Crime: A New Deal* (Milton Keynes; Open University Press, pp. 40–6.

Steele, B. F. and Pollock, C. B. (1968), 'General characteristics of abusing parents', in C. M. Lee (ed.), *Child Abuse: A Reader and Sourcebook* (Milton Keynes: Open University Press), pp. 116–25.

Sutherland, E. (1949), *White Collar Crime* (New York: Holt, Rhinehart & Winston).

Tarling, R. and Softley, P. (1976), 'Compensation orders in the crown court', *Criminal Law Review*: pp. 422–8.

Taylor, S. (1988), 'Researching child abuse', interview by P. McNeil in *New Society*, 15 January: p. 35.

Van Dijk, J. (1988), 'Ideological trends within the victims' movement: an international perspective', in M. Maguire and J. Pointing (eds), *Victims of Crime: A New Deal* (Milton Keynes: Open University Press), pp. 115–26.

Vanick, C. (1977), 'Corporate tax study 1976', in D. M. Erman and R. J. Lindman (eds), *Corporate Crime and Governmental Deviance* (Oxford: Oxford University Press).

Von Hentig, H. (1948), *The Criminal and his Victim* (New Haven, Conn.: Yale University Press).

Walklate, S. (1984), *S.L.V.S.S.: A Consumer Evaluation*, report of the Crime, Justice and Welfare Unit, Liverpool Polytechnic.

Walklate, S. (1986), 'Reparation; a Merseyside view', *British Journal of Criminology*, vol. 26: pp. 287–98.

Waller, I. (1988), 'International standards, national trail-blazing, and the next steps', in M. Maguire and J. Pointing (eds), *Victims of Crime: A New Deal* (Milton Keynes: Open University Press), pp. 195–203.

Weisstraub, D. (1986), 'On the rights of victims', in E. A. Fattah (ed.), *From Crime Policy to Victim Policy* (London: Macmillan), pp. 317–22.

West, D. J. (1987), *Sexual Crimes and Confrontations* (Aldershot: Gower).

Willmott, P. (1987), 'Introduction', in P. Willmott (ed.), *Policing and the Community* (London: PSI), pp. 1–7.

Wilson, E. (1983), *What is to be done about violence against women?* (Harmondsworth: Penguin).

Wolfgang, M. E. (1958), *Patterns in Criminal Homicide* (Philadelphia, Pa: University of Pennsylvania Press).

Worrall, A. and Pease, K. (1986), 'Personal crime against women', *Howard Journal of Criminal Justice*, vol. 25, no. 2: pp. 118–24.

Wright, M. (1982), *Making Good: Prisons, Punishment and Beyond* (London: Burnett).

Wright, M. (1985), 'The impact of victim/offender mediation on the victim', *Victimology*, vol. 10: pp. 631–45.

Young, J. (1986), 'The failure of criminology: the need for a radical realism', in R. Matthews and J. Young (eds), *Confronting Crime* (London: Sage), pp. 4–30.

Young, J. (1988a), 'Risk of crime and fear of crime: a realist critique of survey-based assumptions', in M. Maguire and J. Pointing (eds), *Victims of Crime: A New Deal* (Milton Keynes: Open University Press), pp. 164–76.

Young, J. (1988b), 'Radical criminology in Britain: the emergence of a competing paradigm', *British Journal of Criminology*, vol. 28: pp. 159–83.

Index

abuse
  distinguished from neglect   53–4
  a social problem   56, 58
accidents at work   90–1
adaptation   12
ageism, and child abuse   73
ageist assumptions   78, 79
air traffic controllers   103
Alexander Kielland disaster   95–8
anal abuse   67
anger   44
assault   26, 36, 110
  fear of   159
Associations for the Prosecution of Felons   110–11
attractiveness   14–15, 17
avoidance strategy   173

battered baby syndrome   58
battered child syndrome   53
battered women's refuges   138, 139–40, 151
behaviour, crime-related   40
Boesky affair   93, 94
bounding periods   29–30
British Crime Surveys   27–8, 30–1, 35, 119, 121, 164–5, 179
  and specific survey findings   42–3
buggery   65, 67
built environment, and private and public space   160
burglary   14, 34, 36–7, 38, 39, 45, 122, 159, 177
business corporations, power of   81–4

Canada
  needs assessment   149
  victims of crime initiative   137
capital accumulation   102, 103
capitalism   104, 178
car theft   26, 36, 122
child abuse   12, 24, 57–8, 61–2, 170

  toward an explanation   72–4
child abuse figures   54–5
child abuse registers   54
child physical abuse   53–8, 64, 67, 80
  disease model   71–2
child as seducer   69
child sexual abuse   21, 58–63, 64–5, 68, 78, 80, 141–2, 179
  clarification of   59–61
  explanations   69–70
  feminist dilemma   174
  incidence and prevalence   60–2, 67
child victims in the criminal justice process   74–6
childhood, current notions of   68–9
childhood innocence   68–72, 78
Childline   142
children   20, 44
  in care   54
  position in society   73
  structural powerlessness of   73
  as victims   153
  as witnesses   75
Children and Young Persons Act (1969)   57–8
Cleveland affair   65–8, 72–3
collusion   104
  of mother   70
commercial fraud   86, 94, 106
community, definitions   163, 166
community blaming   157, 158, 163–70, 176–7
community cohesion   164
community crime reduction   157, 161
community initiatives   171–2
community safety   165–6, 169
community service   121, 122
compensation   93, 108, 109, 118, 151
  public support for   120–5
  for victims of child abuse   76
  for victims of violent crime   113–17
compensation orders   117–18

195

Index